Art in WORLD HISTORY

BERKSHIRE Essentials
Art in WORLD HISTORY

宝库山精选：艺术在世界历史

William H. McNeill

Jerry H. Bentley, David Christian,
Ralph C. Croizier, J. R. McNeill,
Heidi Roupp, and Judith P. Zinsser

Editors

Brett Bowden

Associate Editor

Copyright © 2012 by Berkshire Publishing Group LLC

 All rights reserved. Permission to copy articles for internal or personal noncommercial use is hereby granted on the condition that appropriate fees are paid to the Copyright Clearance Center, 222 Rosewood Drive, Danvers, MA 01923, U.S.A., telephone +1 978 750 8400, fax +1 978 646 8600, email info@copyright.com. Teachers at institutions that own a print copy or license a digital edition of *Art in World History* may use at no charge up to ten copies of no more than two articles (per course or program).

Digital editions
Art in World History is available through most major e-book and database services (please check with them for pricing).

For information, contact:
Berkshire Publishing Group LLC
122 Castle Street
Great Barrington, Massachusetts 01230
www.berkshirepublishing.com
Printed in the United States of America

Library of Congress Cataloging-in-Publication Data

Art in world history / Ralph C. Croizier ... [et al.], editors. — 1st.
    p. cm.
"Illustrated selections from the Berkshire Encyclopedia of World History, 2nd edition."
Includes bibliographical references and index.
ISBN 978-1-933782-91-1 (pbk. : alk. paper) — ISBN 978-1-61472-999-0 (e-book)
1. Art and history. I. Croizier, Ralph C. II. Berkshire encyclopedia of world history.
N72.H58A78 2011
709—dc23
                    2011021126

Top left: Mary Cassatt, *The Bath*. (1891–1892). Oil on canvas. By the 1890s Cassatt's compositions and color schemes showed a Japanese influence.

Second row left: Unknown Mughal court artist, *Emperor Aurangzeb*. Opaque watercolor and gold. Ackland Art Museum.

Bottom left: Jan Asselyn (1610–1652), *Italian Landscape with the Ruins of a Roman Bridge and Aqueduct*. Oil on canvas.

Center top: Detail of silk banner from the tomb of Lady Dai, burial site at Mawangdui, on the outskirts of present-day Changsha, China. Second century BCE.

Center: Mandala of the Single-Syllable Golden Wheel. (Heian period, twelfth century.) Nara National Museum.

Center bottom: The intricately carved, massive Stone of Sun, or Aztec calendar, in Mexico City. Photo by Arturo Delfin (www.morguefile.com).

Top right: One of the earliest depictions of the Virgin and Child, from the Catacomb of Priscilla, draws upon Egyptian images of Isis suckling Horus.

Second row right: Sergei Gerasimov, *Collective Farm Festival* (1937). The painting exemplifies the Socialist Realism movement.

Bottom right: Helmet Mask, "Mulwalwa." Democratic Republic of Kongo, Southern Kuba, nineteenth or early twentieth century. Wood, paint, raffia, brass nails. Collection of the Ethnological Museum, Berlin-Dahlem.

THE **BERKSHIRE** *Essentials* SERIES

From the *Berkshire Encyclopedia of World History*, 2nd Edition:

- *Africa in World History*
- *Art in World History*
- *Big History*
- *Religion and Belief Systems in World History*
- *War, Diplomacy, and Peacemaking*
- *Women's and Gender History*
- *World Environmental History*

Distilled for the classroom from Berkshire's award-winning encyclopedias

BERKSHIRE *Essentials* **from the *Berkshire Encyclopedia of China* and the *Berkshire Encyclopedia of Sustainability* also available.**

About this "Berkshire Essentials" Volume

For more than a decade Berkshire Publishing has collaborated with an extraordinary worldwide network of scholars and editors to produce award-winning academic resources on cutting-edge subjects that appeal to a broad audience. With our Berkshire Essentials series—inspired by requests from teachers, curriculum planners, and professors who praise the encyclopedic approach we often use, but who still crave single volumes for course use—we at Berkshire have designed a series that "concentrates" our content.

Each Essentials series draws from Berkshire publications on a wide-ranging topic—world history, Chinese studies, and environmental sustainability, for starters—to provide theme-related volumes that can be purchased alone, in any combination, or as a set. (For example, individual volumes of the Essentials in World History series take a global approach to art; big history; religion and belief systems; war, diplomacy, and peacemaking; women and gender studies; world environmental history; and of course, with this volume, Africa.) Teachers will find the insightful, illustrated articles indispensable for jump-starting classroom discussion or independent study. Individuals—whether students, professionals, or general readers—will discover the articles invaluable when exploring a new line of research or an abiding interest.

The Berkshire Essentials volume *Art in World History* contains twenty-two color-illustrated articles; most of them logistically focus on a geographic area but nevertheless balance and interweave their regional coverage with cross-cultural perspectives: "Contact and comparison—the warp and the woof of the new world history," advised our volume editor Ralph C. Crozier, "not just a Cooke's travelogue of what happened where." Robert Poor's "Art—East Asian and European Connections," for instance, begins when trade brought Chinese silk to Roman weavers, circa 100 CE, and continues through the centuries to examine other East–West connections, such as how the celebrated nineteenth-century Japanese printmakers, Hokusai and Hiroshige, used one-point perspective, a Western technique.

Wilfried Van Damme's "Art—Paleolithic" explains how recent archaeological discoveries in Africa have prompted scholars in a growing number of disciplines to revive their interest in Paleolithic-era art—and thus to open up debate on fundamental world history

Vincent van Gogh, *Portrait of Père Tanguy* (1887). Oil on canvas. The rise of modernism in late nineteenth-century Europe embraced Japonisme. In the background van Gogh includes some of his *ukiyo-e* (woodblock) collection, or perhaps his take on the medium.

This mammoth, one of the world's earliest ceramic figurines, was excavated at Pavlov (Czech Republic), a site that reveals the hunting and tool-making skills of its Upper Paleolithic–period inhabitants.

questions that involve the origins of art making; the physical, mental, social, and cultural conditions that made it possible; and the fact that creating art has endured and become increasingly integral to our existence. Kathleen Kimball, in "Art—World Art Studies," discusses how studying world art—objects and technologies humans have made from their earliest days to the present—takes a similar interdisciplinary approach, mining such fields as archaeology, anthropology, art history, and, perhaps surprisingly but significantly, neurobiology.

Overviews on vernacular architecture and textiles examine how the study of these art forms can provide insight on a people's aesthetic sense and development, as well as on the cultural, political, and socioeconomic aspects of their lives, while Robert Finlay chronicles how China's millennium-long dominance of international porcelain production and trade declined and gave way in the mid-eighteenth century to the British manufactory owned by the "pottery baron" Josiah Wedgwood.

Kate Ezra's "Art—Africa" provides a panorama of ancient rock paintings; abstract representations of the human body in the first centuries CE; terracotta sculptures, bronze casts, and ivory carvings of the thirteenth to sixteenth centuries; nineteenth-century ritual masks—some caked with mud, animal blood (or other sacrificial material) and adorned with tusks, horns, woven raffia, feathers, and beads—and the conceptual work of the postcolonial world explored in performance art, video, photography, and installation. The article focuses throughout on cultural exchange—from earliest days of trade routes, to the influence of Christianity and Islam on art and architecture, to the Cubist's and German expressionist's inspiration by African artists' geometrical forms, vivid colors, and freedom from naturalistic representations.

Ralph Crozier's introduction, "Art—World History and Art," addresses the gradual disconnection of visual studies from world history that began in the 1960s with the growing emphasis of historians' research on trade and trading patterns, and on the transfer of technologies and their environmental impacts. Crozier goes on to raise provocative questions: Is art illustration or content? In world history research, where is the art? If world history has always been undisciplined, Crozier asks—that is to say, not confined within the bounds of normal academic history, but drawing data and ideas from cultural anthropology, the natural sciences, and even economics—is there hope that other these academic disciplines might bring more visuality to world history? Crozier explains how, at least to some extent, this hope is being fulfilled.

We at Berkshire appreciate comments and questions from our readers. Please send suggestions for other Essential volumes you'd like to see in this world history–themed series. And do check our website for news about our other Essential volumes on China and environmental sustainability.

Karen Christensen
CEO and Publisher
Great Barrington, Massachusetts

Contents

About this "Berkshire Essentials" Volume VII
Introduction: Art in World History XI

Architecture 1
Architecture, Vernacular 12
Art—Africa 17
Art—Ancient Greece and Rome 23
Art—Central Asia 31
Art—China 40
Art—East Asian and European Connections 57
Art—Europe 63
Art—Japan 74
Art—Native North America 84
Art—Paleolithic 92
Art—Pre-Columbian Central and South America 101
Art—Russia 112
Art—South Asia 121
Art—Southeast Asia 130
Art—West Asia 136
Art—World Art Studies 143
Leonardo da Vinci 151

Museums 155
Porcelain 160
Textiles 162
Index 171
Editorial Board and Staff 181
Author Credits 182

Introduction: Art in World History

World history, almost by necessity, is often interdisciplinary in its approach and research methods. So far, however, it has not connected very closely with the visual studies disciplines, especially art history. Some recent scholarship suggests this might be changing and non-textual evidence will play a larger role in how we see world history.

The great pioneers and popularizers of world history in the first half of the twentieth century—Arnold Toynbee in *A Study of History*; Oswald Spengler in *The Decline of the West*—reified the visual arts as a unique expression of the animating spirit of the "Great Civilizations," whose rise and fall was the core of world history. Art measured and reflected those life cycles.

The new world history taught in the United States since the 1960s has largely abandoned a separate-civilizations approach to world history in favor of interconnections and comparisons, especially more material ones—trade, the transfer of technologies, the spread of disease, and impacts on the environment. The importance of art in this new context has consequently declined. Does art have any significant role to play in world history in the twenty-first century other than as textbook illustration?

Art: Illustration or Content?

In his enormously influential though misleadingly titled *The Rise of the West* (1963), a comprehensive one-volume survey of the entire human past, William H. McNeill strove to give art and visual material a meaningful presence in a global narrative that still used civilizations as its basic building blocks but made cultural diffusion between civilizations the real motor of historical change—with art being a prominent part of that story. McNeill not only insisted on illustrations—these were lesser-quality, black-and-white photos compared to the lavish color that would become de rigueur once world history had established a large textbook market—but they were tightly linked to the historical narrative. He also made his publisher (University of Chicago Press) commission the Hungarian-born artist Bela Petheo, who drew a series of diagrammatic maps and sketches to convey some of the book's interpretations and narratives—particularly those having to do with contact and diffusion. Petho's illustrations combined words and symbols with the gestures of, and the spatial relationships among, simply rendered human figures.

Subsequent world history textbooks, including McNeill's, developed the use of art as illustration but seldom as an integral part of the narrative itself. As material history became more important the emphasis on nonmaterial culture declined. Illustrations functioned more as vehicles to break up large blocks of text, and the lessons art could teach about history, including the history of cultural diffusion, seemingly diminished. When McNeill co-authored his next venture into macro-history, *The Human Web* (2003), art had shrunk to a few passing one-line references. This is not so surprising, for the many subjects McNeill tackled in influential books and lecture series during the years after *The Rise of the West* dealt with "harder" fields of history—military power, demography, disease, and the environment, for instance—topics seldom interpreted through the visual enhancement (or evidence) provided by art.

Johannes Vermeer, *Officer and Laughing Girl* (c. 1655–1660). Oil on canvas. The beaver fur hat inspired the title for Timothy Brook's episodic study on the effects of seventeenth-century trade. The Frick Collection, New York.

This should not be interpreted as criticism. It reflects the general interest of McNeill's time in questions of economic development, of power and organization, and of material culture. The other influential world historians of the last fifty years, from Leften Stavrianos to David Christian, pacesetters in the development of world history as a respectable field of intellectual inquiry, followed similar paths, or rather blazed new trails, but none explored the visual dimensions of world history. Patrick Manning's *Navigating World History: Historians Create a Global Past* makes this point clear. Manning's volume, which in his preface he calls "an overview and critique of world history as a field of scholarship and teaching" (2003, ix), includes a chapter called "Cultural History." A discussion of nonmaterial culture is part of that chapter, but it draws heavily on anthropology; so art is once again marginalized—not necessarily because of any anti-artistic prejudice on the part of the author—but perhaps reflecting the author's Africanist background.

World History Research: Where is the Art?

Surveying research publications in the field of world history one finds very few books, monographs, or scholarly articles by historians that have anything to do with art. The *Journal of World History*, an official publication of the World History Association, has run exactly two articles with an art theme—"The Pilgrim's Art: The Culture of Porcelain," and "Weaving the Rainbow: Visions of Color in World History," both by Robert Finlay—in its twenty years of publication. A newer journal, the U.K.-published *Journal of Global History*, appeared to be following the same track in its first four years until in the July 2009 issue it published "Dionysus and Drama in the Buddhist Art of Gandhara," co-authored by the art historian Pia Brancaccio and the world historian Xinru Liu. The article is a model of what interdisciplinary scholarship can do to draw more cultural and social history out of a topic, especially one so well covered as Greek influence (between the first and third centuries CE), in what is now northern India and eastern Afghanistan. But its interpretive use of artistic evidence (sculpture) is very much the exception in world history research.

One other seeming exception should be mentioned. Timothy Brook, a globally conscious historian of Ming China, takes the seventeenth-century Dutch artist Johannes Vermeer as the starting point for his 2008 book, *Vermeer's Hat*. But the art is almost incidental to the episodic story Brook tells of how in the seventeenth century the European search for the riches of the Orient, with China at its center, started to build the interconnected world of modern times. He focuses on one small object in several paintings (the beaver fur hat of a Dutch officer in one of them provides the title), to explain where these items came from and the history of how they got to Holland—from the opening of the New World and the exposure to furs, tobacco, and silver; to trade with Asia and the spice islands; and to changes in European customs, habits, and life styles. It is definitely world history told with grace, charm, and wit. But it does not use the art to explain the history; it is not world history as seen through art.

A more recent but better example of the historian crossing over into art history—but still asking world-history-type questions about complicated cross cultural connections or networks—is Robert Finlay's book (expanding on the article mentioned above) *The Pilgrim Art: Cultures of Porcelain in World History*. He traces the invention of true porcelain in China, explains why other pottery-making cultures (and who didn't make pottery?) had such trouble matching the Chinese combination of extremely high kiln temperatures and special types of clay seldom found elsewhere, and why this created a unique worldwide trade network when European maritime expansion connected all the continents. Most significant for cultural history, fine porcelain was an artistic product that carried all kinds of cultural baggage. East met West, China and Europe but also everywhere in between, in the pictures and designs on a Chinese china cup. It is the furthest we have come so far in making art a meaningful part of truly global history.

Still, when we turn from the research monographs to the world history textbooks it is apparent that much more needs to be done. Despite attempts at stimulating interest with attractive illustrations and graphics, they seldom integrate the art or explain why it was created, who its intended audience was, or what impact it had on the history being illustrated. In fact, rarely is any information given about the artist, or even the present location of the work of art, making art seem more like eye candy than an aspect of history. The frequent use of sidebars or "insets" to explain an illustration further separates the visual from the historical narrative rather than integrating it.

There are, of course, some exceptions: mainly textbooks that move away from the more conventional area-by-area chronology toward thematic organization. A pioneering text of this type, Kevin Reilly's *The West and the World: The History of Civilization from the Ancient World to 1700*, makes a serious effort to integrate art into the history rather than just decorate it. From erotic painted scenes on ancient Greek vases in his chapter on "Love and Sex" to his final chapter on "Citizens and Subjects," he uses a range of visual material to illuminate major social, political, and cultural developments. (A subsequent edition published in 2003 brings the reader up to the twenty-first century and ends with the chapter "Identity and Global Culture.")

An even more thematically organized text, *In the Balance: Themes in Global History* by Candice Goucher, Charles Le Guin, and Linda Walton (1998), has several special sections on the arts. For instance, "The Deadly Arts: Expressions of Death in World Arts before 1500," ranges around the globe to touch on religious and cultural beliefs surrounding this universal human dilemma. Another section, "Cultural Creativity and Borrowed Art," meaningfully illustrates the fundamental theme of the new world history—cross-cultural borrowing and innovation.

Still, even these textbooks only scratch the surface of how it is possible to use art—and especially in these modern times, a broader visual culture—for historical analysis. But this will only be possible when the research side of world history generates more articles, monographs, and detailed case studies showing where and how art can be integrated into world history.

This rather negative appraisal of the presently existing role of art in world history scholarship needs to be balanced by two other factors: (1) the greater presence of art and visuality in the teaching of world history, and (2) the potential for help from other academic disciplines.

Art in the World History Classroom

Two publications indicate that art is finding a more prominent place in world history classrooms. In 1997, Heidi Roupp, a high school teacher and president-elect of the World History Association, edited a volume called *Teaching World History: A Resource Book*, part the M. E. Sharpe series *Sources and Studies in World History*. Of the fifty essays on teaching strategies and resources, three involved visual art. Although 6 percent may not seem like a large share,

it is significant compared to the *Journal of World History*'s record of two art articles in twenty years (less than 1 percent). It also is significant that the other WHA publication, the *Bulletin of World History*, more teaching-oriented than the *Journal*, does intermittently have articles dealing with art's role in world history education. That, as well as the greater interest high school teachers show in art panels at the annual and regional meetings of the WHA, seems to indicate that a movement to put more art in world history might come more from practice (teaching) than theory (scholarly research).

But this contradicts one of the fundamental principles of the WHA and the world history movement in general: the teaching needs to be informed by new scholarship and the scholarship should be relevant to the teaching. Since world historians are not producing much scholarship on art in world history, where will such research come from? The most hopeful source may be other academic disciplines with a better eye for nonwritten sources.

Interdisciplinary Solutions?

World history has always been undisciplined—that is to say, not confined within the bounds of normal academic history. The key historians in the intellectual evolution of the new world history all drew ideas and data from other disciplines: William H. McNeill from cultural anthropology, for instance, and the world economic historians—Kenneth Pomeranz, Bin Wong, and Andre Gunder Frank—from economics. David Christian, for his *Big History*, the twenty-first-century continuation of the meta-history tradition, turned to the natural sciences: evolutionary biology, geology, and astronomy. Is there, then, hope that other academic disciplines might bring more visuality to world history? If so, why hasn't it already happened? To some extent it has.

Archeology

The broad vision of world history, going back at least to the agricultural revolution and preliterate societies, means that archaeological evidence has been essential for reconstructing the distant global past. Few, if any world historians, have got their own fingers dirty at digs, but they have certainly made use of what archaeologists have uncovered, from crude stone and pottery "Venus figures" in Paleolithic Europe to lost cities in Africa or ancient graves along the Silk Road(s). The new journal *Silk Road* is a particularly rich source for archaeologically discovered evidence of trans-Eurasian contacts and cultural exchanges.

But the most startling recent research on pan-Eurasian patterns and possible connections goes back long before silk linked the far parts of what William H. McNeill called "the global eucumene." Two philologists, Victor Mair and Miriam Robbins Dexter (2010), have produced a little book, *Sacred Display: Divine and Magical Female Figures of Eurasia*, with startling implications about the prominence of the feminine in very ancient Eurasian religion and society from China to Scandinavia. Their research uses textual as well as visual evidence, but the book is a striking example of what can be done when text and image are combined and disciplinary boundaries are ignored.

For modern times, with such variety of art and its intermixing in the age of globalization, cultural anthropology is the field that has done the most significant work. In studying mainly nonliterate small societies, anthropology has always turned to art as a vital part of "symbolic culture" and has been global in its scope. More recently, realizing that autonomous native cultures were almost all involved in global exchanges, cultural anthropology has looked at the interaction between different societies and cultures—exactly what world history does—but has given more focus to art than world history has. It has been to world history's disadvantage that there has not been more dialogue between the two disciplines. The recent volume of collected essays, *Exploring World Art* (Venbrux et al. 2005), would be a good place for world historians to begin, even if most of its case studies deal with small societies—the Sepik River valley in Papua New Guinea, for instance, not China or Japan.

Cultural, Visual, and Media Studies

Some anthropologists look at art in larger societies, and they are in much closer touch with the new fields of cultural studies, visual studies, and media studies than most historians are. Those fields, products of the age of an electronically interconnected world, would seem to be more promising for world history than has been the case so far. But from a world historian's viewpoint most of their intellectual production has been disappointing or irrelevant. There are several reasons for this.

First, the scholarship is so heavily suffused with theoretical concerns—poststructuralist, Lacanian, psychoanalytic, deconstructivist—that they literally speak a different language, one foreign to most practicing world historians. More seriously, as the polymath art historian and world art theorist James Elkins has lamented (2003, 36), they show very little interest in "history," that is, what happened before the advent of electronic images. And finally, a problem for fact-grubbing historians, there is very little first-hand research on non-Western visual cultures in the new fields' leading journals, which are long on postmodernist theorists and short on facts or even images.

World historians should not ignore these new fields of inquiry into global culture, especially when they are really global, but the most likely source of help with visual evidence still lies in art history. How promising is that older and well-established discipline as a source of allies, ideas, and material?

Art History

Although "world art" as a conscious intellectual enterprise and curriculum component is still very much in its infancy, the last few decades have seen considerable changes in the way art history is conceptualized, researched, and taught. Most relevant for world history, it has become less Eurocentric and less focused on stylistic development and "great artists and masterpieces."

The extent of this progress should not be exaggerated. Many art history surveys and textbooks now incorporate the word *world* into their title as global consciousness spreads along with economic and cultural globalization. But coverage is still much more comprehensive for the Western canon, from Mesopotamia and Egypt, through Greece and Rome, the Middle Ages, Renaissance, modern Europe, and America. "The rest"—almost all of Asia, Africa, pre-Columbian Americas, Australia, and Oceania—on average gets one-quarter to one-third the total number of pages. Still, this is a considerable improvement over just a few decades ago.

Global coverage in itself may not be terribly useful for a world history agenda. Often written by multiple authors, these thousand-page or more tomes are organized by era and area with not much attention to connections and comparisons between them. That is not to say that the diligent world historian cannot find some examples to use in illustrating cultural contact between different civilizations. Almost all the art history textbooks discuss, more or less adequately, Greco-Roman influence in Gandharan Buddhist art and its spread from northern India to China as one of the most striking cases of long-distance transmission of artistic style and ideals. Similarly, *japonisme* usually figures prominently in the rise of modernism in late-nineteenth-century Europe.

Still, these beautifully illustrated textbooks and the online image banks designed for art history are strongest on the Western art canon, not yet free of "the West and the rest" approach. They remain more useful as a source of illustrations for teachers and scholars of world history. For ideas, world historians will have to search through some of the newer trends and publications in art history.

The two leading professional art history journals, *Art Bulletin* in the United States and *Art History* in Great Britain, still publish heavily on "Western art." Since the 1990s, the number of articles on other parts of the world has risen to about 12 percent of the total, far less than in the textbooks, which give more weight to course enrollments than art historians' professional interests. More to the point, however, very few articles in that 12 percent touch on the themes of cross-cultural contacts and comparisons which are so important to world historians. Conceptually, the discipline of art history still seems uninterested in a global approach. But is it?

Perhaps more than history, art history is a discipline in the throes of theoretical change. Much of this theory—semiotics, poststructuralism, and so forth—seems irrelevant for down-to-earth, fact-seeking, narrative-constructing historians. Since the turn of the century, however, there have been several major works by prominent art historians that attempt new approaches to "global art."

John Onians and his School of World Art Studies at East Anglia University (in the United Kingdom) may be the most significant for world history. His massive, multi-authored *Atlas of World Art* is more truly global in its coverage than any of the standard art history textbooks. Whether or not world historians find his neurologically based theory of universals in art useful, they could benefit from his pioneering work in the discipline of art history.

More active in Europe than America, the world art studies "movement" is very broad in its vision, encompassing the world from the earliest paleo-archaeological evidence of hominid artistic creation to the present, and all relevant disciplines from philosophy to neurobiology. Judging from published essays deriving from a number of workshops held at the University of Leiden—in a 2008 volume, *World Art Studies: Exploring Concepts and Approaches*, edited by Kitty Zijlmans and Wilfried van Damme—cultural anthropology seems to be the closest ally to world art history. There were no historians included, perhaps more a comment on historians' lack of interest in the visual than any exclusion by world art studies.

On the other side of the Atlantic, two American art historians have seriously engaged the problem of a global art history on the theoretical level. David Summers, in *Real Spaces: World Art History and the Rise of Western Modernism* (2003), tries to come to terms with what new theories of the visual and heightened global awareness mean for the study of art history. He believes those different "real spaces" around the world can be brought into a non-Western-centric universal art history. James Elkins, equally dissatisfied with the lingering elitist and culture-bound narratives of art history in the West, is much more skeptical about the possibility of constructing a universal narrative out of the world's various traditions of art and art history. Of his many publications, *Stories of Art* (2002) is probably most relevant for theories of world art history and, by implication, world history.

Three Rubrics for Research

This kind of new thinking by art historians such as Onians, Summers, and Elkins is important for connecting art history to world history, but practicing world historians might find more limited studies that examine specific cases of cross-cultural contacts and comparisons more immediately useful. Much of this closely focused research comes from younger art historians and fits easily under the three large rubrics of world history research—connections, comparisons, and global patterns.

Connections

A few examples of "connections"—cross-cultural influences in art, especially where the art is part of larger cultural, economic, and even political patterns—follow.

The Silk Roads, networks of trade and travel linking East Asia with western Asia and Europe, figure large in both world history and recent art history. The roots of this Western romance with the caravan routes go back to late-nineteenth-century European explorers like Sven Hedin and Aurel Stein, who brought the desert-preserved artistic and archaeological treasures of Central Asia to the world's attention. More recent archaeological work and art studies have shown how much cultural contact flowed through central Asia on the long-distance trade routes. The artistic record for the transmission of Buddhism from its northern Indian birthplace to East Asia is well known, but new discoveries suggest far more contact between China and Europe in the Middle Ages than had previously been imagined. (The journal *Silk Road* publishes much of this scholarship.) Lauren Arnold describes in detail one particular "Silk Road journey" in her book *Princely Gifts and Papal Treasures: The Franciscan Mission to China 1250–1350 and Its Influence on the Art of the West*. For influence flowing the other way, Arnold has shown how the image of the Virgin Mary with the baby Jesus, brought to China by fourteenth-century Franciscan missionaries, was transferred into Chinese portrayals of the child-giving goddess, Guan Yin.

The question of Chinese contributions to European Renaissance art is still contentious with most art historians not accepting Arnold's views or those postulating Chinese influence on Giotto published earlier by the Japanese art historian, Hidemichi Tanaka. But mainstream Western art history has recognized that the Renaissance was not entirely a European affair as several well-received books have appeared in the last decade or so showing the connections in art, architecture and culture between Italy, particularly Venice, and its Eastern Mediterranean trading partners in Istanbul, Cairo, and elsewhere. (See Jerry Brotton's *Renaissance Bazaar*, 2002, and his collaboration with Lisa Jardine,

Lauren Arnold, author of *Princely Gifts and Papal Treasures*, noticed a striking similarity between a scroll (left) signed by Tang Yin (1470–1523) and the famous eighth-century painting (right), *Salus Populi Romani*, in Rome's Santa Maria Maggiore. Most likely missionaries had carried a copy of the iconic Roman work to China, where Tang Yin was inspired to adapt the image of the goddess Guan Yin in his portrayal of the Virgin Mary. Nishio Conservation Studio.

Global Interests: Renaissance Art between East and West, 1996).

In the ensuing age of European maritime expansion these cross-cultural connections expand beyond the Silk Roads and the Mediterranean to become global, especially with the spread of the Jesuit mission. *Art and the Jesuit Missions in Asia and Latin America, 1542–1773*, by Gauvin Alexander Bailey (2001), and *The Jesuits and the Arts*, edited by Bailey and John W. O'Malley, deal with the visual arts in this premodern occurrence of globalization. Another art historian, Michael Sullivan (1973), looks beyond the Jesuits and brings the interchange between European and East Asian art (Japan as well as China) up to the twentieth century in his pioneering study *The Meeting of Eastern and Western Art*.

In the four decades since Sullivan's broad-gauged survey, other art historians have conducted more focused research on particular cases of East–West contact and intra-Asian interactions. One example is the work of Aida Wong, now a resident in the United States but significantly from Hong Kong, that meeting place of international and transnational influences. Wong's recent book, *Parting the Mists: Discovering Japan and the Rise of National-Style Painting in China* (2006), internationalizes the art history and cultural history of twentieth-century East Asia. A shorter work of Wong's, "Landscapes of Nandal Bose (1882–1966): Japanism and Populism in Modern India," published in *Shadows of the Past: Okakura Tenshin and Pan-Asianism* and edited by Brij Tankha, is even more clearly world history, or world history through art, with its revelations of how pan-Asian thought arose in reaction to Western colonial dominance.

Later in the globalized twentieth century, these connections are even more obvious. To take just three of many art histories dealing with East–West artistic interchange in the last century, there is Shiji Takashima and Thomas Rimer's *Paris in Japan*, published by the Japan Foundation in 1987; Partha Mitter's *Art and Nationalism in Modern India* (1995), and Liliane Karnouk's 2004 study *Modern Egyptian Art, 1910–2003*.

Utagawa Sadahide (1807–1873). This *ukiyo-e* style Japanese print shows a Dutch family along the shoreline in Yokohama; a Dutch ship is at anchor in the background. As an example of a European subject rendered in traditional Japanese style, the print attests to the East–West cultural exchange. Library of Congress.

Such studies can contribute significantly to world historian's efforts to trace the emergence of global styles, global culture, and the complex questions of cultural identity they produce. This is also the area where visual and cultural studies may be most useful, and world historians should not ignore the work on small societies by cultural anthropologists well represented in the essay collection, *Exploring World Art* (Ventrux et al. 2006). Beyond the small societies and tourist art described in those essays, there are other examples of globally circulating pop culture and art, such as the spread of Japanese anime and other elements of cross-Pacific pop largely through the Internet.

Comparisons

Comparative studies, at least in art, are less popular than they once were and perhaps not as obviously useful for world historians looking for a "web" of global connections rather than distinctly different civilizations. In 1954, the Harvard art historian Benjamin Rowland wrote in the introduction to his little book (at 140 pages, it's an easy-to-handle volume compared to some of its thousand-page successors), *Art in East and West: An Introduction Through Comparisons*, that he was looking for, "accidental parallels . . . not designed to illustrate the influence of one culture upon the other" (1954, vii).

Since then, awareness of cultural influences has grown and broad categories like "East" and "West" have been much refined. But there still are comparative questions where the interests of the art historian, the social scientist, and the world historian overlap. How, in different societies at different times, does art work as an instrument for cultural cohesion, religious belief, and political control? Answering such questions requires some understanding of "style" (the language of art), as well as of social theory. For instance, look at monumentality and political authority in both the sphinxes and pyramids of Pharonic Egypt and the relief sculpture of ancient Mesopotamia—or, for the modern revolutionary period, how art was used to mobilize and indoctrinate the masses in Fascist Italy, Nazi Germany, Soviet Russia, and Communist China. (See Igor Golomstock's 1990 book *Totalitarian Art*.) Religion, of course, is another promising field for an interdisciplinary approach: the ideological functions of icons, holy sites and architecture, art and the missionary enterprise—all the numerous areas where art is a basic source for the history of belief.

Global Patterns

Finally, stopping just short of meta-projects (Onian's atlas or Summers' global art theory) there is the search for global patterns. There surely are others, but one of the most obvious is the virtually worldwide spread of post-Renaissance Western "realist" art in the late nineteenth and early twentieth centuries when, from Teheran to Tokyo, or from Moscow to Bangkok, it was seen as an essential component of modernity. (See John Clarke's 1998 work, *Modern Asian Art*.) Closely behind that wave of Westernization comes the fusion of art and identity politics in the postmodern, postcolonial era. These are not national topics, and they are not just art history topics.

At the other end of recorded history with the emergence of cities, states, and empires there may also be similarities in the functions of art that go beyond comparison of the particularities of form and style. There may be patterns, if not one line of development, and art may be the key to unlocking them. Again, it is essential for world historians to engage in dialog with archaeologists and art historians, not just read the results of their research. Art and visual evidence in general are too important, too relevant to history everywhere to be neglected as world history goes forward in its task of creating a global past for an increasingly globalized future.

Ralph C. CROIZIER
University of Victoria

Further Reading

Arnold, L. (1999). *Princely gifts and papal treasures: The Franciscan mission to China and its influence on the art of the West, 1250–1350*. San Francisco: Desiderata Press.

Bailey, G. A. (2001). *Art on the Jesuit missions in Asia and Latin America, 1547–1773*. Toronto: Toronto University Press.

Brancaccio, P. & Liu, X. (2009). Dionysus and drama in the Buddhist art of Gandhara. *Journal of Global History, 4*, 219–244.

Brook T. (2008). *Vermeer's hat: The seventeenth century and the dawn of the global world*. London: Bloomsbury Press.

Brotton, J. (2002). *The Renaissance bazaar: From the Silk Road to Michelangelo*. Oxford, U.K.: Oxford University Press.

Brotton, J. & Jardine, L. (1996). *Worldly goods: A new history of the Renaissance*. Ithaca, NY: Cornell University Press.

Clark, J. (1993). *Modernity in Asian art*. Broadway, Australia: Wild Peony Lt'd.

Clark, J. (1998). *Modern Asian art*. Honolulu: University of Hawaii Press.

Elkins, J. (2002). *Stories of art*. London: Routledge.

Elkins, J. (2003). *Visual studies: A skeptical introduction*. London: Routledge.

Elkins, J. (2007). *Is art history global?* London: Routledge.

Finlay, R. (2010). *The pilgrim art: Cultures of porcelain in world history*. Berkeley: University of California Press.

Golomstock, I. (1990). *Totalitarian art in the Soviet Union, the Third Reich, Fascist Italy and the People's Republic of China*. New York: Harper Collins.

Goucher, C., Le Guin. C., & Walton, L. (1998). *In the Balance: Themes in Global History*. Boston: McGraw Hill.

Haskell, F. (1993). *History and its images*. New Haven, CT: Yale University Press.

Levenson, J. (1991). *Circa 1492: Art in the age of exploration*. New Haven: Yale University Press.

Mair, V. & Dexter, M. R. (2010) *Sacred display: Divine and magical female figures of Eurasia*. Amherst, NY: Cambria.

Manning, P. (2003). *Navigating world history: Historians create a global past*. New York: Palgrave Macmillan.

Mitter, P. (1995). *Art and nationalism in colonial India, 1850–1922, occidental orientations*. Cambridge, U.K.: Cambridge University Press.

Marceau, J. (1998). *Art: A world history*. New York: DK Publishing.

Onians, J. (2006). *Compression versus expression: Containing and explaining the world's art*. Williamstown, MA: Clark Visual Studies in the Arts.

Onians, J. (Ed.). (2004). *Atlas of world art*. London: Oxford University Press

Parry, K., Gardener, I., & Lieu, S. (Eds.). (2005). *From Palmyra to Zayton: Epigraphy and Iconography*. Turnhout, Belgium: Brepolis.

Pasztory, E. (2005). *Thinking with things*. Austin: University of Texas Press.

Reilly, K. (2003). *The West and the world: The history of civilization from 1400 to the present*. Princeton, NJ: Markus Wiener.

Rowland, B. (1954). *Art in East and West: An introduction through comparisons*. Cambridge, MA: Harvard University Press.

Sullivan, M. (1973). *The meeting of Eastern and Western art*. London: Thames and Hudson.

Summers, D. (2003). *Real spaces: World art history and the rise of western modernism*. London: Phaidon.

Venbrux, E., Sheffield Rosi, P., & Welsch, R. L. (Eds.). (2005). *Exploring world art*. Long Grove: Waveland Press.

Wong, A. (2006). *Parting the mists: Discovering Japan and the rise of national-style painting in China*. Honolulu: University of Hawaii Press.

Winegar, D. (2006). *Creative reckonings: The politics of art and culture in contemporary Egypt*. Palo Alto, CA: Stanford University Press.

Architecture

In the practice of architecture, the art and science of building environments for human needs, architects strive to design structures that are sound, useful to their inhabitants, and aesthetically pleasing to society—whether starkly monumental in structure (like ancient Stonehenge and the modern skyscraper) or elaborately embellished (like the Parthenon in Greece and Córdoba's Great Mosque).

Since prehistoric times, people have created architecture to shelter their activities and to express societal or personal values. Usually the term *architecture* refers to a building or group of buildings, but the field overlaps with interior design and with landscape and urban design. Many architects agree with the ancient Roman architect Vitruvius (c. 90–c. 20 BCE), who wrote that architecture must be stable, useful, and beautiful. To accomplish this architects must understand (a) how to employ one or more structural systems to support the design, (b) how the design will be used once it is built, and (c) what a client or society will find visually pleasing. Therefore, architects are faced with choices regarding approaches to the building site, available materials, and building technologies.

Prehistoric and Nonurban Architecture

Nomadic humans of the foraging (Paleolithic) era (c. 35,000–8000 BCE) lived in caves and rock shelters, but they also created portable woven architecture—oval huts of vertical poles that were covered with hides or thatched reeds. In the Neolithic era (c. 8000–1500 BCE), herders and farmers erected permanent settlements, including monumental buildings that merged with surrounding landscapes. They crudely quarried large stones (megaliths), moved them by barge and by sled on rollers, and raised them on earthen ramps to create

Stonehenge, the best-known monument of the Neolithic era, dramatically illustrates the concept of trabeated architecture—construction based on a post-and-lintel system. Photo by Carol Hermann.

trabeated (or post-and-lintel) structures (dolmens) of vertical columns supporting horizontal beams. The most famous example of such a structure, located on Salisbury Plain, England, is Stonehenge (c. 2750–1500 BCE), a series of concentric circles probably built to accommodate festivals held by related warrior tribes. The more common dolmen was a sepulchral chamber built of megaliths and buried within an artificial hill, called a cairn.

Little remains of more humble buildings, except their influence on the surviving vernacular architecture of villages around the world, rooted in the myths and traditions of the people. In African Cameroon each Bamileke village has a central open space, chosen as sacred by the ancestors. The adjacent chief's house, an aggrandized version of the others in the village, has bamboo walls fronted by a porch and sheltered by a thatched conical roof. In Cameroon's Fali culture, forms, orientation, and dimensions of the ideal human body inspire the design of residential compounds. The Dogon culture of Mali builds men's assembly houses, open-sided huts in which anthropomorphic wooden pillars, representing the ancestors, support a thick roof of dried vegetation that shades the interior but allows air to circulate.

A similar situation is found in North America, where the Anasazi people constructed "Great Houses," of which Pueblo Bonito in Chaco Canyon, New Mexico, is the largest known. Built in stages from the tenth to the mid-thirteenth century CE, the quarrying, timber cutting, and transport during the construction were done without metal tools, wheelbarrows, or draft animals. In its final form Pueblo Bonito resembled a "D" with a perimeter wall approximately 400 meters (about 1,300 feet) long. Sandstone walls defined adjacent living units accessed from openings in the wooden roofs. Hundreds of units encircled central plazas under which the Anasazi built subterranean sacred gathering places (kivas). Men entered a kiva—women were forbidden—through a hole in a domed ceiling of interlocking pine logs. Because the number of rooms at Pueblo Bonito far exceeds evidence of human habitation, and the desert locale made obtaining food a constant challenge, archaeologists believe that the Anasazi devoted many of the rooms to food storage. When threatened by enemies, the Anasazi abandoned the Great Houses for dwellings built into the sides of easily defensible, south-facing cliffs, such as those at Mesa Verde, Colorado (twelfth–thirteenth centuries CE).

Ancient Temple Ziggurats, Tombs, and Palaces

Urban civilization—dependent on the development of writing, trade, diversified employment, and a centralized government—produced a variety of monumental building types, generally to glorify gods and god-kings. In the first cities of Mesopotamia, temples were raised heavenward on giant stepped platforms called ziggurats. Both temple and ziggurat were built of sun-dried mud brick using bearing-wall construction. The Ziggurat of Ur-Nammu (c. 2100 BCE) in Ur, Iraq, was faced in a more durable kiln-dried brick laid in a bitumen mortar. In Central America the stepped pyramids of the grand city of Teotihuacán (c. 250 BCE–650 CE), near present-day Mexico City, were faced with volcanic stone and stucco and probably painted bright colors. They formed the backdrop for the rituals and public events associated with the temples, which took place on the top platforms.

Of the monumental tombs, the most famous are the three Great Pyramids of Giza (c. 2551–2490 BCE) in Egypt, which exhibited ashlar masonry (carefully cut stone blocks), piled in tight rows and faced in polished limestone. Workers probably used wooden rollers and sleds on earthen ramps to elevate the heavy stone blocks, and levers to place them in their final locations. These tombs memorialized god-kings for eternity and were seen as ladders for royal spirits to reach the heavens. In Greece beehive-shaped tombs survive, such as the Treasury of Atreus (c. 1300–1200 BCE) at Mycenae, where a vault of corbelled stone (formed by laying each course of stone slightly inward and beyond the previous row until it forms a narrow arch) capped the subterranean main circular chamber. The tomb, half buried until excavated in 1878, remained the largest uninterrupted interior space in Europe for over a thousand years, until the Pantheon in Rome (built in the first century CE), exceeded it in size.

A third type of monument served rulers during their lives. The enormous Assyrian Palace of King Sargon II (c. 720–705 BCE) at Dur Sharrukin, modern Khorsabad, Iraq, represented his combined secular and sacred authority and intimidated his foes with the carved imaginary beasts and scenes of military prowess that decorated its mud-brick walls.

The Greek Temple

The ancient Greeks influenced later Western builders with their post-and-lintel building tradition. Their three types of orders—systems of columns supporting entablatures—were distinguished by proportion and decoration, Doric being the most simple, Ionic more elegant in proportion than the Doric, and the Corinthian the most elaborate. Stone blocks of limestone and marble were held in place by metal clamps and dowels, and terracotta tiles covered the sloping wooden roof rafters. The apex of Greek architecture, the Parthenon temple (448–32 BCE), designed by Kallikrates, redesigned by Iktinos, with construction supervised by the sculptor Pheidias, was meant to be the focal point of Athens's raised sacred precinct, the Acropolis. The Parthenon featured a stepped platform and an exterior row of columns (or colonnade) that sheltered a central room housing a gigantic statue of Athena. The temple's proportions, determined by harmonious numerical ratios, were given life by the slight curvature of lines (called entasis), so components appeared to resist the weight imposed on them from above. (The entire temple was marble, even the roof.) Surfaces were stuccoed, painted, and embellished with colorful relief sculpture and friezes much admired for their graceful naturalism.

Roman Innovations and Their Eastern Progeny

Ancient Roman buildings, complexes, and new towns were regimented by simple geometric spaces related along clear axes and were often constructed using new materials and technologies. Voluminous interiors were created by using the semicircular arch, a method of spanning space with many small wedge-shaped elements that balanced against one another. Three-dimensional extrusions of the arch formed tunnels, rings, domes, and other types of spaces. The Romans employed concrete—a mixture of cement, water, and aggregate that can take on many

The architects who designed the Parthenon as the focal point of the Athenian Acropolis perfected an anthropometric approach to design, including its proportioning system and subtle optical refinements.
Photo by David M. Breiner.

flowing shapes—and faced it in stone or coursed brick and tile. The best-known examples of Roman architecture, the Pantheon temple (117–126 CE) and the Colosseum amphitheater (c. 70–80 CE), both in Rome, had interiors that were spatially exciting, their concrete surfaces lavishly finished with multicolored marbles, gilding, and sculpted detailing. The Pantheon, the result of sophisticated engineering despite its apparently simple dome shape, is one of the most remarkable structures existing in Rome today; from the inside the eye is drawn by a circular pattern of coffers (recessed panels) toward the ceiling (about 43 meters, or 143 feet, high at the summit), where light flows through a 9-meter- (29-foot)-wide oculus (central opening).

During the waning years of the Roman Empire in Western Europe, Christians adopted the multipurpose basilica as the model for their churches, such as Old Saint Peter's (begun c. 320 CE) in Rome. This multi-aisled building featured parallel stone colonnades that supported the masonry walls above. Those in turn held up a roof structure of wooden trusses, rigid triangular frames that resulted in the typical gabled roof form. The glittering, glass mosaic surfaces of the interior were hidden by a bare brick exterior. Byzantine Christians in the eastern half of the empire chose Roman vaulted structures as their models, resulting in the Cathedral of Constantinople, Hagia Sophia (532–537 CE), by Anthemios of Tralles and Isidorus of Miletus. The enormous masonry dome, though it rested on four curved triangular surfaces (called pendentives) seemed to float unsupported above the interior, thanks to the ring of windows at the base of the dome and the light-reflecting surfaces of mosaic and marble throughout the vast interior. Also inspired by Rome, Islamic builders developed a new building type for communal worship, the mosque. The Great Mosque (eighth–tenth centuries CE) in Córdoba, Spain, exhibited the horseshoe-shaped arches of alternating stone and brick bands that became typically Islamic, while innovatively stacking the arches in two levels, thereby creating a limitless sense of space. Dazzling marble and mosaic decoration was limited to stylized vegetation and other nonrepresentational patterns, according to Muslim practice.

Beyond Rome's orbit, in the Buddhist monastery at Sanchi in India, the dome of the Great Stupa (first century BCE–first century CE) enshrined important relics. (Stupas, religious structures fundamental to the Buddhist world, were first constructed to house the cremated remains of the Buddha after his death in 483 BCE.) Protected within a wall featuring four elaborate gateways, the earth-and-rubble-filled dome of the Great Stupa represented the mountain of the world. Pilgrim worshippers circumambulated the building on walkways at two levels, reflecting the Buddhist belief in cyclical Earthly suffering that was only relieved upon reaching nirvana.

The Middle Ages

In the centuries after the Roman Empire, European Christians supported powerful monasteries, whose builders turned to bearing-wall construction in limestone, granite, and sandstone. Master builders maintained the basilican church form (a rectangular building with side aisles separated from the center nave by colonnades), but ultimately they replaced the simple plan and trussed roof with more complex solutions to the problems presented by increasing numbers of pilgrims and concerns over fire safety. During the Romanesque Era (c. 1050–1200), so called due to the revival of Roman (that is, semicircular) vaulting techniques, builders experimented with heavy stone-vaulted ceilings and extended side aisles around the church's perimeter to improve circulation for pilgrims. Extensive sculpted ornament in abstracted forms greeted visitors with Christian lessons of good versus evil. The French church of Saint-Sernin (c. 1070–1120) in Toulouse exemplified this movement.

Structural experiments coalesced in the later twelfth century and throughout the thirteenth, during the Gothic era, led by northern France, which dominated Europe at that time. Gothic verticality, aspiring to express divine loftiness, combined with great visual coherence at Chartres Cathedral (1194–1220), where the minimal stone skeleton supported walls of stained glass illustrating sacred and secular themes. This effect was made possible through the combined use of the structurally efficient pointed arch, the framework of arched ribs (rib vaults) that allowed lighter vault panels, and the flying buttress that supported the vaults outside the building. Broad and steep roofs of innovative wood truss design protected the church vaults. A very high level of roofing technology was also evident in the contemporary wooden stave churches (using post-and-beam construction) of Norway.

Around the same time, builders in south and east Asia likewise developed impressively tall structures to house images of their gods and to visually connect Earth with heaven. Hindu Indians created the Visvanatha Temple to Siva (c. 1000) at Khajuraho, in the state of Madhya Pradesh. Inspired in design by a mandala (cosmic diagram), the temple's "grid plan" featured a sequence of increasingly important spaces, concluding at the inner sanctum with its image of Siva. Seemingly countless voluptuous sculptures covered the exterior surfaces that climaxed at the mountain-like tower over the inner sanctum. In China and Japan, Buddhist pagodas served similar uses but were characterized by their winged eaves and centralized plans.

In Europe continued insecurity encouraged the powerful to live in fortified castles. A moat and high walls with towers protected inner courts and the main multistoried residence, called a keep or donjon (the word *dungeon* is a derivative). By the latter Middle Ages, improved security fostered the development of the less-fortified, but still grand, manor house; the main room, or great hall, a multifunctional entertainment space, required sturdy roof support in the form of various trussed solutions. The Islamic rulers of Spain produced luxurious, sprawling palace complexes, such as the Alhambra (thirteenth–fourteenth centuries) in Granada. The gardens interspersed throughout the complex provided refreshing water, fragrant plants, and soft, indirect lighting. Rooms had ethereal domes, whose structure was veiled by *muqarnas*, open, honeycomb-like cells made from stucco or wood.

Idealized Plans and the Renaissance

Beginning in the fifteenth-century Italian Renaissance, men with humanistic educations, not just practical building experience, aided by familiarity with classical antiquity, mathematics, and orthogonal drawing, won many architectural commissions. Their buildings and publications argued for the unity of architectural practice and theory. Filippo Brunelleschi's Cupola (1417–1434), or dome and lantern, for the Cathedral of Florence combined a Gothic pointed profile and a

The Villa Rotonda (or Villa Capra) merges religious and domestic symbols. Its domed central hall and four matching porticoes dominate the bucolic site and make it among the most memorable achievements of the Italian Renaissance. Photo by David M. Breiner.

Pantheon-like concentric grid with his original ideas of a double shell, interlocking brick pattern, and inventive construction mechanisms. Sophisticated uses of Roman ideas also characterized the work of Leon Battista Alberti, whose classically grand Church of Sant'Andrea (begun c. 1470) in Mantua, Italy, derived from ancient building types, proportional systems, and the classical orders. Its façade—a classical temple front and triumphal arch, with two sets of Corinthian pilasters on the porch—belies the grand interior: an immense barrel-vaulted nave flanked by tall chapels.

Efforts to supersede classical accomplishments were evident in the contemporary architecture of Rome. The first grand scheme by Donato Bramante (1505) for rebuilding the Basilica of St. Peter affirmed the humanist interest in the idealized centralized church plan. Under Michelangelo's guidance the design of the basilica's cupola (1546–1564) was largely resolved, producing a cohesive and influential scheme that was the last of the great purely masonry domes. Michelangelo also designed a monumental civic center, the Campidoglio (begun 1538), its complexity organized by a strong central axis, colossal pilasters on the building facades, and the view over the city.

Renaissance ideas spread from Florence and Rome. Near Venice, Andrea Palladio, an experienced stonemason and a humanist scholar, advanced his own influential architectural treatise; by the eighteenth century most educated people (including Thomas Jefferson in America) had his *Four Books of Architecture* in their libraries. In his design for a suburban residence near Vicenza, Italy, the Villa Rotonda (begun 1566), he appropriated the portico (four, actually, one on each side of the square structure) and central domed hall formerly associated with religious buildings. The building is famous for its idealized siting, harmonic proportions, simple geometries, and clear axial relationships. Venice's powerful nemesis, the Ottoman Empire, produced Palladio's counterpart, the architect Sinan, whose skillful designs for central-domed mosques with stunning tile work were represented by his Mosque of Selim II (1568–1575) in Edirne, Turkey.

Idealized masonry monuments of the West contrasted with the idealized wooden post-and-lintel structures of the East, climaxing in Ming dynasty (1368–1644) China. The focal point of Beijing's monumental Forbidden City was the emperor's principal throne room, the Hall of Supreme Harmony (begun 1627). Though grander in size and ornament than other Chinese halls, its arrangement of standardized interchangeable parts was similar. A grid of wooden columns supported fingerlike brackets, which in turn held boxlike truss beams (or stepped roof trusses) that produced the characteristic curve of the tiled roof. Japanese builders transformed the Chinese architectural system by favoring more subtle asymmetrical arrangements and indirect paths of circulation, from Sen no Rikyu's intentionally rustic Tai-an tearoom, Myoki-an Temple (c. 1582) to the impressive Imperial Katsura Palace (largely c. 1615–1663), both in Kyoto.

Baroque Vitality

In the seventeenth-century West, Renaissance priorities blended with the dynamic growth of science, nationalism, and religious fervor. Designs, often structurally and spatially complex and characterized by illusionistic effects, were best appreciated by a person moving through them, for example, Gianlorenzo Bernini's Piazza (1656–1667) at St. Peter's in Rome. Intense ornamentation was common during the period and spread to Spanish and Portuguese colonies in Latin America. The monumental enlargement of the Château at Versailles (1667–1710), for France's autocratic "Sun-King" Louis XIV, had a network of axial pathways that led to the king's central bedchamber. In the château's Hall of Mirrors, innovative large mirrors created infinitely reflecting vistas of the vast gardens. Christopher Wren, who was a scientist before becoming an architect, reworked continental influences in his redesign for St. Paul's Cathedral (1675–1711) in London, where the cupola combined an inner masonry shell with a lightweight outer dome and lantern. In Bavaria structural experimentation, illusionism, and spatial complexity climaxed in works such as the Residence of the Prince-Bishops (1719–1753) in Würzburg, by Johann Balthasar Neumann.

Historical Revivals

Eighteenth-century architectural influences included the Enlightenment, which emphasized the individual person; increased historical scholarship, especially archaeology; and the Industrial Revolution. Giambattista Piranesi's widely disseminated, imaginative views and reconstructions of ancient Roman ruins aroused awe. In England, Robert Adam's renovation of Syon House (1760–1769) in Middlesex sought to authentically re-create the architecture of classical Rome. Yet with Horace Walpole, Adam also created the mysterious, picturesquely asymmetrical Gothic Revival Strawberry Hill (1749–1763) at Twickenham, its different parts appearing to be centuries-old accretions. French architect Jacques-Germain Soufflot combined Gothic structural lightness with classical spatial purity in his Church of Ste.-Geneviève (1755–1780) in Paris. Étienne-Louis Boullée drew unbuildable projects, like the Cenotaph to Isaac Newton (1783–1784), a classical but sublime giant hollow sphere that celebrated the achievements of the great physicist. It connected use and form in a direct manner called "architecture *parlante*." The mining of historical styles for contemporary projects continued into the nineteenth century, highlighted by Karl Friedrich Schinkel's Greek Revival Altes Museum (1824–1830) in Berlin, and the Gothic Revival Houses of Parliament (begun 1835) in London, by Charles Barry and A. W. N. Pugin.

By the mid-eighteenth century, Europeans began to seek increasingly private and comfortable residences. Renovated (1732–1739) in the delicate Rococo style by Germain Boffrand, the Hôtel de Soubise in Paris incorporated intimate interiors that were easily heated by improved fireplace design and easily illuminated by large windows and mirrors. Residences of the wealthy incorporated dumbwaiters and corridors to allow greater separation between masters and their servants. The English aristocracy and North American colonists also turned to making more comfortable buildings, typically favoring a restrained neo-Palladian approach to design, such as Thomas Jefferson's Monticello (1768–1782) in Charlottesville, Virginia.

Early Modernism

In the nineteenth century, the Industrial Revolution expanded its impact on European architecture. France's

Frank Lloyd Wright's Robie House adapts horizontal lines of the prairie into long brick planes, continuous window bands, and deep overhangs. Photo by David M. Breiner.

Architecture is the art of how to waste space. • **Philip Johnson (1906–2005)**

official architectural school, the École des Beaux-Arts, emphasized "universal" architectural ideals found in primarily classical models, but the buildings of its alumni, including Charles Garnier's exuberant Opéra (1860–1875) and Henri Labrouste's Bibliothèque Ste.-Geneviéve (1838–1850), both in Paris, united those lessons with contemporary technology. The Eiffel Tower (1887–1889), by Gustave Eiffel, epitomized the celebration of modern materials and their logical assembly. Conversely, William Morris, the most significant British voice at the time, protested against the social upheaval and shoddy craftsmanship associated with the Industrial Revolution. His own home, The Red House (1859–1860) in Bexleyheath, Kent, designed by Philip Webb, exemplified his Arts and Crafts Movement with informal, vernacularly derived forms and materials that hearkened back to a simpler time.

American architects adapted these British ideas to their own context. Balloon-frame construction (pre-cut timber studs connected by machine-made nails), which was sheathed with wooden shingles, allowed more informal, open interior layouts that were easy to heat with American central heating systems and easy to cool during the hot American summers. The epitome of the American Shingle Style was the Mrs. M. F. Stoughton House (1882–1883) in Cambridge, Massachusetts, by Henry H. Richardson. Americans continued to take the lead in residential design with the work of Frank Lloyd Wright, whose inspiration came from nature, simple geometries, and exotic cultures. Wright's F. C. Robie House (1908–1910) in Chicago climaxed his search for the "Prairie House." The building's strong horizontality and locally inspired ornament harmonized with the prairie of the Midwest. Abstracting Japanese and other prototypes, he created transitional zones that wove together exterior and interior space and effortlessly connected interior spaces around the central hearth.

Modernism

Seeking to express contemporary life and technology, modern architects increasingly relied on modern

The Seagram Building relies on a limited palette of exquisite materials arranged according to a strict three-dimensional grid, thereby demonstrating Mies van der Rohe's maxim "less is more." Photo by David M. Breiner.

materials, exposed structure, and undecorated compositions that were open and asymmetrical. Many designers searched for schemes that would be universally valid in a world made more homogeneous by technology. The results spanned from a machine-like precision to an organic expression of use and/or place.

Iron and steel structural frames increasingly transformed architecture beginning in the late nineteenth century. European Art Nouveau designers copied natural forms and exposed the sinuous iron structure in their glass-filled buildings, such as Victor Horta's Tassel House (1892–1893) in Brussels,

Belgium. In American cities the demand for space, the need to cluster offices, and the desire to create bold symbols of business set the stage for modern skyscraper construction. Tall buildings depended on the passenger elevator and the development of metallic cage construction that was fireproofed, insulated, and ornamented in brick, stone, or terracotta. Louis Sullivan's Guaranty Building (1894–1895) in Buffalo, New York, exemplified early attempts to devise a visually coherent solution to a new building type. Ludwig Mies van der Rohe, the master of the steel and glass skyscraper, pared away visual clutter to express the purity and careful proportions of the steel skeletons, as exhibited in his Seagram Building (1954–1958) in New York City. Other building types were similarly transformed by metal construction, for example Kenzo Tange's steel tensile suspension design for the National Gymnasium (1961–1964) in Tokyo, Japan.

The rediscovery of concrete as a primary building material and the innovative addition of metal bars to create reinforced concrete structures expanded the scope of modern architecture. Le Corbusier (born Charles-Edouard Jeanneret) established his international reputation with machine-age designs like the pristine concrete box of the Villa Savoye (1928–1929), near Paris; and later he led the expressionistic Brutalist movement with the aggressive, roughly finished concrete forms of the Capitol Complex (1950–1965) in Chandigarh, India. The contours and textures of subsequent reinforced concrete buildings ranged from the soaring openness of Jørn Utzon's Opera House (1956–1973) in Sydney, Australia, to the contemplative enclosure of Tadao Ando's Koshino House (1979–1981) in Hyogo, Japan.

Over time architects increased their use of glass from the exterior "curtain" (non-load-bearing) walls of Walter Gropius's Bauhaus Building (1925–1926) in Dessau, Germany, to the strut- and mullion-free glazed exterior of Norman Foster's Willis Faber Dumas Office Building (1975) in Ipswich, United Kingdom.

Some highly successful twentieth-century architects gained respect by adapting modern, universal themes to local conditions and cultures in their work. Among the most noteworthy were Alvar Aalto's Civic Center (1949–1952) in Säynätsalo, Finland; Louis Kahn's National Assembly Building (1962–1974) in Dacca, Bangladesh; and Renzo Piano's Jean-Marie Tjibaou Cultural Center (1991–1998) in Nouméa, New Caledonia.

Architecture Enters the Twenty-First Century

Contemporary architectural trends continue to respond to the issues of culture and technology.

An example of tensile architecture: the Elrey Jeppesen Terminal at Denver's International Airport uses steel cables and Teflon-coated fiberglass to create an airy interior, while the exterior mimics nearby peaks of the Rockies. Photo by David M. Breiner.

The Jean-Marie Tjibaou Cultural Center is an exemplar of contemporary hybrid solutions, combining diverse perspectives of design and the shell-like vernacular huts of local villages. Photo by Susan I. Frostén.

Like many leading architects, Rem Koolhaas has questioned societal beliefs and institutions in his Netherlands Dance Theater (1987), The Hague. Innovative solutions for structure and interior illumination aided the design of Norman Foster Associates giant Hong Kong Bank (1986) in Hong Kong, China. Tensile membrane structure, such as the Denver (Colorado) International Airport (1994) by C. W. Fentress, J. H. Bradburn & Associates, allows large spaces to be enclosed, while the curving structural steel columns of Beijing's National Stadium (the Bird's Nest)—designed for the 2008 Olympics by the Swiss firm Herzog & de Meuron in collaboration with Chinese artist and architect Ai Weiwei—weave a permeable outer layer that can be crossed or even climbed, allowing people to feel absorbed rather than smothered by the enormous structure. Digitized imaging software facilitated the titanium-clad design of Frank Gehry's Guggenheim Museum (1997) in Bilbao, Spain.

In the growing trend of "green" or ecologically sustainable design, designers conserve materials and energy, provide occupants with abundant fresh air and natural light, and carefully manage waste. Among the best-known examples is William McDonough & Associates Offices for Gap, Inc. (1997) in San Bruno, California, with its careful siting, vegetated roof, and other "green" elements. Kenneth Yeang's Menara Mesiniaga Building (1991) in Kuala Lumpur, Malaysia, connects sustainable design with the local traditions of Southeast Asia.

A third trend is the revival in vernacular traditions that has been building since at least Hassan Fathy's design for the Village of New Gourna (1945–1948) at Luxor, Egypt. In the United States vernacularism has inspired the pedestrian-friendly "new urbanism" movement publicized by the design of Seaside, Florida (begun 1981), by Andres Duany and Elizabeth Plater-Zyberk.

David M. BREINER
Philadelphia University

See also Architecture, Vernacular; Art—Ancient Greece and Rome; Art—European; Art—Japan; Art—Pre-Columbian Central and South America

Further Reading

Benevolo, L. (1978). *The architecture of the Renaissance* (2 vols.). (J. Landry, Trans). Boulder, CO: Westview.

Blunt, A. (Ed.). (1988). *Baroque and Rococo architecture and decoration*. Hertfordshire, U.K.: Wordsworth Editions.

Conant, K. J. (1987). *Carolingian and Romanesque architecture: 800–1200*. Baltimore, MD: Penguin.

Curtis, J. W. R. (1996). *Modern architecture since 1900* (3rd ed.). Oxford, U.K.: Phaidon.

Doordan, D. P. (2001). *Twentieth-century architecture.* Upper Saddle River, NJ: Prentice Hall/Harry N. Abrams.

Fletcher,B. (1996). *A history of architecture* (Rev. ed.). Oxford, U.K. and Boston: Architectural Press.

Grodecki, L. (1977). *Gothic architecture.* (I. M. Paris, Trans.). New York: Harry N. Abrams.

Kostof, S. (1995). *A history of architecture* (2nd ed.). New York: Oxford University Press.

Krautheimer, R. (1986). *Early Christian and Byzantine architecture.* Harmondsworth, U.K. and Baltimore: Penguin.

Kruft, H.-W. (1994). *A history of architectural theory from Vitruvius to the present* (R. Taylor, Trans.). London: Zwemmer; New York: Princeton Architectural Press.

Lloyd, S., Müller, H. W., & Martin, R. (1974). *Ancient architecture: Mesopotamia, Egypt, Crete, Greece.* New York: Harry N. Abrams.

MacDonald, W. (1982/1986). *The architecture of the Roman Empire.* (Rev. ed., 2 vols.). New Haven, CT: Yale University Press.

Mainstone, R. (1998). *Developments in structural form.* Oxford, U.K. and Boston: Architectural Press.

Mark, R. (Ed.). (1993). *Architectural technology up to the Scientific Revolution: The art and structure of large-scale buildings.* Cambridge, MA: MIT Press.

Middleton, R., & Watkin, D. (1987). *Neoclassical and 19th century architecture.* (Rev. ed.). New York: Harry N. Abrams.

Moffett, M., Fazio, M., & Wodehouse, L. *Buildings across time: An introduction to world architecture.* London: McGraw-Hill.

Oliver, P. (Ed.). (1997). *Encyclopedia of vernacular architecture of the world* (3 vols.). New York: Cambridge University Press.

Placzek, A. K., (Ed.). (1982). *Macmillan encyclopedia of architects* (4 vols.). New York: Macmillan.

Raeburn, M. (Ed.). (1988). *Architecture of the Western World.* Leicester, U.K.: Popular Press.

Salvadori, M., & Heller, R. (1986). *Structure in architecture.* Englewood Cliffs, NJ: Prentice-Hall.

Trachtenberg, M., & Hyman, I. (2002). *Architecture from prehistory to postmodernity* (2nd ed.). Upper Saddle River, NJ: Prentice-Hall.

Turner, J. (Ed.). (1959–1987). *Encyclopedia of world art* (16 vols.). New York: McGraw-Hill.

Architecture, Vernacular

The term *vernacular architecture* applies to structures built based on local traditions and skills passed down through generations, not on the designs of professional architects. Building techniques vary widely depending on function, location, and available materials. Although historians and educators have largely overlooked vernacular architecture, its practice today continues to shape most of the world's built environment.

Vernacular architecture is the term now internationally applied to buildings that are constructed according to indigenous traditions rather than a professional design. Most of the world's buildings fall into this category; people of innumerable cultures have built structures to meet their physical, social, economic, and spiritual needs. Because many cultures have not been literate, or literacy has been confined to the elites, vernacular traditions have often remained unrecorded and their history is difficult to ascertain. Archaeological excavations have frequently concentrated on religious, palatial, and military sites, but at Sumer for example, the ancient Mesopotamian region of southern Iraq, archaeologists have uncovered dwellings dating back to the fifth millennium BCE, revealing plans, structures, and spatial organization that are similar to settlements extant today.

Certain examples of early art, such as tomb paintings of Middle Egypt or Roman mosaics in Carthage, on the gulf of Tunis, depict the materials indigenous peoples used in their buildings, including reed thatch, earthen bricks, and clay tiles. Ancient artifacts may also illustrate vernacular building styles; a third-century-CE bronze mirror from Nara, Japan, bears images of house and granary types that are still built in Southeast Asia. Clay models of houses placed in graves in Greece, Mesopotamia, and China, some including figurines, show their structure and indicate how they were used. While unbroken sequences of the history of buildings have sometimes been hard to establish, dendrochronology (tree-ring dating) and carbon dating have been applied in European vernacular studies to give a record spanning two millennia. In some countries, wills, inventories, and other documents have disclosed details that relate to property. Inevitably however, the history of vernacular building in much of the world is undocumented, and there is much room for research in the field.

Built to Meet Needs

Building traditions differ widely across the globe, but some requirements are common, mainly the provision of shelter for families. It is not known how many dwellings currently exist in the world; estimates range between 800 million and 1 billion to accommodate the 2009 population of more than 6 billion people. Of these, over three-fourths are vernacular, built by the owners or by skilled members of their communities, whose traditions in building have been passed from generation to generation.

Caves may have provided the earliest dwellings; evidence of cave occupancy in Spain and France dates from Paleolithic times. (In 2009, some 50 million people live in caves, particularly in China, but also in Europe, North Africa, and the Middle East.) Other peoples who hunted game and gathered fruits lived in the forests where they made temporary shelters of branches and leaves, as the Orang Asli of Malaysia or the East African Hadza still do. Adapting to local conditions, peoples such as the Evenki of Siberia made their huts of wood from the taiga, or in the case of the seal-hunting Inuit of northern Canada, built domes of snow blocks.

Traveling in more arid regions, many tribes camped under tents made from strips of woven goat's hair; such "black tents" are still used by the Bedouin of Arabia. Desert nomads move with flocks of camels or goats, often by prearranged routes so that the sparse vegetation is not overgrazed and may recover. In more fertile regions such as the grasslands of Central Asia, the Kyrgyz and Mongols live in the yurt or *ger*, a dome raised on a cylinder of lattices covered with large felts that are tied in place. After a stay of weeks they dismantle the domes and move to new pastures where the women, who make all the components, rapidly re-erect them. As the examples of nomads indicate, the kind of dwelling used by a culture is partly conditioned by the economy in which its makers subsist.

Mankind cannot survive without water, and many cultures live close to rivers, often in the valleys or near the sea. Fishing peoples may construct dwellings on stilts or piles over the water, enabling them to protect their fishing grounds. Some, like sea nomads of the Philippines, live on boats as much as on land. The majority of vernacular buildings, however, are built by sedentary peoples who live in one place and who may be engaged in agriculture, livestock-raising, and the marketing of produce, or in craft occupations such as pottery or weaving, that meet material needs.

Although some vernacular buildings, including farmhouses, are found in relative isolation, most are located in hamlets and villages or in small towns and urban neighborhoods. They may house nuclear families of parents and children, common in North America or Western Europe. In much of the world, however, extended families of three generations, or the spouses and children of siblings, all live together. Suitably large houses may be built for them, as in

Nomadic tribes in fertile regions live in dwellings such as yurts, with easy-to-assemble components that allow for quick moves to new pastures.

Kashmir or western Anatolia, or several single-cell huts may be enclosed in compounds, as is common in West Africa.

Within the farmyard or compound, economic functions are accommodated in special structures. Among the most frequent are granaries, raised above ground to repel damp and rodents. Stables for horses and barns for draft animals or for wintering cattle are customary, though recently many have been adapted to take mechanical equipment. Among vernacular buildings that functioned until the early twentieth century were blacksmith's workshops and outdoor baking ovens, while watermills and windmills were widely used in Europe to provide the power for grinding corn or pigments, draining wetlands, and sawing timber. Many of these functional buildings were lost with industrialization, but others, such as potteries and carpenters' workshops, continue to be productive in many parts of the world.

Numerous vernacular buildings are constructed for social functions that relate to status, power, or belief. A special residence may be constructed by some cultures in honor of a chief, a prince, or a spiritual leader, perhaps as a larger version of the customary dwelling. In some instances, such as the Dyak peoples of Borneo or the indigenous forest cultures of western Amazonia, whole villages are accommodated in single buildings, usually called longhouses, in which all the families occupy spaces beneath one roof. Often the families belong to one clan, and the spaces may be arranged in hierarchical order.

Some buildings may have a ceremonial function, and in settlements the world over prominence is given to buildings that relate to religious beliefs. Temples, mosques, and churches house worshippers, while shrines protect votive objects or mark sacred sites. Priests from such religions may officiate at the selection of a site, bless the stages in the building of a house, and preside at a ceremony to mark its completion. Often the dwelling is itself symbolic, being perceived as having cosmic or anthropomorphic associations, as is the case in Hindu tradition. This serves the important function of reaffirming for the occupants the spiritual values of the culture to which they belong.

The great variety in the size, forms, and construction of houses and related buildings throughout the world is largely due to the diverse nature of specific cultures. Some require communal rooms in which whole families live together, while others have separate entrances to distinct living areas for males and females. The differences are also attributable to respective economies: Chinese hill farmers require accommodation for their livestock and their families, and the structures they build are quite different from the narrow frontages of shophouses—usually two stories high, and built in rows connected by deep courtyards—that are typical of Chinese urban neighborhoods. But whatever the culture and its people's needs, buildings are strongly conditioned by the environments in which they are situated.

Responding to the Environment

Vernacular buildings reflect the peculiarities of their locations, from grassland steppes, deserts, and plains to forests, valleys, lakesides, or mountains. Where land is freely available compounds may spread, but where sites are constricted houses of two or three stories may be constructed, some having stepped levels where gradients are steep. While the majority of circular-plan buildings have a conical roof of poles converging at the apex, the roofs of rectangular and square-plan buildings are pitched to a central ridge. With modifications in plan, such as a T, an L, a square, or a rectangle defining a courtyard, the majority of pitched-roof vernacular buildings take forms that are found with many variants worldwide. In tropical Sumatra (in Southeast Asia), for example, upswept roof ridges on the houses of the Minangkabau end in finials or small spires (a symbol of the horns of the sacred water buffalo). These roofs are effective in expelling warm air and keeping the interiors cool.

Climate is an important environmental factor in the design of vernacular buildings, but extremes of climate and natural hazards can do structural damage, with high winds lifting off roof cladding in the Caribbean and flood waters reducing clay walls in

ARCHITECTURE, VERNACULAR · 15

Houses are built to live in, not to look on; therefore, let use be preferred before uniformity, except where both may be had. • **Francis Bacon (1561–1626)**

Bangladesh. Volcanic eruptions threaten Central America and earthquakes reduce literally thousands of buildings to rubble in Turkey and other seismic regions, though frequently it is the vernacular buildings rather than the concrete ones that enable people to survive a major disaster. In Kashmir and Peru, technologies have been developed that permit buildings to be flexible in earthquakes, but as natural disasters are unpredictable and may not recur, the main concern of most builders is to cope with the vagaries of the seasons and the weather.

In humid tropical climates, houses are constructed so as to encourage air circulation, while those in arid climates may be sited to reduce exposure to the sun; buildings placed around courtyards, for instance, offer continual shade during the day. In temperate and cold regions thick earth walls retain solar heat and warm the interiors; deep layers of insulating thatch are also used. Passive cooling devices such as wind scoops are used in the Middle East, while radiant stoves keep houses warm in the extreme winters of Central Europe. By such means builders have been able to create comfortable internal conditions. Even so, they are dependent on the material resources available to them, and these also exert their influence on the forms of the building.

Perhaps the most widely used material in vernacular building is earth. Whether it is molded to shape, rammed between wooden planked molds, mixed with straw and compressed in adobe blocks, or fired in kilns and made into bricks, earth is ubiquitous and employed in every continent. Factors such as particle size affect its suitability but in some regions, such as Yemen or southern Morocco, multistoried buildings of rammed earth have lasted centuries and are still being constructed. Clay is also used in combination with interwoven panels of willow or hazel wood in the technique, common in Britain, known as wattle-and-daub. Although techniques of molded mud can be used to make vaults, flat roofs on clay buildings are usually constructed with log poles, such as in the pueblos of the southwestern United States. In regions such as Tunisia or Egypt, where there is little wood, palm trunks are used.

Stone is strong and suitable for constructing walls when pieces of manageable size can be found, but it less widely employed than clay. Time-consuming to quarry and heavy to transport, stone has been principally used in elite architecture rather than in the vernacular. Brick is an economic alternative to stone, with standardized sizes and techniques for laying courses, and the use of mortar to ensure stability. Brick building came to England from the Netherlands, and later the British introduced the technique to Africa. Brick and tile traditions were developed independently in China, where the weight of roofs was often borne by internal wood frames rather than by brick walls.

Although a material may be accessible another may take preference over it for economic reasons, or on account of its relative suitability. Finland, for instance, has immense resources of granite but its vernacular buildings were built of wood from the vast forests. Japanese builders constructed their traditional *minka* houses in timber, even though stone was available; for adherents of the Japanese Shinto religion the choice of a living material was a spiritual matter.

Timber has been extensively used and is renewable over time, though the destruction of the forests makes building wood structures unfeasible in many countries. Log construction, with round or squared timber notched to provide secure and interlocking corner joints, is basic to the vernacular traditions of Scandinavia, eastern Europe, and the Alps, from where it was brought by migrants to the United States. An alternative system is timber framing, in which a box-like skeleton is made of jointed wood, the panels being filled with wattle-and-daub, or with bricks laid in patterns as they are in northern Germany.

In some tropical regions timber is less readily obtainable, so bamboo, which is technically a grass, is grown and used for building. Fast growing and flexible, it is employed as a structural material in Southeast Asia and Indonesia, but it is also stripped and made into matting for lightweight walls and roof covering. Palm leaves are often used for wall cladding and for thatching roofs in the Pacific islands, but the principal thatching materials in much of the world are grass or reed. Bundled and secured in overlapping layers, thatch provides a water-resistant cover as effectively for a rectangular plan as for a circular one. Vernacular builders have employed natural materials for centuries, but by replanting and recycling them, and by passing on their practices to succeeding generations, they have been able to remain in the same locations without depleting the resources of their environments.

Vernacular architecture has shaped the buildings of the world's peoples throughout history, but it has been largely overlooked by architectural historians and educators who may dismiss it as primitive. Though most traditions could benefit from improved servicing with electricity, piped water, and modern sanitation, vernacular architecture still has a major part to play in the development of a built environment that is both responsive and responsible in an era of rapid population growth.

Paul OLIVER
University of Huddersfield

See also Architecture

Further Reading

Bourdier, J. P., & Al-Sayyad, N. (Eds.). (1989). *Dwellings, settlements and tradition: Cross-cultural perspectives.* Lanham, MD: United Press of America.

Bourgeois, J. L., & Pelos, C. (1996). *Spectacular vernacular: The adobe tradition.* New York: Aperture Foundation.

Fathy, H. (1986). *Natural energy and vernacular architecture: Principles and examples with reference to hot arid climates.* Chicago: University of Chicago Press.

Oliver, P. (2002). *Dwellings: The vernacular house world-wide.* London: Phaidon Press

Oliver, P. (Ed.). (1997). *The encyclopedia of vernacular architecture of the world (3 vols.).* Cambridge, U.K.: Cambridge University Press.

Rapoport, A. (1969). *House form and culture.* Englewood Cliffs, NJ: Prentice Hall.

Spence, R., & Cook, D. J. (1983). *Building materials in developing countries.* New York: John Wiley & Sons.

Waterson, R. (1990). *The living house: An anthropology of architecture in south-east Asia.* Singapore: Oxford University Press.

Art—Africa

Since ancient times trade routes from Europe, the Middle East, and Asia disseminated ideas, objects, and cultures—as well as Christianity and Islam—to the African continent. African art, which reflects all of these influences and exchanges, is an important lens through which to view world history, and an important field of study in its own right.

Africa, a participant in the global spread of objects, ideas, and people that characterizes the world today, has produced some of the world's earliest preserved works of art and some of its most exciting contemporary ones. The study of African art began in the early twentieth century, and for much of its development focused solely on the area south of the Sahara and on art forms rooted in precolonial culture, which was seen as static and timeless. Egypt and northern Africa were seen as separate entities. The colonial and postcolonial eras were viewed as periods of decline in African art, due to what were seen as negative outside influences in materials, techniques, subject matter, style, and patronage. In contrast, recent scholarship takes a more inclusive and historically dynamic view. The continent is treated as an integrated whole and the changes of the past century are seen as continuing the evolution that African art has experienced throughout its history. Research today focuses on the artistic interconnections between geographic regions, ethnic groups, and time periods, and contemporary art is given equal footing with so-called traditional forms.

Ancient African Art

The earliest known works of art from Africa are the paintings of animals found on rocks in the Apollo 11 cave in southern Namibia (so-named because they were discovered in July 1969 when the spacecraft landed on the moon). These have been dated 26,500–24,300 BCE, making them as old or older than the Paleolithic cave paintings of western Europe. Rock paintings and engravings are also found in East Africa and North Africa, particularly in what is now the Sahara; these depictions of animals and humans document the change from the lush, well-watered grasslands of around 8000 BCE to the arid conditions we know today. As the Sahara became drier, its human inhabitants were forced to move, and many of them settled in the Nile Valley, where they contributed to the development of ancient Egyptian and Nubian culture and art.

The earliest known sculptures from Africa south of the Sahara are those from the Nok culture of northern Nigeria, dated 800 BCE to 200 CE. Despite their early date, the Nok sculptures already show visual elements characteristic of African art from later periods. They depict facial features and body parts as abstract geometric shapes, and they alter the natural proportions of the body to emphasize the head. They portray the elaborate hairstyles and beaded body ornaments that are also an important part of the dress of many later African peoples.

During the first millennium CE the cultural features that characterized sub-Saharan African societies until the late nineteenth century were established, such as states based on sacred kingship, long-distance trade, urbanism (especially in west Africa), and various forms of social and religious organization. All of these contributed to the evolution of African visual arts.

West Africa's first city, Jenne-Jeno, was well established by 800 CE in the inland delta region of the

Niger River in present-day Mali. Sophisticated and expressive terracotta sculptures were produced there, primarily between the thirteenth and sixteenth centuries. Some depict figures with the trappings of leadership, others are possibly in positions of prayer, and still others appears tormented by diseases or snakes. Little is known about the function of these figures, since the majority of them have been illicitly excavated. Archaeologists believe they were used in domestic rituals, perhaps to ensure the solid foundation of a house and the family within it. Jenne-Jeno was part of a vast trading network that stretched north across the Sahara and south to the forests along the coast of west Africa. There, the site of Igbo-Ukwu in southeastern Nigeria produced lavishly decorated bronze objects using an indigenously developed lost-wax technique. (The technique involves coating a wax model in plaster and clay, leaving a small hole in the bottom; when the model is heated, the clay and plaster harden, and the wax melts (i.e., gets "lost" through the hole. Then the sculptor pours molten bronze into the cavity, and when the bronze cools, chips away the outer layer of plaster and clay.) Made in the ninth or tenth century, these were the regalia of a local priest-king. The city of Ile-Ife in southwestern Nigeria, still a political and spiritual center today, had its artistic flowering between 1000 and 1400. During that period the city's artists created sculptures whose pronounced naturalism stands out from most other African art, past or present. Most of these idealized portraits were made of clay, but others were made of brass and copper (which is not found naturally in Nigeria), demonstrating Ile-Ife's long-distance trading connections.

Christianity and Islam were introduced into Africa soon after their inception and quickly found expression in African art and architecture. At first African Christianity was limited to Egypt and Ethiopia, where the rock-cut churches of Lalibela (in Ethiopia) and boldly colored illuminated manuscripts and icons constitute important contributions to Christian art. The Great Mosque at Kairouan in Tunisia, built of stone in the ninth century, is one of the oldest mosques in existence. The Great

Frédéric Christol, *Animal Engraved on a Stone* (an early twentieth-century drawing of an artifact in the Museum of Cape Town). From *South Africa. With 150 Drawings and Sketches by the Author.*

Mosque at Jenne, the Muslim city that arose next to Jenne-Jeno, is typical of west African Islamic architecture in its use of sun-dried mud bricks and strongly projecting engaged pillars and towers along its facade.

When the earliest European explorers arrived in Africa in the fifteenth and sixteenth centuries, they found several thriving kingdoms as well as smaller social units producing notable works of art. In the Kingdom of Benin in Nigeria, ivory carvers and brass casters produced thousands of works of art for use in court rituals that strengthened the spiritual power, authority, and grandeur of the Oba, or divine king. Notable among these were brass heads representing ancestors, ivory tusks carved in relief with figures from Benin history, and brass palace plaques that depicted the panoply of the Benin court hierarchy. In the Kongo Kingdom luxurious textiles of raffia fiber and fly whisks made of ivory distinguished the rulers and other wealthy and powerful people. Brass crucifixes modeled after European prototypes testified to the adaptation to local styles and ideology of objects introduced by Christian missionaries. At Great Zimbabwe, monumental stone buildings, rare elsewhere in sub-Saharan Africa, were created as the residences and ritual centers for rulers from 1300 to 1450.

The Modern Era

Most of the African art known today through museum collections and publications was made in the nineteenth and twentieth centuries. This was a period of great change in Africa, as political, religious, and cultural practices were forced to adapt to new conditions brought about by colonialism and, later, independence. Nevertheless, the art made at this time, and the context in which it was used, have formed the image of "traditional" African art that has dominated the study of the field. The following examples provide only a brief glimpse of the variety and complexity of African art in this period. Many of these art forms still thrive, although they continue to change, as they always have, in response to new circumstances.

The Bamana people of Mali are primarily subsistence farmers who live in independent villages led by male elders. Their art consists of wooden masks and sculptures made for the performances and rituals of men's initiation associations. These associations embody spiritual powers, and their members wield social and political authority within Bamana villages. One such association, Komo, utilizes large wooden helmet masks depicting fantastic animals with projecting jaws and domed heads. Komo masks are covered with a thick crust of sacrificial materials, such as animal blood, plant matter, and sacred earths. These materials, along with added animal parts such as horns, tusks, feathers, and quills, imbue Komo masks with spiritual force and refer to secret knowledge used to keep the village safe from physical or spiritual harm. In contrast to the mask's intimidating appearance and serious function, the wooden headdresses of the Chi Wara association are intricate and elegant, and the performances in which they are worn entertaining. They represent stylized antelopes that honor the mythical being that brought agriculture to the Bamana.

Unlike the Bamana, the Akan people of Ghana are organized into highly centralized and hierarchical states headed by hereditary chiefs who have maintained their status and authority, although much of

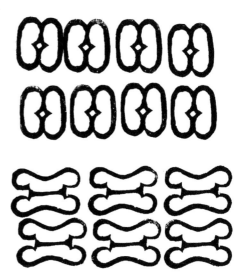

Ancient stamp-pattern designs from Ghana lend themselves for use in both fabric and paper printmaking.

their power has been taken over by Ghana's national government. Akan arts reflect the wealth derived from the region's vast gold deposits and the multifaceted concepts of power associated with Akan chiefs. Prominent among Akan art forms intended for use by chiefs: cast-gold ornaments and staffs, and other regalia covered with gold leaf—all of which depict animals, humans, and objects that illustrate proverbs concerning the nature and responsibilities of leadership. Brilliantly colored and elaborately woven silk and, more recently, rayon textiles called *kente* are also worn by Akan elite to signify their power, wealth, and status.

The arts of the Kuba people of the Democratic Republic of the Kongo are similarly focused on leadership and power. Kuba kings are depicted in idealized portraits carved of wood that are believed to house their spiritual essence. Titleholders wear elaborate garments made of woven, appliquéd, and embroidered raffia fiber textiles along with accessories and regalia covered with cowrie shells, glass beads, and feathers. Kuba wood masks, worn at initiations and funerals, are similarly covered with a dazzling profusion of colors, patterns, and textures. It should be noted that versions of all the art forms mentioned in this article—including the regalia intended only for Kuba titleholders—are made for the foreign market.

Works made by the Zulu people of South Africa, pastoralists who rose to power in the early nineteenth century on the basis of their military strength, reflect yet another aspect of African art. The Zulu rarely make masks or sculptures; utilitarian objects, such as wooden headrests, milk pails, meat plates, and ceramic beer vessels, predominate. These are often decorated with chevron patterns or raised bumps that refer to the ancestors and to herds of cattle that confer wealth and status. Garments and ornaments decorated with colorful glass beads in geometric patterns express the wearer's prestige, gender, and marital status. During the struggle against apartheid, some black South Africans wore beaded garments and ornaments to express their opposition to the white government's ethnic and racial policies. More recently beaded objects have been made as part of the effort to promote awareness of the problem of HIV/AIDS in South Africa.

At the beginning of the twentieth century European avant-garde artists, such as Pablo Picasso and Henri Matisse in France and Ernst Ludwig Kirchner and Max Pechstein in Germany, discovered works of African art in ethnographic museums and curio shops. The geometric forms, freedom from naturalistic representations, and vibrant colors of the African objects corresponded to artistic concerns in their own work, and provided a source of inspiration for European art movements such as Cubism and German Expressionism.

During the colonial period, government policies, the spread of Christianity and Islam, and new forms of education, employment, and health care often undermined the structures of political, economic, religious, and family life that had been the context for creating and using art in Africa. Art forms and cultural practices adapted to the new circumstances.

Helmet Mask, "Mulwalwa." Democratic Republic of Kongo, Southern Kuba, nineteenth or early twentieth century. Wood, paint, raffia, brass nails. Collection of the Ethnological Museum, Berlin-Dahlem.

Artists began to incorporate newly available materials (such as oil-based enamel paints, factory-woven cloth, and chemical dyes) and newly observed imagery (such as Western-style clothing and automobiles). These innovations demonstrate the vitality and resilience of African art and exemplify its long history of adapting to changing circumstances.

Trends and New Expressions

These developments intensified after World War II as the movement for liberation from colonial rule gained

strength and finally culminated in independence for most African nations around 1960. As more and more Africans were exposed to European modes of education and art production in the second half of the twentieth century, distinctive new forms of (and contexts for) African art emerged. Expatriate Europeans in the 1960s established artist workshops in several parts of Africa. The Mbari Mbayo workshop in Oshogbo, Nigeria, and a workshop founded at the National Gallery of Salisbury, Rhodesia (now Harare, Zimbabwe), are prime examples. Participants were provided with materials and studio space, but training was deliberately minimal to allow the artists' innate creativity to emerge. The results, by artists such as Twins Seven Seven of Nigeria (b. 1944) and Thomas Mukarobgwa of Zimbabwe (1924–1999), emphasize abstraction, expressive color or form, and mythic subject matter.

Another trend in modern African art developed out of the painted shop signs ubiquitous in African towns and cities. In the genre known as "urban popular painting," works are often mass-produced and sold to African patrons as home decorations. They share the flat colors, emphasis on consumer goods, and incorporation of text seen in advertising art, and the intuitive perspective and inconsistent shading and scale of artists without formal art education. Tshibumba Kanda Matulu (b. mid-1940s; missing since early 1980s) of the Democratic Republic of Kongo is one of the most accomplished of the urban popular artists. In addition to landscapes and other idealized subjects, he produced a moving series of paintings on the history of his country.

An increasing number of African artists have studied art in colleges or art schools either in Africa or abroad; their work reflects trends in art that are international in scope. In the 1960s, Bruce Onobrakpeya (b. 1932), Uche Okeke (b. 1933), and other Nigerian artists developed a philosophy of art called "natural synthesis" that was based on the fusion of indigenous African and modern European art styles. Their works expressed both the modernity of their newly independent nation and the traditions of African culture. Similar movements arose across Africa.

Since the 1990s, African artists have questioned the relevance of ethnic or national labels and even the relevance of African origin itself. Artists such as Yinka Shonibare (b. 1962 in London, to Nigerian parents), Ghada Amer (b. 1963 in Cairo, Egypt), and Berni Searle (b. 1964 in South Africa) investigate these and other concerns of the postcolonial and postmodern world through the means of conceptual art, using installation, performance, video, photography, and other worldwide contemporary art practices. When seen in its entirety, African art at the beginning of the twenty-first century is a complex mixture of local and global concerns, and ancient and innovative forms.

Kate EZRA
Columbia College, Chicago

Further Reading

Ben-Amos, P. G. (1995). *The art of Benin.* Washington, DC: Smithsonian Institution Press.

Beumers, E., & Koloss, H.-J. (Eds.). (1992). *Kings of Africa: Art and authority in central Africa.* Utrecht, The Netherlands: Foundation Kings of Africa.

Blier, S. P. (1998). *The royal arts of Africa: The majesty of form.* New York: Harry N. Abrams.

Bravmann, R. (1983). *African Islam.* Washington, DC: Smithsonian Institution Press.

Cole, H. C., & Ross, D. H. (1977). *The arts of Ghana.* Los Angeles: Fowler Museum of Cultural History, University of California at Los Angeles.

Colleyn, J.-P. (Ed.). (2001). *Bamana: The art of existence in Mali.* New York: Museum for African Art.

Coulson, D., & Campbell, A. (2001). *African rock art: Paintings and engravings on stone.* New York: Harry N. Abrams.

Enwezor, O. (Ed.). (2001). *The short century: Independence and liberation movements in Africa, 1945–1994.* Munich, Germany: Prestel Verlag and Museum Villag Stuck.

Eyo, E., & Willett, F. (1980). *Treasures of ancient Nigeria.* New York: Alfred A. Knopf, in association with the Detroit Institute of Arts.

Ezra, K. (1992). *The royal art of Benin: The Perls Collection in the Metropolitan Museum of Art*. New York: Metropolitan Museum of Art.

Garlake, P. (2002). *Early art and architecture of Africa*. Oxford, U.K.: Oxford University Press.

Hassan, S., & Oguibe, O. (2001). *Authentic ex-centric: Conceptualism in contemporary African art*. Ithaca, NY: Forum for African Arts.

Heldman, M., & Munro-Hay, S. C. (1993). *African Zion: The sacred art of Ethiopia*. New Haven, CT: Yale University Press.

Kasfir, S. L. (1999). *Contemporary African art*. London: Thames & Hudson.

Nettleton, A., & Hammond-Tooke, D. (Eds.). (1989). *African art in southern Africa. From tradition to township*. Johannesburg, South Africa: Ad. Donker.

Oguibe, O., & Enwezor, O. (Eds.). (1999). *Reading the contemporary: African art from theory to the marketplace*. London: Institute of International Visual Arts.

Phillips, T. (Ed.). (1995). *Africa: The art of a continent*. Munich, Germany: Prestel Verlag.

Sieber, R., & Walker, R. A. (1988). *African art in the cycle of life*. Washington, DC: National Museum of African Art, Smithsonian Institution Press.

Visona, M., Poyner, R., Cole, H. M., & Harris, M. D. (2001). *A history of art in Africa*. New York: Harry N. Abrams.

Art—Ancient Greece and Rome

Concepts of strength and dignity—and of ideal human beauty—inspired the sculptors who shaped early Greek monumental architecture and sculpture from marble. Romans, heavily influenced by the Etruscans (who themselves had borrowed from the Greeks), evoked traditional characteristics of the republic—economical, practical, structural—using concrete. Thus the art of both cultures embodies their age-old values.

The earliest monumental creations of classical Greece are the eighth-century BCE grave markers found in the Dipylon cemetery on the outskirts of ancient Athens. Their forms were familiar to everyone and had been for centuries as ordinary household pots used for storing food or mixing and decanting wine and water. Yet in their new context and in the hand of a truly inspired designer the experience created by them was of the very highest drama: these are not normal kitchen pots. They stand as tall as a man and as broad as a temple column. The drama of these monuments is generated by an unbelievable transformation in scale and is delivered to the viewer by a shocking disconnection between the expected and the experienced. The great Dipylon pots are uniquely valuable for understanding the most basic principles of Greek monumentality, because they represent first attempts. First attempts are significant because they represent conscious choices, not simply the repetition of tradition. And wherever conscious choice can be isolated there is the opportunity of uncovering meaning, for the question can be profitably asked, "Why did they solve the problem in this particular manner?"

The master of the first giant Dipylon pot might have asked himself the question, "How can I best design a monument that is suitable for marking and acknowledging the most profound of human transitions and transformations, from life to death, from flesh and blood to spiritual, from ephemeral to everlasting?" His answer was to create a monument that embodied a similarly incomprehensible transformation, both physical and functional, whose drama disorients the viewer, takes the viewer out of any normal, everyday frame of reference—transforms the viewer, and speaks through unambiguous metaphor of the passage from one state of being to the next. The transformation in scale and function of these great Dipylon pots lifts them out of the realm of everyday utility and into a higher, more symbolic, more universal realm. Their common reference to Homeric heroes in their painted decoration further monumentalizes these pots, further elevates them beyond the everyday.

Transformative Power: The Greek Temple

A similar conception of monumentality is expressed in Greek temple architecture, through the monumental transformation of the temple in the early seventh century BCE from a thatched and mud hut to a solid stone and terracotta colossus. This transformation first takes place in Corinth, which develops a distinctive style of pre-Doric monumental architecture that gradually evolves into the first full-fledged representative of the Doric order, the Temple of Artemis at Corfu (c. 580 BCE), a colony and dependency of Corinth. The transformative nature of Greek monumental architecture is enhanced by the innovation of the sculpted pediment, an invention attributed to the Corinthians by the poet Pindar (522–443 BCE) and seemingly confirmed by its earliest appearance on Corfu, a Corinthian colony and dependency. More than any other feature the early sculpted pediments with their great frontal monsters condition the spirit of approach to the temple: if the approach to the temple was intended to reflect the approach to divinity, the purpose of the monsters was to transform any pilgrims who dared approach, to transport them beyond the protective boundaries of everyday life and into the contemplation of the terrifying nature of divinity and their relationship to it. The purpose of the great emblematic sculptural groups in the pediments was—like religious ritual—the spiritual transformation of the worshipper. Over the course of the sixth century BCE the pedimental instruments of engagement and confrontation become diluted, metamorphose from monsters to more familiar, less intimidating, human-shaped figures, indicating a change in the conception of temple divinity, from abstract, nonanthropomorphic, and chthonic (relating to the underworld) to anthropomorphic Olympian sky gods. This gradual humanization of divinity and consequent divinization of humanity is a theme that unites much of Greek art.

Egyptian Influences

The nature of monumental Greek art and architecture was profoundly affected by the opening of the trading colony Naukratis in Egypt in the later seventh century BCE. From this new and intense contact with Egypt came the inspiration for the peristyle (the continuous colonnade) in Greek temple architecture. The peristyle gave architectural expression to one of the most basic rituals of Ionian cult activity, religious procession: like pedimental sculpture, religious procession serves as a transforming ritual that prepares the worshipper for the approach to divinity. Emulating the processional function of Egyptian colonnades, the colossal peristyles of Ionia led through their formal arrangement to the front of the temple, then to the axis, then to the interior. Peristyles were also adopted on the Doric mainland,

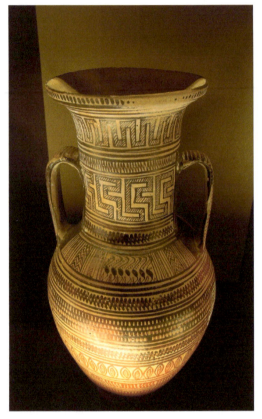

A late Attic amphora, or wine jug, dating to the eighth century BCE, exhibits geometric designs. Louvre, Sully Wing, Campagna Gallery. Photo by Marie-Lan Nguyen.

but in that context their nature was not processional. Instead, a sense of hieratic direction and procession was lent to early Doric architecture by its pedimental sculpture, which followed and further established the early Greek hierarchy of narrative and emblem in religious art: storytelling is associated with a secondary position, the more human realm, at the back of the temple, while the more abstract convention, the emblem, is appropriate for the suggestion of divinity at the front of the temple.

It was also through Naukratis that the Egyptian conception and technique of monumental freestanding

An ancient mural depicting a scene from Homer's *Odyssey*, one of many such Hellenistic works found on the Esquiline Hill, Rome.

sculpture was introduced to Greece. Beginning in the late seventh century, kouroi (male) and korai (female) appear as votives and grave markers and, perhaps, as cult images. There is probably a causal relationship between the appearance of this sculpture and the coincidental relegation of pottery to an almost exclusively non-monumental realm. The physical nature of kouroi and korai makes them particularly appropriate as indicators and inspirers of spiritual transition. Like the religious sculpture of Egypt, they are represented as highly formalized compositions, more religious emblem or hieroglyph than naturalistic representation of humans. Their tight symmetry and stylization intentionally and effectively separates them from the strictly human realm, removes them from the everyday, and places them in a mediating position between human and divine. On the other hand, as in vase painting and pedimental sculpture, an increasing interest in the examination of things human is witnessed in sixth-century freestanding sculpture in the increasingly naturalistic modeling of the body. This parallels the change to the more human conception of temple divinity as represented in pedimental sculpture, and reflects the increasingly central role humans play in the Greek conception of the cosmos.

The Classical Period

The increasingly detailed examination in art of the human condition, physical and emotional, continued unbroken into the classical period (beginning in 480 BCE with the Persian sack of the Athenian Acropolis). This movement toward naturalism, however, was potentially inimical to the goals of monumentality, as the goals of monumental art and architecture had always been to lift viewers out of the ordinary, beyond the everyday, and into the contemplation of forces greater than themselves: how could increasingly human representations lift humans beyond their own environment, inspire in them the contemplation and understanding of something superhuman, of the divine realm? This seems to have been recognized by the mid-fifth-century sculptor Polykleitos, who reintroduced the formal symmetry of kouroi to his compositions, though along diagonal axes rather than in the strictly vertical and horizontal framework of sixth-century sculpture. The decision of Phidias, the sculptor of the Parthenon, to ignore the developing techniques of representing individual characteristics of age, emotion, and character in favor of uniformly abstracted, ageless, "idealized" figures similarly indicates an analytical appreciation of the traditional character and techniques of monumental Greek art.

The Periclean building program on the Athenian Acropolis, undertaken in the aftermath of the Persian destruction of Athens, is perhaps the most elaborate expression of monumental art and architecture ever created in Greece. Its religious roots and purpose are evident in the detailed expression of religious procession through the organization of building types, the organization of their pedimental sculpture, and the incorporation of the processional language of Ionic temple architecture into the Doric tradition of the Acropolis. Its political and historical context and tradition are expressed through the many references to the Persian War, both metaphorical and literal, through the cults of legendary heroes, and through the use of the Ionic order as a reflection of Athens's ancient genetic and linguistic connections with Ionia and of its present position at the head of an Ionian alliance against the Persians. The explicit celebration of the accomplishments and traditions of the Athenians in the religious monuments of their central sanctuary is a remarkable deviation from canon and represents an extreme evolution of the humanization of divinity and divinization of humanity in Greek art and architecture.

After the hiatus of Phidian sculpture, the examination of the human condition in ever-increasing detail recommenced with renewed energy in the fourth century BCE and soon resulted in the monumental representation of generalized but, nevertheless, individual human beings. In the Hellenistic Age (the period beginning with the death of Alexander III of Macedon [Alexander the Great] in 323 BCE and ending with the Battle of Actium in 31 BCE) the gradual humanization of divinity in Greek art culminated in the worship and monumental representation of Hellenistic rulers as gods. Similarly, while mythical or divine representation or reference served as an elevating agent of monumentality in earlier Greek art, reference to, or even quotation of, the buildings and sculpture of the Periclean Acropolis became a common agent of monumentality in the official art and architecture of the Hellenistic kingdoms of Greece, particularly of Pergamon.

Corinth and the Etruscans: Greek Influence on Rome

The connections between Greece and Rome are almost as old as the cultures themselves, and the Romans themselves traced the origins of monumental temple architecture in Rome back to mid-seventh-century Corinth. Around the time that the Corinthians were designing and building the first truly monumental temple in Greece, the old ruling oligarchy was overthrown and expelled from Corinth. When one of the deposed oligarchs, Damaratus, fled by ship from Corinth he carried with him a host of artisans, including terracotta workers, craftsmen we now know were most responsible for the monumental character of that temple—through their invention of the tiled roof. Damaratus sailed with them to the west coast of Italy and settled in the Etruscan town of Tarquinia, where Damaratus's artisans introduced the Etruscans—who became the greatest terracotta sculptors of the Mediterranean—to the art of molding terracotta. So, in addition to developing the first tradition of monumental architecture in Greece, Corinth was also a crucial source for the origins of monumental sculpture and architecture in Etruria. Damaratus then extended Corinth's artistic and cultural influence to Rome itself through his half-Etruscan son

The Gorgon medusa from the Temple of Artemis, Corfu. Early, sculpted pediments were adorned with frontal views of mythological monsters.

Lucumo, who later took the name Lucius Tarquinius Priscus and became the first Etruscan king of Rome. On the heights of the Capitoline Hill in Rome, the central peak and religious center of Etruscan and Latin Rome, Tarquinius initiated the construction of the first monumental temple in Rome, dedicated to Jupiter, Juno, and Minerva, the same three divinities that in their Greek guise of Zeus, Hera, and Athena dominated the central height and religious center of Corinth. This cult of the Capitoline Triad became the central cult of the Roman republic and empire, and the triple-chambered plan of their temple, completed after the Etruscans were expelled from Rome at the end of the sixth century BCE, formed the template for all subsequent Capitolia.

From the Etruscans the Romans inherited the tradition of monumental wood and terracotta temple architecture. They were also deeply influenced by Etruscan sculpture, painting, and religious and political institutions. The tradition of Roman portraiture, a paradigmatic manifestation of an innate Roman fascination with the literal details of history, finds its roots in Etruscan funerary sculpture that goes back to the seventh century BCE. As much as any other art form, the super-realistic, warts-and-all portraiture of republican Rome (509–27 BCE) embodies the traditional Roman dedication to history, family, and age-old values. And as much as any other art form, the conception and appearance of Roman republican portraiture stands in opposition to the traditional Greek conception of monumental art. Through generalization and stylization monumental Greek art was intended to lift the viewer out of the everyday and into the consideration of superhuman forms and forces; Roman republican portraiture encouraged the contemplation of the thoughts and actions of specific, individual human beings through the reproduction of their most individualized, idiosyncratic physical attributes. A similar dichotomy is expressed in the contrast between the native tradition of Roman historical relief sculpture, which depicts the literal details of actual historical events, and the more generalized, emblematic references to history made in the monuments of the Greeks.

The owl, signifying strength and wisdom, is the symbol of Athena, the patron goddess of Athens. Photo taken in 2003.

An Evolving Balance

The most profound wave of Greek influence on the Romans came with the Roman sack of Corinth in 146 BCE. The city was stripped of its sculpture and painting and almost any movable object of value, and it was all shipped to Rome, where it kindled a mighty taste for things Greek and antique and injected a permanent and powerful strain of Hellenism into the art and architecture of Rome. From the second century BCE Roman art and architecture can be read as a constant and intentional shifting—depending upon the specific purpose of the monument—of the balance of native Italic elements and those adopted from classical Greece. The Romans continue to build their temples according to their own traditional Tuscan plan (adopted from the Etruscans), but they consistently monumentalize those temples by veneering them with the materials and decorative orders of the Greeks.

A century later the emperor Augustus (reigned 27 BCE–14 CE) claimed to have found Rome a city of brick and left it a city of marble. Augustus's statue at Prima Porta illustrates well the early integration of Hellenic and Italic forms and spirit in the service of the official message of the state. It combines a recognizable portrait head of Augustus with the body of the famous Doryphoros, the "Spearbearer" of the fifth-century BCE Greek sculptor Polykleitos. The Doryphoros is presented in the armor of a Roman general, the commander in chief, and wears a cuirass that carries the representation in relief of a historical event, a military accomplishment significant to the official image of Augustus. A recognizable, individual human being and a specific historical event are magnified, elevated to the realm of the superhuman through their association with fifth-century Greece, with Periclean Athens and its own remarkable cultural and military accomplishments, the apex, in the Roman mind, of human achievement. The same mixture and purpose is found in Augustus's Altar of Peace (the *Ara pacis*), which presents a historical procession of individually recognizable Romans in the guise of the religious procession depicted on the Ionic frieze of the fifth-century Parthenon in Athens.

Augustus and his Julio-Claudian successors (reigned 14–68 CE) continued to present themselves in official art and architecture in the guise of fifth-century Greece. Even their portrait heads, while recognizable as individual emperors, were generalized and idealized in the manner of classical Greek art. When, however, their grotesque excesses and abuses of power led to the overthrow of Nero (reigned 54–68 CE) and the ruling dynasty, the first Flavian emperor, Vespasian (reigned 69–79 CE), openly distanced himself from the policies and character of his predecessors by changing the balance in the language of official state art. Instead of representing him as Doryphoros, Vespasian's official images returned to the style of the old republican portraits—straightforward, literal, unpretentious, uniquely Roman—and proclaimed a return to the traditional values of the republic. In

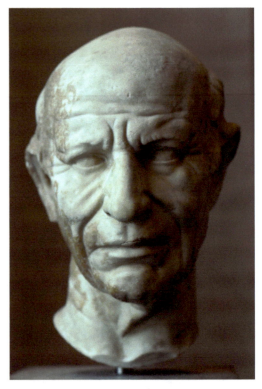

The realistic rendering of an elderly Roman man, circa 60 BCE, embodies the traditional Roman dedication to history, family, and age-old values. Bevilacqua Palace, Verona.

architecture he encouraged the use of concrete, a purely Roman building material and the most important Roman architectural contribution to posterity. The Amphitheatrum Flavium, the Colosseum, was not only the largest and most elaborate concrete structure in Rome, but it also denied the divine pretensions of the Julio-Claudian emperors and their profligate abuse of the Roman treasury for their own individual desires through its function as an entertainment center for the common people and through the site of its construction, on the newly filled-in lake in the center of Nero's notorious Golden House, or Domus Aurea. This structure was built with state funds in the center of Rome as Nero's personal pleasure villa; he appropriated over three hundred acres in the center of the city for its construction. Paradoxically, Nero's architects had also made great use of concrete, but in the private context of Nero's Golden House, where they experimented with the possibilities of concrete for molding interior space in new and fantastic ways. Their discoveries were profoundly influential in creating a Roman architecture of interiors.

The ways in which concrete and marble are used in Roman architecture can serve as a metaphor for the Roman character. In general, concrete formed the structure of the building, marble its veneer: carefully carved marble revetment could make a concrete building look as elegant as the Parthenon. Like the traditional characteristics of the republic—economical, practical, structural—concrete is purely Roman. Marble, on the other hand, as employed in Roman buildings, is expensive, luxurious, superficial, and foreign. While concrete reflects the native character of the Romans, marble reflects the aspirations of the Romans to the cultural heights of Pericles and fifth-century Athens.

Not until the reign of the emperor Trajan (reigned 98–117 CE) is concrete and its protective brick facing presented in unveneered reality as an appropriate surface for monumental architecture. The great curved façade of the Markets of Trajan reflects the molded nature of concrete, and the unstuccoed, unveneered brick surface reveals the fabric and techniques of its structure and initiates a new aesthetic in Roman architecture. Appropriately, this vast concrete building is dedicated to the practical pursuit of business; immediately next door, the contemporary Forum of Trajan, whose function is the symbolic representation of the aspirations and accomplishments of the Roman state under Trajan, is presented in the full glory of the classical Greek marble architectural orders.

Perhaps the most remarkable integration of traditional Roman and classical Greek architectural forms and symbols is found in the Pantheon of Trajan's successor Hadrian (reigned 117–138 CE). Here the façade of a Greek temple is wedded to a completely un-Greek and purely Roman structure, a concrete, domed cylinder. In addition, the most elaborate architectural symbol of religious transition ever created in Greece, the Propylaia (the great gateway of the Periclean Acropolis), is directly referenced in the stacked pediments of the façade, which, in turn, are combined with the uniquely Roman symbol of transition, the triumphal arch, to form the most explicitly processional temple entrance ever created in the classical world. The entrance leads into an immense open interior whose dome (representing the vault of the heavens) is the culmination of decades of experimentation and mastery of the techniques and design of concrete architecture. Here, rather than emphasizing the distinct natures of Greek and Roman architecture, the expressive potential of both is consciously synthesized to create a temple uniquely appropriate to the inclusive, international worship of "all gods," (pan-theon) and consequently to promote Hadrian's own inclusive, international conception of the Roman Empire.

Succeeding emperors continued to create monumental art and architecture in the tradition of Hadrian and his predecessors, and continued to explore the possibilities of concrete as a monumental architectural medium. Classical Greek and native Italic elements continued to be used to express specific official messages and attitudes, though on the whole that balance shifted toward the Italic over the next two centuries. In sculpture this shift expressed itself in part in the increasing interest in frontal representation and in simple, clearly outlined figures. That, coupled with a new spirituality that increasingly expressed itself in an emphasis on the eyes, gradually led to the more emblematic, iconic relief sculpture and portraits of the late empire. Constantine the Great (Constantine I, reigned 306–337) employed the tools of official art and architecture to great advantage, and as the first of the Roman emperors to convert to Christianity, began to direct those tools toward the glorification and propagation of his new religion.

Robin F. RHODES
University of Notre Dame

30 · ART IN WORLD HISTORY

Pictures should not be given approbation which are not likenesses of reality, even if they are refined creations executed with artistic skill. • **Vitruvius (80/70–25 BCE)**

Further Reading

Berve, H., Gruben, G., & Hirmer, M. (1963). *Greek temples, theaters and shrines*. London: Thames and Hudson.

Biers, W. R. (1996). *Archaeology of Greece: An introduction*. Ithaca, NY: Cornell University Press.

Coulton, J. J. (1977). *Ancient Greek architects at work*. Ithaca, NY: Cornell University Press.

Dinsmoor, W. B. (1975). *The architecture of Ancient Greece* (3rd ed.). New York: Norton.

Hannestad, N. (1986). *Roman art and imperial policy*. Aarhus, Denmark: Aarhus University Press.

Kleiner, D. E. E. (1992). *Roman sculpture*. New Haven, CT: Yale University Press.

Lawrence, A. W. (1983). *Greek Architecture* (4th ed). Harmondsworth, U.K.: Penguin Books.

Ling, R. (1991). *Roman painting*. New York: Cambridge University Press.

MacDonald, W. L. (1982). *The architecture of the Roman Empire* (Rev. ed.). New Haven, CT: Yale University Press.

MacKendrick, P. (1983). *The mute stones speak*. New York: Norton.

Osborne, R. (1998). *Archaic and classical Greek art*. Oxford, U.K.: Oxford University Press.

Pollitt, J. J. (1972). *Art and experience in classical Greece*. New York: Cambridge University Press.

Pollitt, J. J. (1986). *Hellenistic art*. New York: Cambridge University Press.

Ramage, N. H., & Ramage, A. (2001). *Roman art: Romulus to Constantine* (3rd ed.). Upper Saddle River, NJ: Prentice Hall.

Rhodes, R. F. (1995). *Architecture and meaning on the Athenian Acropolis*. New York: Cambridge University Press.

Rhodes, R. F. (2000). The classical world. In D. Cruickshank (Ed.), *Architecture: The critics' choice* (pp. 14–45). New York: Watson-Guptill Publications.

Rhodes, R. F. (forthcoming). *A story of monumental architecture in Greece*. New York: Cambridge University Press.

Scully, V. (1962). *The earth, the temple, and the gods: Greek sacred architecture* (Rev. ed.). New Haven, CT: Yale University Press.

Sear, F. (1983). *Roman architecture*. Ithaca, NY: Cornell University Press.

Stewart, A. (1990). *Greek sculpture, an exploration*. New Haven, CT: Yale University Press.

Art—Central Asia

The art of Central Asia is critically important to world historians because it provides evidence of the extraordinary synthesis of cultural influences that so typify the history of the region. This blending of Mediterranean, Iranian, Indian, Chinese, steppe nomadic, and local techniques and motifs that occurred at the "crossroads of Eurasia" resulted in the emergence of several major syncretistic schools of art.

Central Asian art needs to be clearly distinguished from the other artistic traditions of Inner Eurasia. Geographically, the term denotes the arts of modern-day Afghanistan, Pakistan, northern India, Nepal, Xinjiang Province in northwestern China, Tajikistan, Kyrgyzstan, Uzbekistan, and Turkmenistan, whereas Inner Eurasia also includes Mongolia, the Gobi, and central Siberia. It is culturally and stylistically different from Islamic, Indian, Chinese, and Russian arts, although these styles have all been practiced within the region. Historically, Central Asian art dates from prehistoric times to the present, with the ancient Silk Roads era being the most significant. Media have included sculpture and engraving in a variety of stone and stucco, as well as wall paintings, coin engravings, and textiles.

In the oasis towns of Central Asia, artists from a variety of cultures worked together to produce both sacred and secular art, which was then transported along the trade routes to profoundly influence the subsequent art of East Asia in particular. This essay offers a brief survey of Central Asian art in a chronological framework.

Pre-Achaemenid

The history of Central Asia from the late Neolithic period (c. 6000–3000 BCE) until quite recently has been characterized by the interaction between sedentary agrarian and nomadic pastoralist communities. The original inhabitants of the region lived in small semi-sedentary settlements. More substantial colonization followed as a direct result of the migration of Indo-European- and Indo-Iranian-speaking pastoralists into the region in three waves from approximately 4000 BCE. An important urban civilization emerged in the valleys of the Amu Dar'ya and Zeravshan rivers late in the third millennium BCE, originally known as the Bactrian-Margiana archaeological complex (BMAC), but "Oxus Civilization" is the term now more commonly used. Oxus Civilization oasis sites were probably agricultural communities developed to facilitate trade and exchange between the indigenous sedentary agriculturists and the neighboring steppe-nomadic pastoralists, evidence of the early emergence of a tradition of cultural exchange.

Artifacts discovered in Oxus Civilization sites—particularly battle-axes with cross-guards, mirrors, pins, bracelets, and rings—demonstrate high levels of craftsmanship and the borrowing of styles. Oxus Civilization potters used the wheel from as early as the third millennium BCE and decorated their works with geometric designs or stylized renderings of large animals and goats. The iconography of seals, cylinders, and metal ornaments is clearly of steppe-nomadic tradition—which includes both

31

realistic and fantastic animal images (particularly horses), mythical raptor-headed creatures, hunting and riding images, and some abstract symbol—while later artifacts are more Iranian in appearance, featuring human figures in full-frontal or profile poses, often sacrificing before a small fire altar. The Oxus Civilization declined late in the second millennium, although soon after 1000 BCE there is evidence of renewed urbanization and the construction of extensive irrigation systems. These settlements were extensively fortified, providing evidence of increased levels of conflict during what is known as the Scythian era (c. 1000–200 BCE).

The militarized Scythian tribes, who were active in Central Asia from the seventh century BCE, were responsible for the production of superbly decorative objects, particularly jewelry and trappings on horses, tents, and wagons. Scythic representations of real or imagined beasts were worked into a wide range of materials, including wood, leather, bone, appliqué felt, bronze, iron, silver, gold, and electrum. Outstanding examples are gold belt buckles, often with turquoise inlay, and 30-centimeter-long gold stags with their legs tucked under them, which may have been used as central ornaments on shields. The 1979 discovery at Tillya Tepe in Afghanistan of six royal graves replete with magnificent gold and lapis lazuli jewelry and weapons demonstrates the extraordinary artistic achievements of (probably) Scythian craftsmanship. The easternmost outpost of Scythian culture was the Ili River valley (in present-day southeastern Kazakhstan and northwestern Xinjiang Province, China), where they may have influenced the artistic tastes of the Xiongnu tribal confederation. A range of personal ornaments discovered at the major Xiongnu site of Noin-Ula depict fantastic animals with raptor-headed appendages, similar to those created by steppe-nomadic peoples from further west.

An important sedentary civilization also emerged in the Indus Valley during the third millennium BCE. The excavation of large cities such as Mohenjo Daro and Harappa provides evidence of a tightly organized, architecturally sophisticated urban society with straight streets intersecting at right angles,

This gold ram, a headdress ornament, displays the extraordinary craftsmanship of the Scythians. From Tillya Tepe, Tomb IV (first century BCE–first century CE). National Museum of Afghanistan ©Thierry Ollivier / Musée Guimet (www.nga.gov).

sophisticated drainage systems, and high standards of pottery production. Venus fertility figurines have been found at various sites, demonstrating extensive levels of cultural exchange with the civilizations of southwestern Asia. Stamps and seals from the Indus civilization depict naturalistic animals, but also horned humans, unicorns, and other large figures that might be gods, indicating possible steppe-nomadic influence upon artists.

Further north in the Indus Valley some 35,000 petroglyphs and inscriptions have been discovered, and others are known in Afghanistan, Uzbekistan,

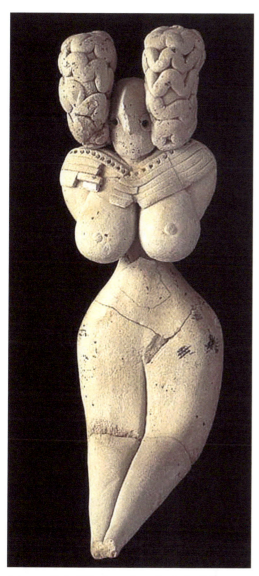

A terracotta fertility figure from the Indus Valley civilization (c. 2200 BCE) provides evidence of cultural exchange with southwestern Asia. The National Fund for Cultural Heritage.

and Tajikistan. The oldest carvings, which are pecked or chiseled into the surface of boulders scattered on the riverbanks and terraces, are prehistoric, mostly depicting animals, hunting scenes, and demon-like creatures. The petroglyphs continued to be cut until the early modern era and provide evidence of the changing religious practices of travelers (notably of Buddhism and Islam) along this branch of the Silk Roads. They depict an astonishing array of stupas (burial mounds and reliquaries) with the Buddha in various poses, and bodhisattva figures; later petroglyphs feature Indian and Iranian iconography, including some Zoroastrian and later Islamic symbols.

Achaemenids and Greeks

The relative isolation of small, fortified city-states in Central Asia made them vulnerable to attacks from the armies of major agrarian civilizations to the west. By the mid-sixth century BCE the Achaemenids (an Iranian dynasty that held power from the seventh century BCE through 330 BCE) had incorporated Bactria (ancient Afghanistan) and Sogdia (ancient Turkmenistan and Uzbekistan) into their empire. These regions were thus exposed to the artistic traditions and belief systems of Iran until the arrival of Alexander III of Macedon (Alexander the Great) in 329 BCE. This long period of incorporation into the durable and tightly organized Persian Empire helped establish the region as part of a Eurasia-wide cultural exchange network. Central Asia was exposed to Zoroastrian iconography, and small votive figurines produced by potters in Bactria and Sogdia were designed to be used in fire-worshipping ceremonies. The Achaemenids also introduced the first coins into Central Asia, establishing a tradition that would culminate under the Greco-Bactrians in arguably the finest example of the coin engravers' art known in the ancient world.

Alexander campaigned in Bactria and Sogdia for two years, establishing a number of cities, including Alexandria-Kapisu (Begram in Afghanistan), which the Kushans later made their summer capital. Alexander's campaign reinforced the process begun by the Achaemenids and further linked Central Asia to the civilizations of southwestern Asia and the Mediterranean. Greek populations flooded into the region during the subsequent Seleucid (Macedonian Greek) era (312–64 BCE), founding a string of Greek towns such as Ay Khanum on the southern banks of the

A rock petroglyph in Kazakhstan, approximately 4,000 years old, partially defaced by scratches. Photo by Jeff Frame.

Amu Dar'ya, complete with classical Greek temples and theaters. The Seleucids also issued tetradrachms that are masterpieces in the Greek tradition of coinage, with superb portraits of kings on the reverse that are sometimes realistic enough to reveal symptoms of disease, such as goiter.

Around 250 BCE Diodotus, the Seleucid satrap of Bactria, revolted and declared Bactria an independent state. During the subsequent Greco-Bactrian era a series of kings expanded their realms into Sogdia and Fergana to the north, Parthia to the west, and Kabul and the Indus Valley to the south. Soon after 190 BCE, Demetrius extended Greek interests into northern India, forging a link between the Hellenistic and Indian cultures that was strengthened under his successors Eucratides and Menander.

As well as establishing a link between Hellenic and Indian culture, the most significant artistic legacy of the Greco-Bactrians is their superb coinage, which was issued in silver and bronze. The royal portraits are masterpieces of coin engraving; facial features are so realistically and individually realized as to surpass even the Seleucids. Euthydemus is depicted with a thick neck, full cheeks and chin, and a determined mouth; Eucratides wears a helmet with bull's horns above his naked torso; Demetrius wears an elephant-scalp headdress and formidable expression; and Antimachus has unique facial features reflecting his mixed Greek and Sogdian blood. The coins strongly influenced the subsequent issues of the Kushans, under whom Central Asian art reached the heights of syncretistic achievement.

The Kushans: Gandharan and Mathuran Art

The invasion of Bactria by the Yuezhi confederation in 130 BCE ushered in a period often described as the Golden Age of ancient Central Asia. By around 45 CE the Yuezhi had transformed themselves into the imperial Kushans, and for much of the subsequent two centuries the stability of their regime facilitated astonishing levels of trans-Eurasian cultural exchange along the various Silk Roads, which linked the Mediterranean, Parthian, Indian, Chinese, and steppe-nomadic worlds into a single world system for the first time in history. Central Asian art was transformed by this interaction, and although a number

This view of the Kazakhstan petrogylph shows a male figure shooting at a wild horse with a bow and arrow. Photo by Jeff Frame.

A Cybele plate from Ai Khanum, Afganistan, shows the Phrygian goddess in her lion-drawn chariot, the Greek sun god Helios, and an Iranian fire altar. Photo by Marco Prins, © Jona Lendering for Livius.Org, 2006.

stair-riser reliefs) depicting both religious and secular scenes. These pieces abound in details from everyday life—comfortable beds, food and wine, dancers and musicians, and realistic portraiture—and their extraordinary mixture of Indian symbolism, Romano-Hellenistic architectural details, and steppe-nomadic costumes are a quintessential example of Central Asian artistic synthesis.

In later phases (Gandharan art continued until the sixth century CE) the remarkable blending of local, of distinctive Kushan styles are known, the most significant are those that emerged at Gandhara and Mathura.

Gandhara (located near Peshawar in Pakistan) had been incorporated into the Greco-Bactrian kingdom, and the art that evolved there owed much to Mediterranean, Indian, and local traditions. Gandharan sculpture (along with Kushan coinage) has long been associated with the earliest depictions of the Buddha, who had previously been represented only by symbols such as footprints or an umbrella. In an attempt to express for the first time the idea of his divinity in human form, Gandharan sculptors (who worked in hard, gray schist) turned to statues of Greek and Roman gods. The earliest Buddhas feature drapery that hangs in loose folds but still outlines the form and movement of the body beneath. Many are similar to the contemporary statues of deified Roman emperors, and the head recalls the Greek god Apollo. Also remarkable in Gandharan art are flat sculptures worked on slabs of schist (often used as

The standing Buddha of Gandharan style, circa first–second century CE, features characteristic loose drapery revealing the form of the body underneath. Tokyo National Museum.

Eastern, and Western styles continues to be found in Buddhas and bodhisattvas that combine Greek symmetry with Indian sensual spirituality and serenity. In turn, these syncretistic images went on to profoundly influence later East Asian images of the Buddha, particularly the Chinese. So stylistically unmistakable is the sculpture of Gandhara that early-twentieth-century archaeologists were able to map the spread of Kushano-Gandharan influences to the eastern edge of the Tarim Basin, based primarily on the continuing Greek and Roman stylistic influences observed in Buddhist sculpture they had unearthed.

Mathuran artists (based on the Jamuna River, a tributary of the Ganges) worked mainly in white-spotted red sandstone and were clearly influenced by the Gandharan synthesis. Whether standing or seated, the Buddha is depicted with broad shoulders and a large chest, and with legs apart and feet firmly planted, conveying a sense of power and energy. Mathuran secular art is notable for its sensual depictions of women and also for a superb series of portraits of the Kushan kings. Particularly impressive is a low-relief (unfortunately headless) sculpture of Kanishka (reigned c. 129–152 CE) in which he is depicted with sword and mace, and with his feet planted in a masterful manner. The king wears nomadic dress, and although the work was undertaken in Mathura (the Kushan winter capital), the style and concept seem to stem more from a Scythic-Parthian tradition than an Indian one. However, the arts of both Gandhara and Mathura did contribute profoundly to the formation of the classic style of Indian art, which reached its maturity during the three-century-long Guptan period.

First Millennium of the Common Era

Following the death of the Kushan ruler Vasudeva around 228, the Kushans were rapidly replaced in

This fragment from the "Swimmers" wall fresco in Kizil, Cave of the Seafarers (c. 500 CE), was pillaged, like many other "portable" works, by nineteenth-century European archaelogists. Collection of the Museum of Asian Art, Berlin.

Central Asia by the Iranian Sasanians, who later established strong trade contacts with Tang-dynasty China (the Tang were in power from 618 to 907) that ensured the continuation of the tradition of artistic synthesis. Tang art—including flasks and pottery figurines—was clearly influenced by Central Asian and Western prototypes brought to China by pilgrims and traders. Mahayana Buddhism was by now firmly entrenched in Central Asia, and much of the art created during the first millennium CE was produced in monasteries across the Tarim Basin. Many of the more portable pieces were pillaged by European archaeologists in the nineteenth and twentieth centuries and now reside in institutions all over the globe. Notable are the superb wall frescoes produced around 500 to 800 at Kizil, which demonstrate Sasanian, Indian, and Chinese influences; Buddhist wall paintings from Kuqa (from around 900 to 1000) in west central Xinjiang and Uygur frescoes from Bezeklik and Sorcuk (both displaying Sogdian, Persian, and Indian influences); and the astonishing library of illustrated scrolls discovered by the archaeologist Aurel Stein in the Monastery of a Thousand Buddhas near Dunhuang in north central China. Included among the latter was the oldest block-printed book so far known, a copy of the Diamond Sutra dating from approximately 860 CE. Cultural and stylistic influences continued to move in both directions. The sculpture and painting produced in monasteries in Turpan in Xinjiang, for example, influenced the subsequent Buddhist art

The archaeological remains of the Bamiyan Valley represent rich artistic and religious exchanges among cultures. The Buddha pictured here in 1976 was one of two destroyed by the Taliban in 2001. Photo by Marco Bonavoglia.

of Tibet, while the funeral art of the Uygurs deeply affected Mongolian painting. Many superb examples of Manichaean art are also known throughout Central Asia, documenting the spread of the "religion of light" eastward from the Sasanian realm as far as the Tang capital of Xi'an.

Not all the art of Central Asia was so easily transportable. In the high Bamiyan valley in northern Afghanistan, at a crossroads of two Silk Roads routes, a large monastic complex was responsible for the carving of monumental figures of the Buddha. Until just prior to its destruction in 2001 by the Taliban regime, the tallest of the colossal statues (52.5 meters) was the single largest Buddha known in the world. The Bamiyan Buddhas were massive reliefs set deep in the side of a cliff, inspired by the Indian rock-cut architecture of Ajanta in south central India. They were completed in a naturalistic, post-Gandharan style strongly influenced by both Parthian and local traditions, and in turn inspired the carving of another group of colossal Buddhas at Yungang in the Chinese province of Shanxi (northeastern China), completed late in the fifth century.

Modern Era

Outside of the scope of this brief outline is a consideration of the splendid cultural legacy of Islam that has been such a dominant influence upon Central Asian art from late in the first millennium CE until today. The textile arts of the region also deserve an essay to themselves, particularly as the great trade routes were named after silk. Textiles are of paramount importance to world historians because of the role they have played as mediums of exchange and as indicators of social position, ethnicity, and religion. Textiles were used as currency, to pay taxes, and as symbols of imperial patronage, and yet the fragile nature of the medium has meant that only a fraction of those produced have survived. One of the largest collections of ancient Central Asian textiles so far discovered are those associated with the desiccated mummies found at sites all over Xinjiang, analysis of which has been tentatively used to suggest a historical connection between the Tarim Basin mummies and the Bronze Age migration of Indo-European-speaking migrants into the region.

The richness of color, pattern, and texture that so distinguishes the region's textiles is a product of the intense transfer and blending of ideas, motifs, techniques, and materials between nomadic and sedentary peoples, a tradition that continues in the twenty-first century. In the contemporary nations of post-Soviet Central Asia, weavers, potters, ceramic masters, jewelers, and painters from both

Thus shall ye think of all this fleeting world: A star at dawn, a bubble in a stream, A flash of lightning in a summer cloud, A flickering lamp, a phantom, and a dream. • **Diamond Sutra (868 CE)**

A Tarim Basin mummy photographed by the archaeologist Aurel Stein circa 1910.

Since the Central Asian republics gained independence in the 1990s, nongovernmental organizations such as UNESCO have played an important role in the renaissance of traditional arts and crafts through grants to artists and assistance in the international marketing of their works. One result of this well-intentioned strategy has been that many artists now concentrate on producing commercial works for foreign buyers as they adjust to market realities, and the creative process, particularly in terms of original modern art, has suffered. Of course, Central Asia has always been a region characterized by the tensions between local ethnic traditions on the one hand and a diverse range of foreign influences on the other, as a result of its geographical location as a hub for trans-Eurasian cultural exchange. It remains to be seen how Central Asian artists of the twenty-first century will balance the seemingly opposing forces of tradition and foreign influence, although it has been this very dynamic that for over five thousand years has resulted in the production of some of the most profoundly influential art in world history.

Craig BENJAMIN
Grand Valley State University

sedentary and seminomadic traditions continue to practice their art. But the Soviet policy of forcing artists and craftspeople to work in collective factories and prohibiting the production of individual work had a devastating effect on many of the traditional arts of Uzbekistan, Turkmenistan, Kyrgyzstan, and Tajikistan. In some cases, archaeologists of the era also destroyed later layers of artistic artifacts in the process of excavating older periods. As a result, the few masters who remain in the region today carry a precious living legacy of tradition and technique.

Further Reading

Barber, E. J. (1991). *Prehistoric textiles.* Princeton, NJ: Princeton University Press.

Benjamin, C. (1998). An introduction to Kushan research. In D. Christian & C. Benjamin (Eds.), *Worlds of the silk roads: Ancient and modern* (Silk Roads Studies Series No. 2, p. 31–49). Turnhout, Belgium: Brepols.

Bunker, E. C., Watt, J. C. Y., & Sun, X. (2002). *Nomadic art from the eastern Eurasian steppes: The Eugene v. Thaw and other New York collections.* New York: Yale University Press.

Christian, D. (1998). *A history of Russia, Central Asia and Mongolia: Vol. 1. Inner Eurasia from prehistory to the Mongol Empire.* Oxford, U.K.: Blackwell.

Errington, E., & Cribb, J. (Eds.). (1992). *The crossroads of Asia: Transformation in image and symbol in the art of ancient Afghanistan and Pakistan.* Cambridge, U.K.: Ancient India and Iran Trust.

Frye, R. N. (1996). *The heritage of Central Asia*. Princeton, NJ: Princeton University Press.

Hiebert, F., & Cambon, P. (Eds.). (2008). *Afghanistan: Hidden treasures from the National Museum, Kabul*. Washington, DC: National Geographic.

Litvinsky, B. A., & Altman-Bromberg, C. (1994). The archaeology and art of Central Asia: Studies from the former Soviet Union. *Bulletin of the Asia Institute, 8*, 47.

Pugachenkova, G. A., Dar, S. R., Sharma, R. C., Joyenda, M. A., & Siddiqi, H. (1994). Kushan art. In J. Harmatta, B. N. Puri, & G. F. Etemadi (Eds.), *History of civilizations of Central Asia: Vol. 2. The development of sedentary and nomadic civilizations: 700 b.c. to a.d. 250* (pp. 331–395). Paris: UNESCO.

Stein, A. (1933). *On Central Asian tracks*. London: Macmillan.

Tanabe, K. (1993). *Silk road coins: The Hirayama collection*. London: British Museum.

Art—China

The breathtaking scope of Chinese art—highly decorated Bronze Age vessels, exquisitely executed calligraphy, monumental Buddhas carved from rock cliffs, landscape paintings brushed in ink on silk scrolls, the Socialist Realism of the Mao years, and even the fireworks display at the 2008 Beijing Olympics (designed by a renowned Chinese artist)—comprise remarkable works from several millennia that developed both in response to and isolated from other countries and cultures.

Chinese art, as part of China's culture, can claim to be one of the world's oldest and continuous traditions—existing in relative isolation at times, at other times heavily influenced by outside elements. It deserves respect for extraordinary achievements, especially in calligraphy and pictorial art, and for a more than one-thousand-year-old tradition of landscape painting, through which Chinese painters have used art to come to terms with human life and nature. Although Chinese artists in the twenty-first century have absorbed Western ideas, many still continue to draw upon their tradition.

Pre-Imperial Era: circa 3000–221 BCE

The origins of Chinese art date to the third millennium BCE with the emergence of settled agricultural communities, mainly in the North China plain. Since early in the twentieth century archeologists have unearthed many pieces of finely built, wedged and coiled ceramic pottery in a variety of regional, cultural styles. Early artisans embellished their bowls and flasks with brushwork in abstract designs or with depictions of fish and other creatures. This tension between stylized and more naturalistic representations remains an enduring feature of Chinese art throughout history, from the Neolithic period on.

With the emergence of cities and dynasties by the second millennium BCE (Shang dynasty, 1766–1045 BCE; Zhou dynasty, 1045–256 BCE), a highly stratified society appeared in which the royal house and nobility patronized artisans who produced luxury goods, some for personal consumption and many for ceremonial purposes, especially rituals having to do with the emerging cult of the ancestors. Tombs from the period are full of items—jade, ivory, and lacquer objects; gold and silver ornaments; and bronze eating and drinking vessels in particular—made by highly

Bronze ax head. Late Shang dynasty (1766–1045 BCE). Imperial Palace, Beijing. The strange combination of features in the monster face of this ax head is characteristic of Shang design. Photo by Joan Lebold Cohen.

skilled craftspeople to serve the deceased in the afterworld (and perhaps to appease vengeful spirits who might harm the living). During the Shang dynasty large-scale human and animal sacrifices were included in these burial treasure troves, but under the influence of Confucian humanism by the late first millennium BCE, this practice was replaced by the use of substitute figures (*ming qi*) fashioned in clay, metal, or wood.

The utilitarian but highly decorated bronze vessels, the most admired and studied of these artifacts, signified the wealth and power of the families who owned (and were buried with) them. The vessels evolved in a basic repertoire of about thirty shapes, with the three-legged bowl (ding) being the favored form. Some vessels were very large, weighing over 100 kilograms (about 225 pounds); some derived from earlier pottery forms; others were sculptural and took the shape of composite animals. The artistry and technical virtuosity that went into these ritual bronzes has seldom been equaled and never surpassed in bronze casting anywhere. The outside surfaces were highly decorated with rigid bands of semi-abstract relief sculpture—some suggesting feathers and scroll patterns, and others depicting birds, dragons, animals, and mythical figures, many of which reflect Shang attitudes to the supernatural world. Most famous is the "monster face" (*taotie*), a mask-like, double-profile motif with eyes and curlicue brows but no lower jaw. The image evokes the shaman's costumed face in pre-Confucian religion; even in the twenty-first century shamans wear animal skins that are missing the lower jaw.

The ceremonial and burial use of bronzes continued throughout this period but by the late Zhou, especially after 600 BCE, styles reflected changes in Chinese society and culture. Warring states and disunity brought social unrest; the era of China's great philosophers—Confucius, the legendary Laozi, and Mozi—arose. Thus the intricate scroll patterns and monster faces of earlier times lost the energy and mystery of the old shaman rituals. Bronze vessels still used in burial sites were adorned with a looser, decorative elegance, and they have become treasured collector's items in the twenty-first century.

Early Imperial China: 221 BCE–220 CE

Archaeological finds, mainly from tombs, remain the best source for studying the development of art in the era beginning with the Qin (221–206 BCE) and Han (206 BCE–220 CE) dynasties. The most spectacular find in recent years was the huge, 2,200-year-old army of terracotta soldiers buried to guard the tomb of the Qin emperor Shi Huangdi, the "First Emperor" to unify China. In 1974, a farmer digging a well near the modern city of Xi'an stumbled upon some of these slightly larger-than-life-sized statues. Subsequent excavations showed not only the highly developed skill in clay sculpture of the time but amazingly realistic detail and individual facial features.

This realism also appears in miniature clay figures, notably of dancers and entertainers, found in less grandiose tombs from the Han period. Han funerary traditions also included burying clay models of houses, some with realistic details such as penned enclosures for pigs and hutches for chickens. A scene depicting two crows perched on the branches of a tree, part of the decorative embellishments painted on the exterior walls of such a model (now at the Nelson-Atkins Museum of Art in Kansas

Flying horse from Wuwei, Gansu Province. Eastern Han dynasty (25–220 CE). This sculpted bronze steed suggests mythically divine qualities attributed to the horse.
Photo by Joan Lebold Cohen.

City, Missouri) is a precursor to tenth-century flower and bird painting—the first extant example, in fact, of what would become in the tenth century an important and independent genre in Chinese art.

More luxurious tomb items forged from precious and semiprecious metals (gold and silver as well as bronze) further attest to the high skill of workmanship and the tendency toward realistic representation. A highly detailed bronze—a miniature horse and chariot, complete with driver, umbrella, and reins, which was found in Gansu Province along the ancient Silk Roads route—is very different from the massive, symbolically decorated bronze vessels of the previous era. Even more striking is the bronze "Flying Horse of Gansu," in which the horse, depicted in full gallop, is poised on just one hoof. Here, spirit as well as naturalism animates the creation of this long-dead anonymous sculptor.

Archaeologists have uncovered an example of one of China's unique contributions to world art and commerce—silk fabric art—in a burial site at Mawangdui, on the outskirts of present-day Changsha. Bog-like conditions helped preserved artifacts in the tomb of the Marquise of Dai (Lady Dai), including the noblewoman's clothing and body (found in a semi-mummified state), and a large T-shaped silk banner. Painted scenes on the banner, dating to the second century BCE and now in the Hunan Provincial Museum, represent hierarchical levels of the cosmos—heaven, Earth, and underworld—and reflect the early Han belief in the close relationship between the human and supernatural worlds.

Departing from traditional views that interpret the banner based on three sections of equal proportion in the composition, Wu Hung (1992), in his study "Art in a Ritual Context: Rethinking Mawangdui," sees the scene comprising four parts. Heaven, predictably occupying the top (i.e., the "crossbar" of the T), contains a sun (superimposed with the image of a crow) in the right corner, a crescent-shaped moon with a perching toad on the left, and the Han imagining of the Great Ancestor (a primordial deity depicted as a man with a serpent's tail) in the middle. Among the constellations immediately below swarm dragons and fantastic

The T-shaped banner from Lady Dai's tomb is covered with images that reflect the early Han belief in the close relationship between the human and supernatural worlds.

snakes. Positioned at the place where this horizontal heaven is connected to the T's stem, two doorkeepers eagerly wait to admit Lady Dai. All the figures are painted energetically, in an almost cartoon-like style, combining human and capricious animal forms floating in the ether.

In the two "earthly" sections below heaven, which occupy more than a third of the banner's total space, Lady Dai prepares for entry to the afterlife—underneath a high ceiling that signifies the difficulty of entering heaven, and above the section where family members offer sacrifices to her. In the lowest and fourth part of the composition an underworld creature holds up the world like a Hercules. Coiling snake-like dragons enclose each of these four sections. At the dramatic center they crisscross threading through a circular jade *bi* disc (a symbol of heaven). The artist's skill in organizing such a complex story in a series of space cells reveals an early mastery of a narrative form and an approach to image making that moves toward "realism."

Painting and Calligraphy: 220–589 CE

Relics such as Lady Dai's banner provide tantalizing glimpses not only into the society and belief system of the age but also into the early development of two-dimensional Chinese art—painting. The Chinese invention of paper and ink is of enormous significance to the world as papermaking techniques and brush writing also moved west along the Silk Roads. (At the same time outside influences, specifically Buddhism and its art, moved eastward along the same route.) Paper and the writing brush hugely influenced the development of China's centralized bureaucratic form of government and the high culture of its literati class. Painting and calligraphy would develop in China as "high art" forms.

Abundant Chinese literary sources and histories state that the post-Han era—a period of disunity before the Sui dynasty began in 589 CE—was an important one for painting. But because works of art were destroyed in periods of social unrest and political upheaval, few paintings of the period survive. One of the most important that does, a silk handscroll called *Admonitions of the Instructress to the Ladies of the Palace* and attributed to Gu Kaishi (c. 344–c. 406), illustrates the already centuries-old Confucian view of art as didactic and morally enriching: the narrative defines wifely virtues, filial piety, and rules for proper behavior. In one scene an empress resolutely places herself between her frightened emperor husband, his frantic courtiers, and a charging bear; in another, servants groom and dress royal children while their indulgent parents look on. The figures, outlined in even brushstrokes with only a few areas of color filled in, show detailed facial expressions, especially on the men. Handscrolls (this one some 3.5 meters (11 feet long), were meant for intimate viewing, with three of four people looking on as the person holding the scroll revealed small sections at a time.

For Daoists of the period, whose ancient traditions fostered connections to nature, art had spiritual value; thus landscape, later a major theme in Chinese painting, emerged as a subject. The quality of brushstrokes, as vehicles of expression and as the "bones" giving a work its primary structure, became the benchmark by which the Chinese judged a painting. This combination had already found its purest embodiment in calligraphy, a form of expressive handwriting in a variety of styles that would carry on pedigrees of famous scholars. Wang Xichi (c. 303–361 CE), one of the most renowned practitioners of his day, became the model for many later calligraphers and literati elite.

Buddhism and Chinese Art

The arrival of Buddhism, which started as a trickle of monks with sutras and images in the late Han dynasty and built to a flood by the sixth century CE, was the major foreign influence on Chinese art before the global reach of European culture and power in recent times. Buddhism, brought by Indian monks traders, entered China by two routes: maritime via the Indian Ocean and Southeast Asia, and overland by the Silk Roads into northwestern China, which was still the center of the empire. The visual stimuli initially arrived through illustrated scriptures and small portable images and shrines, but soon Chinese created their own larger Buddhist sculpture and mural painting.

Attributed to Gu Kaishi (c. 344–406), *Admonitions of the Instructress to the Ladies of the Palace* (detail). Scroll, ink on silk. In this scene nannies groom royal children as parents look on indulgently. Collection of the British Museum.

After the fall of the Han dynasty, the disintegration of central political authority, ensuing social chaos, and invasions from the north greatly facilitated the acceptance of this otherworldly religion in both the North China plain and the Yangzi (Chang) Valley; Buddhism offered consolation in life and the promise of salvation after death. The carving of huge caves and monumental statues from solid rock cliffs, an art form established in India, migrated with Buddhism to China and punctuated the landscape en route. (The huge standing statue of the Buddha in Afghanistan, destroyed in 2001 by the Taliban, is such an example.)

The rulers of the Northern Wei dynasty (386–535 CE), who made Buddhism a state religion in the large part of northern China they ruled, became important patrons of Buddhist sculpture. In the first Northern Wei capital at Datong (Shanxi Province), in the shadow of the Great Wall, they sponsored the construction of cave temples with large stone statues and brightly painted murals inspired by the Gandharian style of northwestern India and Afghanistan, which itself had borrowed heavily from Greco-Roman sculpture. In the great cave complex at Yungang magisterial images of the Buddha and his pantheon still exist; some, over thirty feet high, depict stories of his lives drawn from the *Jataka Tales*. Originally painted with gold and vivid colors on living rock, they now stand largely intact but weathered into a more austere, colorless appearance not unlike that of the once-painted classical architecture and statuary of ancient Greece.

Images of the Buddha (and the practices of Buddhism) changed as they traveled east. Already at Yungang, Chinese aesthetic and social values made their mark on the foreign religion and its art. Here the full bodied, curvaceous Indian Buddhist images assumed a newly sinicized form and were flattened and hidden under robes, according to Chinese Confucian propriety, to avoid any corporeal impropriety. When the Northern Wei emperor moved his capital south to Luoyang in 494 CE, a former co-capital with

Li Zhaodao (c. 675–730), *Emperor Ming Huang's Journey to Shu*. Colors and ink on silk. Although attributed to Li, the silk hanging scroll is almost certainly a Song-dynasty copy.

Xi'an, he decreed that evermore magnificent caves be carved out of the living rock at nearby Longmen Grottoes on the bank of the Yi River; they were also painted with scenes from the Buddha's lives. The stone at Longmen—a hard, closely grained, and dense limestone, quite different from the sandstone at Yungang—allowed for more detailed carving.

After the reunification of the Chinese Empire under the Sui (589–618 CE) and Tang (618–907 CE) dynasties, Chinese rulers continued imperial patronage by building additional cave temples at Longmen. (With more than 2,300 caves, and 100,000 statues and relief sculptures carved over a 250-year period, Longmen contains some of the finest examples of large-scale Buddhist carvings in China.) The style of Buddhist imagery was transformed again by a new wave of Indian influence, as the Buddha and his heavenly host had lost their stiff, disembodied poses and were refigured with softer, rounder, even sensuous bodies, sometimes in other materials such as wood and bronze.

Cave-temple paintings created from the fifth through the twelfth centuries, with their Indian and Central Asian inspirations, trace the evolution of Chinese religious painting over this long period. The largest and best preserved cover the walls and ceilings of 492 caves at the Mogao complex (at the oasis of Dunhuang in the Gobi Desert in Gansu Province). Many murals feature radiant polychrome frontal images of a seated Buddha with his huge bejeweled pantheon hierarchically arranged in paradise. Others draw on the *Jataka Tales*, chronicling the former lives of the Buddha. An exotic motif used in these murals—and, in the context of Confucian morality, an erotic one—are the Flying Apsaras, heavenly (female) beings without wings who nevertheless soar through the sky wearing scanty Indian-style clothing and long diaphanous scarves that help them fly. Mural artists painted the Apsaras in deeply hued colors using some shading to suggest volume.

Two other aspects of these desert-air-preserved paintings deserve mention, not just for the subjects they address but for the backgrounds they place their subjects against. First, such paintings often show the Buddha seated in front of a Chinese-style palace, and these representations are the oldest visual record of Chinese palace-style architecture of wooden construction—more horizontal than vertical, with series of courtyards and distinctively upturned golden tile roofs. The form of architecture persisted, the surviving Qing Imperial Palace in Beijing being its latest reincarnation. Second, more relevant to the development of Chinese painting, Dunhuang paintings sometimes use natural scenery in the background. The color choice is noteworthy, especially in view of later Chinese landscape painting's general preference for monochrome ink or muted color. In the Tang period (618–907 CE), artists painted mountains, valleys, and rivers in brilliant blue and green hues, a color pattern that would predominate as landscape painting, treating nature itself as the main subject, emerged in the late Tang and subsequent dynasties.

The most famous example of this use of blue and green mineral colors in a non-religious context is a silk hanging scroll, *Emperor Ming Huang's Journey to Shu*. Although the painting is attributed to Li Zhaodao (c. 675–730), it is almost certainly a Song dynasty copy. (Chinese reverence for the past made copying artworks a common practice, sometimes as forgery but more often to preserve valued cultural artifacts whose material substance, silk or paper, was prone to decay and disintegration.)

The painting recounts a famous incident in Tang dynasty history, the story of the emperor forced to flee from the capital when a rebel general, who'd had an illicit liaison with the emperor's favorite concubine, Yang Guifei, defeated imperial troops and seized the throne. Accompanying the emperor in exile is a procession of black-hatted courtiers riding through passes between three steep mountains. Women in wide, brimmed hats with veils move in single file along the narrow paths. In the glorious composition, with the picture plane tilted skyward to convey spatial depth, the verdant, pointy peaks poke through layers of clouds.

Emergence of Literati Art: Song–Yuan Period

Chinese society underwent profound changes in this so-called Middle Period of Chinese history. For art, the most important change consolidated social eminence and cultural hegemony with the emergence of the literati (*wen ren*). The term refers to those literate in the classical language who aspired to pass the imperial government's civil-service examination, a system of recruiting officials on merit rather than on family or political connections. Only a small minority of the millions of men who took these rigorous exams actually passed with a score high enough to win them a government post. (Women were not eligible

Fan Kuan (active c. 1023–1031), *Travelers by Streams and Mountains*. Fan's use of perspective in this 7-foot-long hanging scroll suggests humankind's small role in the universe.

to apply for court positions, and thus to take the exams, but they nevertheless studied classical language and parallel subjects in the Confucian spirit to make themselves more worthy to be chosen as wives and mothers.) As a consequence the large pool of male

Xia Gui (c. 1180–1230), *Twelve Views from a Thatched Hut* (detail). Handscroll, ink on silk. Just a few deft brushstrokes capture the details of the scene.

examination "failures" constituted a landowning rural gentry class that preserved largely Confucian values and imperial peace throughout the vast empire. Literati were profoundly "civil" rather than militaristic in their outlook, a sensibility reflected in the art they patronized and produced themselves. Although these trends started in the Han period and continued in the Tang, Confucian ideals of ruling through the pen ("writing brush" in China) were only fully realized in the Song period; there too they remained in dynamic tension with imperial power and the military might behind it.

Literati art is remarkable, almost unique in world history, because the individuals who produced it also consumed or patronized it. Most importantly it was, at least for a time, independent of court influence. The cultural prestige of these gentleman artists became part of their social status. Literati art forms were almost all "arts of the brush"—calligraphy, poetry, and ultimately painting.

During the tenth century a number of subsequently famous landscape masters began to treat "scenery" as more than a background to human activity. Landscape's emergence as the most prestigious genre of painting, often linked to the veneration of nature in Chinese Daoist philosophy, has also been correlated to the Confucian self-esteem of artists who expressed their own feelings rather than cater to the wishes of rich and powerful patrons. Many centuries would pass before anything comparable developed in Europe; thus some art historians acknowledge a precursor to "modernity" in Chinese painting by the end of this period.

The first half of the Song dynasty, noted for large hanging landscape scrolls, is also the earliest period from which survive a reasonable number of original works, although their subsequent prestige and market value has made forgery a thriving industry right down to the twenty-first century. One famous work from the eleventh century, *Travelers by Streams and Mountains* by Fan Kuan (active c. 1023–1031), now at the National Palace Museum, Taipei, Taiwan, is monumental in size (206.3 x 103.3 centimeters, almost seven feet high) and heroic in concept. The three planes of the painting, the smallest in the foreground giving way to immense scale and space beyond, illustrate a particularly Chinese expression of perspective. Inky, textured strokes in the bottom eighth of the picture depict a low-lying group of rocks. In the next section two tiny figures driving a mule team enter from the right; craggy hillsides spanned by a bridge rise above them, on which leafy gnarled trees grow, their trunks outlined in black; a temple roof appears at the timber line of the hill on the right. In the third section, which fills nearly two-thirds of the scroll, a giant mountain looms, rendered with dry-brushed ink strokes pressed closely together to create the illusion of a towering monolith. A waterfall drops from a cleft in the mountain like a decorative ribbon and dances its rhythmic course over rocks at the mountain's base, which is partly obscured by mist. The scene embodies a kind of naturalism—one could imagine standing in this landscape and experiencing the feeling the artist so clearly conveys: the glory of nature within the universe and the small role that humans play in this celestial plan.

A number of artists of the period, such as Guo Xi (c. 1020–1090) and Li Tang (c. 1050–c. 1130) practiced this new form of monumental realism in landscape painting. Emperor Huizong (r. 1101–1126) was a talented painter himself who led the Song dynasty academy. Perhaps his preoccupation with the arts was so intense that he neglected the threat to his empire when the Northern Jin state invaded his capital Bianliang (present-day Kaifeng). Some of the court fled south to Hangzhou, where his son established a temporary capital as the Southern Song (1127–1279).

The Southern Song emperor Gaozong (reigned 1127–1162) reestablished the academy in this milder clime. Living next to the beautiful West Lake surrounded by mountains, lush flora, and trailing mists, artists confronted a new imperial mood and a new way to convey an atmospheric landscape. Song rulers were no longer lords of the "Middle Kingdom," as the Chinese named their country. They were a military failure in flight from the northern conquerors. Having lost their confidence as masters of their world they turned inward, living for the pleasures of the moment, day and night. Moreover, "form likeness," what they called copying from nature, was considered an unworthy goal.

Southern Song paintings were smaller in concept and scale; handscrolls designed for intimate viewing unwound with a cinematic effect, and album leaves (pages) provided yet a smaller scale. Artists no longer attempted to paint towering landscapes that conveyed the precise wonders of a scene; instead they focused on compositions that expressed a lyrical mood, something the art historian James Cahill, a Chinese specialist, calls "a blend of dream and reality." Two outstanding academy artists, Ma Yuan (flourished c. 1190–c. 1225) and Xia Gui (c. 1180–1230) used simplified forms—contrasts of light and dark, and great expanses of blank space—to suggest a fleeting world captured only in glimpses. The extant portions of Xia Gui's *Twelve Views from a Thatched Hut* (handscroll, ink on silk, 28 centimeters [11 inches] high; 2.31 meters [about 7.5 feet] long) show subtly and perfectly modulated ink washes that evoke a landscape veiled in mist; just a few deft brushstrokes indicate details of the scene—grasses, trees, fisherman, and two bent-over human figures carrying heavy pails.

The "Ma-Xia one-cornered style," an innovation named after these Southern Song masters, conveyed a sense of space by using asymmetrical compositions. Ma's *Viewing Plum Blossoms by Moonlight* (Metropolitan Museum of Art), a silk fan mounted on an album leaf, exemplifies this charmingly off-center configuration; an angular landscape of cliff and mountains occupies the space on the lower left, from which white-robed gentlemen gaze at plum branches reaching toward the moon—a small, pale circle counterbalanced and floating in the sense of limitless space on the upper right.

Although the Mongol conquest of China during the Yuan dynasty (1279–1368) devastated the Chinese in many respects, the arts continued to flourish. Many Song scholars refused to serve their new "barbarian" rulers and devoted themselves to literati pursuits of painting, poetry, and calligraphy. One such scholar, Ni Zan (1301–1374), who had grown up in effete luxury but then withdrew from official society, ignored the traditional spatial convention of near, middle, and far distances as they spanned from the bottom of the picture to the top. Scholars interpret Ni Zan's un-peopled compositions—with

Shen Zhou (1427–1509), *Watching the Mid-Autumn Moon*. Ink and colors on paper. Shen was the first to use the motif of a poet dominating the nature he observes instead of being dwarfed by it.

standard-issue trees, rocks and mountains—as an expression of the artist's isolation from his foreign-occupied world, and a longing for a simpler time. James Cahill calls Ni Zan's dry-brushed compositions "unimpassioned, subdued, and static."

The range of landscape styles during the late Yuan dynasty increased as literati pursued and developed painting outside the influence of the court. Wang Meng (ca.1308–1385), another painter whose work conveys an aura of detachment, seemed to fill every square inch of silk with trees, rocks, streams, architecture, animals, and people. Fang Congyi (c.1301–c. 1393) paints in a powerful, individual, and more emotional style, with inky trees and flowing ink lines. His hillside mushrooms up in a powerful explosion of black strokes to an umbrella crest of vegetation, while shadowy mountains rise in the distance.

The restoration of Chinese rule with the Ming dynasty (1368–1644) reinforced literati dominance of high Chinese culture, but such tastes did not totally predominate. The Ming saw a resurgence of popular culture and art with accelerating economic growth and urbanization; like Europe in this period, China too was developing a middle-class culture rather different from rural-based folk culture, itself given a boost by the availability of cheap, popular prints. (Most of the vernacular painting and printmaking for popular or middle-class consumption, however, has been lost.) Yet the history of the period remains associated with upper-class art and, as many art historians agree, that art is one of the most sophisticated traditions in global art history.

The Ming's conscious attempt at summoning leading artists to court resulted in the group informally called the Ming Academy. These artists produced colorful bird-and-flower paintings in dramatically decorative styles as well as portraits, history, and genre paintings. At the same time the rise of amateur literati artists, who had gained recognition in the Southern Song and Yuan, became a more important part of Chinese art. Shen Zhou (1427–1509), a shining example of a literati painter born into a family of scholars-painters, learned many styles by copying. Thus with a mastery of ancient styles he created his own compositions—Shen was the first to use the motif of a poet dominating the nature he observes, not being dwarfed by it—and included poems in a finely wrought calligraphic hand to reinforce the painting's meaning. In *Watching the Mid-Autumn Moon*, (ink and colors on paper, Museum of Fine Arts, Boston), the artist and his friends sit drinking wine in a grass shack across from an expanse of still water, while the harvest moon shines. His heart-felt poem extols enduring friendship and the evanescence of life.

Later in the Ming, Dong Qichang (1555–1636) dominated the scene as scholar-official, painter, and theorist. His view of Chinese art history divided painters into two schools: a northern (conservative) school dominated by professional painters whose often-decorative style emphasized technical skill (something he categorized as "sweet vulgarity"), and a southern (progressive) school whose painters aimed for free, expressive brushstrokes and the development of personal style. (Neither school depended on any

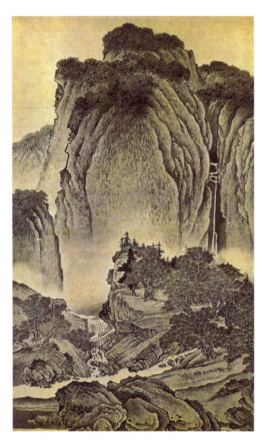

Dong Qichang (1555–1636), *Traveler in the Mountains*. Dong—a Ming court scholar-official, painter, and theorist—advocated preserving the values and traditions of the cultivated scholar.
National Palace Museum, Taipei, Taiwan.

and background; he effectively flattened space so that mountains, trees, and rocks functioned less as representational forms than as semi-abstractions. In *Autumn Mountains* Dong Qichang shows his innovative spirit by arranging his landscape arbitrarily; curving mountains hug the earth and trees march into the distance like soldiers at the painter's command.

The Last Emperors: 1644–1911/12

The Manchu conquerors of China, who ruled as the Qing dynasty (1644–1911/12), went to great lengths to conciliate the Confucian literati class, and they became avid patrons of Chinese high culture. Eventually most Chinese scholar painters were reconciled to Manchu rule, but several "loyalist painters"—because of their creativity, but also perhaps due to their blood ties to the Ming, which appealed to modern Chinese nationalism—have been highly esteemed since the twentieth century. Two worthy of mention are Zhu Da (1626–1705) and Zhu Ruoji (1642–1707), better known by their respective assumed names, Bada Shanren and Shi Tao.

Zhu Da lived in luxury as a Ming prince until the age of eighteen, when the dynasty fell. He joined a Buddhist monastery where, according to some historians, he affected "crazy" behavior to escape Qing persecution. He took the name Bada Shanren (Dweller of Eight Great Mountains) and channeled his despair into painting flowers and birds (the latter usually rendered with angry expressions and only one leg), fish and other creatures, and simple landscapes with powerful inky black strokes that course across the paper in surprising directions. His work falls well within the Chan (Zen) Buddhist tradition of seeking essential truth within a tiny piece of nature. Shi Tao, another relative of the Ming, was only two when the Qing came to power. His principled eremitism earned the respect of Confucian literati and his emphasis on originality has made him an icon for modern Chinese ink painters. At times some of his landscapes approach abstraction; in one, an album leaf simply called *Landscape*, a monk sits in a small hut enveloped by heavily outlined, mountainous terrain dotted with

geographic significance.) Dong introduced ideas used to discuss calligraphy, such as "opening and closing," and "rising and falling," into dialogues about painting. He advocated learning from ancient masters before attempting to paint from nature, cautioning that the excellence of a painting should not be judged by how closely the work resembles nature, but by its evocative power.

Dong's landscapes show deliberate dissonances in the relationship between foreground, middle ground,

Lin Fengmian (1900–1991), *Portrait of a Woman Reading*. Chinese painters in the 1930s who stressed the realism rather than the abstraction of Western art got more support from the Nationalist government. Photo by Joan Lebold Cohen.

vegetation that seems, literally, to swallow him up. Dots, traditionally used to suggest diminutive vegetation on rocks, assume a much more dominant place in this composition; Shi Tao's use of them clearly influenced Wu Guanzhong (b. 1919), whose *Pine Spirit* (1984), with its links to abstract expressionism, still pays homage to Chinese tradition.

The Manchus, who had already adopted many Chinese practices before ruling as the Qing, continued to show respect for Chinese art that was based on the study of old styles and masters. Literati painting in the Qing thus became orthodox and stereotyped, especially as represented by the prestigious "Four Wangs" of the late seventeenth and early eighteenth centuries: Wang Shimin (1592–1680), Wang Jian (1598–1677), Wang Hui (1632–1717), and Wang Yuanqi (1642–1715). But painting was still infused with a current of individualism and the idea that the art represented the moral character of the artist. In the eighteenth century a group known as the "Eight Eccentrics of Yangzhou," named for the prosperous commercial center in the lower Yangzi Valley where they worked, continued in this direction, appealing to the tastes of an audience beyond the court with figural subjects (and more flowers and birds) that were less ponderous and more commercially viable than landscapes.

Many have claimed that, after the trauma of Mongol Yuan, Chinese culture adopted an inward, "Great Wall" mentality. This is only partly true, although "foreign" Buddhist art, long since sinicized, had indeed lost much of its creative force. Systematic contact with maritime Europe started in the sixteenth century and had some influence on some aspects of Chinese art, largely through European prints brought by Jesuit missionaries; such traces can be found in portrait painting from the late 1600s onward, and in efforts at fixed-point perspective in early seventeenth-century landscapes. In general, literati artists regarded European painting as a curiosity rather than serious art, but Qing emperors were enamored of Western representational techniques and the effects of chiaroscuro. The Jesuit missionary Giuseppe Castiglione (1688–1766), who became a court painter for the Qing sometime after 1716 (under the Chinese name Lang Shining), worked to some extent with Chinese assistants to synthesize European methods and traditional Chinese media.

Chinese ceramics, however, made a very significant impact on the rest of the world, including Europe. China's long history of advanced ceramic technique culminated in the perfection of smooth white and green celadon in the Song and true porcelain in the Ming. Appreciated as an object d'art by both court and literati, porcelain was nevertheless a tradesman art. There were famous kilns, like Jingdezhen in Jiangxi Province under imperial control, but no famous potters. Porcelain was a major Chinese contribution to world trade and world culture, but in China it was not an art form in which a gentleman could express his command of high culture.

Art historians have generally regarded the nineteenth century in Chinese art as a period of stasis, if not decline, but this characterization may be oversimplified. The cultural changes that slowly began to influence Chinese artists at the end of the Qing dynasty can best be understood by reviewing the dark period that began with foreign invasions and civil wars in the mid-nineteenth century. After Britain's victory in the First Opium War of 1839–1842 (a second war would follow from 1856 to 1860), the defeated Chinese conceded five treaty ports where foreigners could live and trade. The opening of treaty ports brought new visions of the world through books, magazines, technologies, and materials. Photography and various printing techniques, including Japanese-style woodblock printing, all of which were quite different from methods previously practiced in China, helped to disseminate new views.

In 1864, after the Taiping Rebellion, a prolonged and devastating civil war conducted under the ominous presence of Western troops, Qing imperial forces finally triumphed over peasant forces. Chinese felt increasing pressure after the French conquest of neighboring Vietnam and when Japan defeated China in 1895. The final blow came in 1900 when legions of foreign soldiers defeated the imperial troops in the Boxer Rebellion. At the same time many intellectuals did indeed find nineteenth-century ink painting on silk and paper stagnant. Paintings of idealized mountain landscapes, thought to be without energy and originality, had little relationship to the multiple realities of China—from the increasingly international cities to the decreasingly pristine countryside. But the changes to Chinese traditional painting were subtle in the beginning, introduced one small step at a time. In the second half of the century, a resurgence of calligraphic styles that had been used in ancient "metal and stone" inscriptions revitalized painting in the modern urban center of Shanghai, where the grand literati genre of landscape painting was eclipsed by new vigor in flower-and-bird and some figure painting. It is by no means clear that Chinese art had lost all its creative vitality. In particular, the "Four Rens" in Shanghai (Ren Bonian, Ren Xiong, Ren Yu, and Ren Xun) looked both backward to the grand tradition of ink

Huang Binhong, landscape painting (1982). Even after the end of imperial China, landscape painting continued to develop as artists expressed the new and engaged the old. Photo by Joan Lebold Cohen.

painting and forward to the challenges posed by the coming of the West.

Post-Imperial, Modern China

The movement of reform in Chinese art, connected to the introduction of modern science in China, started before the end of the Qing dynasty with the emergence of the first Western-style schools and the inclusion of Western-style drawing as part of the curriculum. After the establishment of the Republic of China in 1912, a weak government prevented the state from leading this educational reform effectively, although the Minister of Education, Cai Yuanpei, considered art to be an essential part of modern culture and spiritual values. But within several years Liu Haisu (1896–1994), a precocious teenager who would go on to be a leading oil painter and art educator in the

Qi Baishi (1864–1957). A painting of fish and crabs. Qi favored mundane subjects ignored by the elite.
Photo by Joan Lebold Cohen.

Republican era, founded the first private art school in Shanghai. By the 1920s a number of art schools appeared in other major cities such as Guangzhou (Canton) and Beijing, with young artists who had studied in Europe or Japan taking the lead in teaching the new Western art—oil painting, sculpture, design—to an iconoclastic generation eager to rejuvenate Chinese culture.

Their efforts remained a very small part of total Chinese art, confined to major cities and with more effective state support after the establishment of the Nationalist (Guomindang) government in Nanjing in 1927. The next ten years were the most productive period for introducing Western art, both formal academic styles (as represented by the L'Ecole des Beaux Arts–trained oil painter Xu Beihong at the new National University in Nanjing), and by more modernist painters such as Lin Fengmian in Hangzhou and Pang Xunqin in Shanghai. All Western styles were, of course, new and "modern" to China. But there was a sharp difference between two factions: on one side the putative avant-garde who saw the latest styles of Western modernism—post-Impressionism, Expressionism, Surrealism—as the shock treatment needed to stimulate a progressive modern consciousness in China; and on the other side, those who stressed the scientific realism of more conventional Western art as the key to building national strength. The latter would eventually get more support from the Nationalist government and their Communist successors.

Ink painters remained far more numerous and claimed a far larger share of a growing urban art market. Many clung to tradition but others tried to use modern innovations such as galleries and exhibitions to keep the tradition alive and develop it further. Two of the most famous landscape artists, Huang Binhong (1864–1955) and Zhang Daqian (1899–1983), both called on ink painters to be inventive and display a new energy within the old parameters. Huang explored a deeper level of intensity in black ink; Zhang used color with inventive boldness, especially after he toured the Mogao caves in Dunhuang during the 1940s. There he copied the Buddhist cave murals, using the past as inspiration to rejuvenate the present.

Probably the most famous twentieth century artist, however, was the carpenter-turned-literati-painter Qi Baishi. He reinvigorated the literati tradition by painting humble subjects—garden vegetables, fish, shrimp, and baskets—often with splashes of brilliant color. But his calligraphy, poetic inscriptions, and seal carving (an artist's insignia stamped on a painting) were all continuations of that cultural milieu—and his venerable appearance fit the role perfectly. He was lionized in both the Nationalist and Communist eras.

The Japanese invasion in 1937 politicized much of Chinese art, but this trend was apparent even earlier in the left-wing woodcut movement supported by modern China's most famous writer, Lu Xun. The woodcut print was an old medium in China but new movement—its strong and distorted styles inspired by Western artists such as the German Expressionist

Dong Xiwen, *Founding of the Nation* (1954). Oil on canvas. This iconic example of Chinese Socialist Realism depicts Mao on the balcony of Tiananmen Square on 1 October 1949.

Kathe Kollowitz and modernist Russian print makers—introduced themes of social criticism and patriotic resistance against the Japanese. During the War Against Japan (1937–1945) many of these young artists joined the Communist Party in its rural base in the far northwest and shifted their artistic focus to appeal more to peasant tastes. This trend foreshadowed the fate of most Western modernist styles under the People's Republic. Art, in Mao Zedong's words, must "serve the people."

"Serving the people" meant that art and artists had to follow the revolutionary agenda of the Communist Party in a prescribed style called Socialist Realism, a term borrowed from Stalin's Soviet Union. Perhaps the most iconic example of the style was Dong Xiwen's (1914–1973) *Founding of the Nation* (1954), which depicts Mao atop the balcony of Tiananmen Square on 1 October 1949 as he announced the establishment of the People's Republic. The dramatically arranged composition, with the new leadership lined up at Mao's side, inferred infinite control and a great future. The Communist Party distributed reproductions of the painting as a form of propaganda over a period of years, but the copies (and the painting itself) had to be doctored several times as figures present on that historic occasion disappeared when they were removed from power.

Traditional ink painting, linked to feudalism, was condemned as part of the old society in 1949. Not surprisingly, many ink painters fought passionately to restore its status, and it resonated with Chinese cultural nationalism especially after the split with the Soviet Union in 1960. The new compositions retained the Socialist Realist formulae but used ink and watercolor as the media. In one prominent example of this "new red wine in old Chinese bottles," the talented revolutionary woodcut-artist-turned-ink-painter, Shi Lu (1919–1982), created *Fighting in Northern Shaanxi* (1959) in a reprogrammed ink and watercolor style. A small but empathic figure of Mao stands triumphantly peering over the steep drop of rocky mountain dramatically bathed in a revolutionary red–washed landscape.

The politicization of art reached its peak during the Cultural Revolution (1966–1976), the last ten years of Mao's life. For instance, Dong Xiwen had to paint the disgraced president of the People's Republic, Liu Shaoqi, out of *Founding of the Nation*, and Shi Lu was

Liu Haisu (1896–1994), a leading oil painter and art educator in the Republican era, founded the first private art school in Shanghai. Photo by Joan Lebold Cohen.

denounced for making Chairman Mao so small in his *Fighting in Northern Shaanxi*.

For a time Cultural Revolution populism demanded that art be for and by the people, with famous artists denounced either for reactionary feudal thought, bourgeois influences, or both. But by the end of the Cultural Revolution and the beginning of Deng Xiaoping's reform policies both traditional ink painting and less political art came back in all fields.

The first somewhat premature assault on Socialist Realism as a style and doctrine came from a group of young artists in Beijing who took the name "Star Stars." In late September 1979, they created works in previously taboo modernist styles with even more taboo political and sexual content. They hung an unauthorized exhibition outside the National Art Gallery for two days before police removed it.

Though temporarily stalled, the new generation of artists' impulse to explore modern Western styles could no longer be held back as China opened to the world economically and culturally. By the mid-1980s a "New Art Tide" (*xin meishu chao*) was rising, particularly among students at the state's most prestigious art academies. It crested and broke with a privately sponsored exhibition, "China Avant-Garde," at the National art Gallery in 1989.

This large-scale exhibition drawing younger artists from all over China featured Western-inspired art forms—conceptual art, installation art, mixed media, performance art—as well as all manner of twentieth-century Western modernist styles in painting and sculpture. *Dialog* epitomized the confrontational nature of performance art and prompted authorities to close the show. *Dialog*'s two young artists fired pistol shots into a pair of telephone booths they had set up with dummies of a woman and a man connected in their telephone conversation. Five months later the avant-garde's dialog with authorities broke down completely when the more lethal gunfire in Tiananmen Square marked the crushing of the student-led democracy movement.

Democracy may have been stopped in Tiananmen, but new art was not as China became increasingly integrated with the rest of the world at the end of the twentieth century. The 1990s saw the rise of genres popular with foreign buyers, such as "Cynical Realism" and "Political Pop," which turned some younger artists into market superstars. Several who combine painting with installation and/or performance art have become international art celebrities with critical acclaim and exhibitions in the West and subsequent fame in China, especially Gu Wenda and Xu Bing, who both have lived in the United States for long periods. Their deconstruction of the Chinese written language by producing meaningless Chinese characters, either calligraphically or by woodblock printing, has struck a responsive postmodernist cord in the West for toying with the pillars of the

There is in fact no such thing as art for art's sake, art that stands above classes, art that is detached from or independent of politics. Proletarian literature and art are part of the whole proletarian revolutionary cause. • **Mao Zedong (1893–1976)**

established culture, suggesting its impotence and irrelevance. Another émigré, Cai Guo-Qiang, has become famous for his exploitation of gunpowder, another Chinese discovery, in large-scale pyrotechnic displays. He orchestrated the fireworks for the 2008 Beijing Olympics.

The speed of this leap from domestic to global in the early years of the new millennium is an affirmation of China's creativity and innovation. Even if belated, this recognition in the art world has been welcomed by the Chinese, as they achieve a difficult feat: to create new art that is both international and Chinese.

Joan Lebold COHEN
Independent scholar, Fairbank Center for East Asian Studies

Ralph C. CROIZIER
University of Victoria

Further Reading

Andrews, J. & Kuiyi Shen. (1998). *A century in crisis* [exhibition catalogue]. New York: Guggenheim Museum.

Barnhardt, R. M.; Fong, Wen C.; & Hearn, M. (1996). *Mandate of heaven* [exhibition catalogue]. Zurich: Rietberg.

Cahill, J. (1985). *Chinese painting*. New York: Skira/Rizzoli.

Cahill, J. (1976). *Hills beyond a river*. New York: Weatherhill.

Cahill, J. (1978). *Parting at the shore*. New York: Weatherhill.

Cahill, J. (1982). *The compelling image*. Cambridge, MA: Harvard University Press.

Cahill, J. (1982). *The distant mountains*. New York: Weatherhill.

Chang, K. C. (1983). *Art, myth and ritual*. Cambridge, MA: Harvard University Press.

Ch'en, K. K. S. (1973). *The Chinese transformation of Buddhism*. Princeton, NJ: Princeton University Press, Princeton.

Chiu, M. & Zheng Shengtian. (2008). *Art and China's revolution*. New York: Asia Society.

Clunas, C. (1997). *Art in China*. Oxford, U.K.: Oxford University Press.

Cohen, J. L. (1987). *The new Chinese painting, 1949–1986*. New York: Harry N. Abrams.

Hearn, M. K. (2002). *Cultivated landscapes*. New York: Metropolitan Museum.

Hearn, M. K. (1996). *Splendors of Imperial China*. New York: Rizzoli.

King, R. (2009). *Art in turmoil: The Chinese cultural revolution, 1966–1976*. Vancouver: University of British Columbia Press.

Lee, S. E. (1974). *The colors of ink* [exhibition catalogue]. New York: Asia Society.

Puett, M. J. (2002). *To become a god*. Cambridge, MA: Harvard Yenching Institute.

Rogers, H. (Ed.). (1998). *China 5,000 years: Innovation and transformation in the arts* [exhibition catalogue]. New York: Guggenheim Museum Publications.

Sickman, L. & Soper, A. (1960). *The art and architecture of China*. Baltimore, MD: Penguin Books.

Sullivan, M. (1996). *Art and artists of twentieth century China*. Berkeley and Los Angeles: University of California Press.

Wu Hung. (1992). Art in a Ritual Context: Rethinking Mawangdui. *Early China, 17*, 122.

Yang Xin; Barnhart, R. M.; Nie Cheongzheng; Cahill, J.; Shaojun. L.; Wu Hung. (1997). *Three thousand years of Chinese painting*. New Haven, CT: Yale University Press.

Yiu, J. (2009). *Writing modern Chinese art*. Seattle: Seattle Art Museum.

Art—East Asian and European Connections

East Asian and European art intersected around 100 CE, when trade brought Chinese silk to Roman weavers. From 1200 to 1500, Europeans imported Chinese porcelains and founded potteries to create Chinoiserie ceramics. In the 1800s, European artists developed Japonisme, a style mixing Japanese woodblock print and European imagery. The West's further focus on traditional East Asian art and religion during the twentieth century influenced modern Western art.

By the first century CE, imperial Rome was connected to China by a tenuous filament of silk that stretched more than 11,000 kilometers from Luoyang, the capital of the Han dynasty (206 BCE–220 CE), to Rome. Roman weavers, lacking the coveted silkworm, depended on the import of Chinese raw materials to produce the luxury fabric Roman high society so craved. The enormous distances between the two cultural centers inhibited the flow of bulky goods, however, and though the exchange of commodities, medicinal herbs, gemstones, and gold for silk thread flourished, Chinese art had little influence on the arts of Rome or the lands in between.

By the ninth century CE, heavier items, such as Chinese porcelain, were traveling west along maritime trade routes. The Arab traveler Ibn Battuta (1304–1368/69) remarked on the "green pots" shipped from southern China's ports to the homes of affluent merchants on Africa's east coast. Ibn Battuta's description perfectly characterized the gray to yellow-green ware known in later years in the West as celadon. Known simply as *qingci* (green ware) in China, this ancient ceramic was perfected in the third and fourth centuries CE. As the backbone of the Chinese porcelain industry, *qingci* was mass-produced in such huge numbers that the Venetian traveler Marco Polo (1254–1324) marveled over ordinary Chinese eating rice from *porcella* bowls—that is, dishes with the hard, lustrous surface of a cowrie shell (*porcella*). In Europe, celadon's exquisite finish and elusive color promoted this fine ceramic from dinner table to a place of honor in the curio cabinet. Interestingly, these cherished imports were often modified to suit European taste in ways that would have shocked their Chinese makers. Thus, a bowl of "grene pursselyne," reportedly given by the British archbishop of Canterbury William Warham (c. 1504–1532) to New College, Oxford University, was set in silver gilt, signifying its acceptance as an objet d'art fit for display with similar ceramics that had also been privileged with grandiose mounts.

In Asia, fine ceramics for everyday use were the stock-in-trade of massive export programs; as many as forty thousand pieces of various sorts have been recovered from a single shipwreck. Although choice examples may have graced an imperial table as testimony to wealth and good taste, ceramics retained a functional character in Asia until the late nineteenth century, when the collapsing Qing dynasty cut off the flow of patronage that supported the manufacture of the finest wares.

Chinese Blue and White

At the time of Marco Polo's sojourn in Cathay between 1275 and 1292, the domain of the Mongol ruler Khubilai Khan stretched from the Pacific Ocean to the Danube River, from the Himalaya to the Siberian forests. (Cathay, the Anglicized name for China, or Catai, gained currency in Europe when Marco Polo's journals were published.) The Mongol Empire encompassed within its boundaries Beijing, Samarqand, Karakorum, Moscow, all of Korea, parts of Southeast Asia, and Baghdad, the gem in the crown of Islam. This vast empire was one great trading zone where paper money (backed by precious metals and silk) facilitated the exchange of goods, none of which the Mongols made. A new kind of porcelain appeared during the reign of the Khans, one destined to become the most successful invention in ceramic history—Chinese blue and white porcelain.

The cobalt used to paint the vibrant blue designs on the white porcelain ground was originally imported from Persia (Iran). It may be that Persian merchants, residing in the port cities of southern China, were the original market for this ware; the enormous size of some early blue-and-white platters points to clients accustomed to eating off large, common plates, as the Persians did. Regardless, the demand for blue and white porcelain soon spread throughout the world, spawning speculation about the secret of its manufacture. Augustus the Strong (1670–1733), the elector of Saxony and king of Poland, sponsored Johann Friedrich Böttger (1682–1719) in experiments to produce porcelain, efforts that led to the establishment of the works at Meissen, Saxony, in 1710. European manufacture of porcelain did not interrupt the flow from China and Japan. The trade continued through the eighteenth century, with more than a million pieces entering northern Europe in 1774 alone.

Chinoiserie

Painted designs on Chinese porcelain provided an indirect model for the "Anglo-Chinese" gardens that were the rage in England in the early eighteenth century. The small pictures on the porcelain items inspired actual European and American replicas: in England, the pagoda erected in Kew Gardens, the arched fretwork bridge at Hampton Court (now destroyed, but known through an engraving by the Venetian painter Canaletto), and the fretwork arms of a Chippendale chair; and in America, the fence Thomas Jefferson designed for the University of Virginia campus. Views of merchant houses painted on export porcelains were like illustrated postcards providing a glimpse of Chinese interiors and their furnishings. These miniature views, occasionally buttressed by the reports of travelers to Asia, provided the underpinning for the style known as Chinoiserie. The painter and designer François Boucher (1703–1770) was a master of that hybrid manner. Boucher's romantic *Chinese Fishing Party* (1741) melds Asian-looking actors with an ethereal French setting perfectly attuned to the tastes of his patrons, the French king Louis XV and the Marquise de Pompadour.

Chinoiserie does not exclusively depict Chinese subjects. Japanese themes were included in these Rococo fantasies, reflecting the long-standing trade in Japanese goods. By 1639, the Dutch were established at Deshima Island in Nagasaki Harbor, exporting the Arita and Imari porcelain, which Dutch factories sometimes imitated. Deshima remained the exclusive port of call for foreign trade and the only place where enterprising Japanese could gain knowledge of European art, science, and technology.

The arrival of the American admiral Matthew Calbraith Perry (1794–1858) and his sail- and steam-powered ships in Shimoda Harbor in 1853, followed by the successful negotiation of the Kanagawa and Shimoda treaties, guaranteed trade between Japan and the United States. Because of treaties like these, the world became one great trading zone connected by wind and steam, the telegraph, newspapers, and international expositions (really trade shows) advertising a nation's most-prized products. The Asian exhibits included various kinds of porcelain, svelte lacquer boxes, refined metalwork, wonderful fabrics,

The pagoda at London's Kew Gardens. In the nineteenth-century "Anglo-Chinese" gardens were all the rage.

and in some instances replicas of teahouses, gardens, and even miniature villages that gave life to the paper images sold to be viewed with the newly invented stereopticon. The citizens of the world were getting to know one another and to share their finest products as never before.

Japonisme

Japanese woodblock prints were sometimes part of the trade show inventory. Though not valued as fine art in Japan, the colorful pictures of actors, courtesans, and landscapes filtering into Europe had great appeal for artists such as Claude Monet (French; 1840–1926), who found in these prints both inspiration and confirmation of his own efforts to forge a modern style. Monet covered his dining room wall with Japanese prints, built a Japanese garden with an arched wooden bridge, and posed his wife in a bright kimono against a background accented with Japanese fans. That picture, *La Japonaise: Madame Monet in Japanese Costume* (1876), was exhibited alongside other Japonisme-style works by Mary Cassatt (American; 1844–1926) and Paul Gauguin (French; 1848–1903). Some artists drew directly from the print sources. Gauguin incorporated a sketch of wrestling figures, copied from the Manga (Sketchbooks) of Hokusai (1760–1849), into his *Vision after the Sermon* (1888). Vincent van Gogh (Dutch; 1853–1890) made a close copy of

"Evening Shower at Atake and the Great Bridge," number fifty-two in the print series *One Hundred Famous Views of Edo* (c. 1856–1858) by Hiroshige (1797–1858). *Nocturne in Black and Gold: The Falling Rocket* (c. 1875), by James McNeill Whistler (American; 1834–1903), is indebted to Hiroshige's prints of the same subject.

The popularity of the prints among these artists was not solely because of their availability, flat color, lack of modeling, or the choice of unusual points of view. Part of their appeal was on the social level. Their treatment of "low-life" themes in Edo (present-day Tokyo) was in sympathy with depictions of the demimonde in Paris, such as those by Henri Toulouse-Lautrec (French; 1864–1901). The exotic sexuality of the Japanese prints in the *ukiyo-e* style (drawings of Edo's "floating world," or pleasure quarters) found a match in the eroticized novels of the French naval officer Louis-Marie-Julien Viaud (under the pseudonym Pierre Loti; 1850–1923) and the opera *Madame Butterfly* (1904), by the Italian composer Giacomo Puccini (1858–1924). And the fascination of the urban citizen of Edo with landscape was in harmony with the *plein air* (outdoor) movement in European painting.

Curiously, the earlier influence of Western art on these same Japanese printmakers is less well publicized. The most famous of all Japanese prints, Hokusai's "In the Trough of the Great Wave at Kanagawa" (first in the series *Thirty-Six Views of Mt. Fuji*, c. 1827) was derived from earlier studies that Hokusai called the "Great Wave in the Western Manner." And both Hokusai and Hiroshige designed prints illustrating one-point perspective, a Western technique. East and West, artists were looking at one another's work for inspiration and guidance.

Influential Role of Museums

In the latter part of the nineteenth century, adventurous Westerners began to report directly from Asia. The American writer Lafcadio Hearn (1850–1904), fleeing Western materialism, published *Japan, An Attempt at Interpretation*. The Harvard-educated Ernest

Claude Monet, *La Japonaise: Madame Monet in Japanese Costume* (1876). Oil on canvas. Museum of Fine Arts, Boston. Monet, inspired by all things Japanese, also built a Japanese garden with an arched wooden bridge.

Fenollosa (1853–1908) received a professorship in philosophy at Tokyo Imperial Normal School (precursor of Tokyo University), where he lectured (with little effect) on the value of Japanese art, which was depreciated in its homeland in the rush toward all things Western. In this climate of fevered modernization, Fenollosa purchased treasures that became the core of the Japanese collections in the Museum of Fine Arts, Boston. In 1912, Fenollosa published his influential *Epochs of Chinese and Japanese Art*.

Sitting on the floor of a room in Japan, looking out on a small garden with flowers blooming and dragonflies hovering in space, I suddenly felt as if I had been too long above my boots. • **Mark Tobey (1890–1976)**

James McNeill Whistler, *Nocturne in Black and Gold: The Falling Rocket* (c. 1875). Oil on panel. Japanese printmakers, such as Hokusai and Hiroshige, influenced the work of nineteenth-century European and American painters.

arts of different cultures. The painter Mark Tobey (American; 1890–1976) worked in the Seattle Art Museum and became interested in Chinese calligraphy, resulting in his "white writing," exhibited in New York in 1944. Tobey lived for a brief period in a temple on the outskirts of Kyoto, Japan. Morris Graves (American; 1910–2001), famous for his mystical "bird" paintings, visited East Asia several times between 1928 and 1930. Tobey and Graves both had an interest in Eastern religions, Tobey in Baha'i and Graves in Daoism and Zen Buddhism. Each would avow the influence of these spiritual systems on their works, though neither was imitating religious icons. What these artists sought was not just the form of Asian art but the essence of its spirit.

The master potter Bernard Leach (British; 1887–1979) was on the same spiritual quest. Together with Shoji Hamada (1894–1978), Leach brought Japanese ceramic practices, especially raku techniques, into the studio arts tradition. The rough-hewn ordinariness of raku ware and its spontaneous expressionism was the perfect complement to the intuitive experience essential to much mid-twentieth-century Action Painting and compatible with the spiritual intent of painters like Tobey and Graves. With the interest in raku came the tea aesthetic and an appreciation of Korean ceramics, celadon in particular, but also pieces displaying an accidental effect.

The influence of Asian art on Western painters that began with the Impressionists in Paris ended with artists like Tobey and Graves and the Abstract Expressionists, all of whom saw Asian art in the past tense. Van Gogh was copying thirty-year-old prints that were only available because they were devalued in Japan. The calligraphy admired by Tobey or the Zen-inspired painting that caught the attention of Graves and the painter and critic Roger Fry (English; 1866–1934) belonged to centuries-old traditions. The raku techniques introduced by Leach have had the most enduring effect, yet even this tradition is being challenged by a younger generation of studio potters. The Japanese-style gardens re-created in parks around the world echo old forms and not the new designs of the present generation in Japan. In

The public museum emerged as the ultimate market for works of art by the end of the nineteenth century and the beginning of the twentieth. In 1923, the American financier Charles Lang Freer (1856–1919) established a self-named gallery of Asian art in Washington, D.C., the first art museum in the Smithsonian system. And in 1936, the Chinese government staged the first "blockbuster" exhibition of Chinese art at Burlington House in London, giving Western audiences an opportunity to sample the full range of Chinese art.

Influence of Asian Spiritual Systems

The collections of Asian art amassed in the great museums in Europe and North America encouraged the public to pick and choose between the various the twenty-first century, the ease of communication along the World Wide Web—the electronic counterpart to the Silk Roads—has internationalized local East Asian artistic traditions to the point that it is difficult to distinguish the art of one country from another. As Leach would have it, "All from West to furthest East are unitive and not dualistic" (Leach 1988, 9–10).

Robert J. POOR
University of Minnesota

See also Art—China; Porcelain

Further Reading

Carswell, J. (1985). *Blue and white: Chinese porcelain and its impact on the Western world*. Chicago: University of Chicago, The David and Alfred Smart Gallery.

Imprey, O. (1977). *Chinoiserie: The impact of Oriental styles on Western art and decoration*. New York: Charles Scribner's Sons.

Leach, B. (1988). *Drawings, verse and belief*. Rockport, ME: One World Publications.

Phillips, J. G. (1956). *China trade porcelain*. Cambridge, MA: Harvard University Press.

Westgesst, H. (1996). *Zen in the fifties: Interaction in art between East and West*. Zwolle, The Netherlands: Waanders Uitgevers.

Wichmann, S. (1985). *Japonisme: The Japanese influence on Western art in the 19th and 20th centuries*. New York: Park Lane (distributed by Crown).

Willetts, W. (1958). *Chinese art*. New York: George Braziller.

Wood, F. (1996). *Did Marco Polo go to China?* Boulder, CO: Westview Press.

Wood, F. (2003). *The Silk Road: Two thousand years in the heart of Asia*. Berkeley: University of California Press.

Art—Europe

European art evolved as the concept of "Europe" and its culture changed over time—from the beginning of early Christian-era iconography to the changes in visual expression influenced by shifting empires and tribal migrations. The Renaissance and its retro-focus on classical Greece and Rome brought emphasis from the divine to the individual, until, in the modern era, art needed no ulterior meaning or external reference.

The history of European art is related to the idea of Europe itself, an idea that has been in transition during the twenty-first century. Although the ever-evolving boundaries of modern Europe were not delineated until the nineteenth century, well before that people may have considered themselves "European," and important artistic activity occurred on the European continent and the island land masses associated with it. The evolution of European art is characterized by the process of fusion and transmutation, much as the political entities of modern Europe developed from encounters between different migrating cultures. The proliferation of Christianity had an important impact on the development of a specifically European art and on its distinctiveness in world cultures, at least until the nineteenth century.

This article focuses on five historical periods: art of the early Christian era (c. 200–400 CE); art of the migrating tribes (400–800 CE); art during the Middle Ages (500–1400); art during the Renaissance and Baroque (1400–1800); and art of the so-called modern world (1800–2000). Although this discussion begins around the start of the common era and is inextricably bound up with the rise and dissemination of Christianity, important art was produced on the European continent during the Paleolithic and Neolithic periods (cave paintings and sculpture in the former, sculpture and architecture in the latter).

Early Christian Art

The most significant achievement of the early Christian period was the forging of a new iconographic language that expressed the tenets of Christianity from a variety of Mediterranean antecedents: the Greco-Roman world, the Old Testament, and Egyptian art. Christians excelled at appropriation to communicate their message, and the visual tropes that were developed at that time persisted through the later periods of European Art.

Catacomb Painting and Early Christian Iconography

The first art that can be associated with Christianity and the vocabulary of Christian signs was created in the Roman catacombs around 270 CE, when Christianity was one among many cults within the Roman Empire. The catacombs were underground burial sites, used by many sects as well as by Christians; a network of chambers and compartments had been dug under Rome and particularly its outlying areas. Although they were not places of worship, their walls were often covered with imagery that marked the religious affiliation of the deceased.

The chamber devoted to Saint Peter and Saint Marcellinus in the Catacomb of Priscilla (fourth century

CE) provides a good example of how diverse sources were melded together to symbolize Christian resurrection. An image of the Good Shepherd, drawn from classical iconography, occupies the center of the ceiling. In a Christian context, this image represents Christ leading his flock to salvation. Images of salvation drawn from Hebrew scripture surround the central image, such as Jonah being spat out by the whale or Noah relaxing under a vine and fig tree after the flood. New Testament expressions of salvation through Christian sacraments such as the Baptism and the Eucharist (Last Supper) flank the central image of the Good Shepherd in a similar configuration in the Catacomb of Callixtus (second and third centuries CE). In one of the first depictions of the Virgin Mary and the Christ child, a woman nurses her child next to a haloed male figure, most likely Balaam, who points to a star over her head; the image, located in the chamber of the Velatio (veiled woman) in the Catacomb of Priscilla, draws upon Egyptian depictions of Isis suckling Horus.

One of the earliest depictions of the Virgin and Child, from the Catacomb of Priscilla, draws upon Egyptian images of Isis suckling Horus.

Constantine, the Church, and the Empire

In 312, on the night before the battle of the Milvian Bridge, the Roman emperor Constantine allegedly dreamt of an insignia emblazoned with the entwined letters *chi* and *rho*, the first two letters of the word *Christ* in Greek, and the Latin phrase *in hoc signo vinces* (in this sign you will win). While carrying the sign of Christ into battle the following day, he defeated his rival Maxentius. Thus began a series of enactments whereby Christianity went from a persecuted cult to a state religion in a period of ten years. Constantine was a pivotal figure. He came to power as a Roman emperor, became the first Christian emperor, and ultimately was the first Byzantine emperor as well. The visual depictions that were formulated during his reign had an important impact on the development of European art for the next 1,500 years.

When Christianity became the state religion of Rome, the power of the empire was placed behind the church, thus stimulating the construction of large-scale buildings. Classical structures were transformed to fulfill the needs of Christian worship, with two architectural forms becoming dominant. The longitudinal form, derived from the Roman basilica but revised to be oriented from east to west along its vertical axis, became the format for the Eucharistic church, which was designed to hold masses of people: Saint Peter's, Saint John of the Lateran, and Saint Paul Outside the Walls. The centralized form, derived from baths and tombs, became associated with baptisteries and *martyria* (building dedicated to and containing the relics of martyrs).

The power of the empire was also reflected in the developing iconography, particularly as images of Christ portrayed as a Good Shepherd gave way to images with imperial connotations. The depiction of Christ as emperor first appears in Constantinian basilicas of the fourth century; a mosaic in the apse of Santa Pudenziana (390 CE), for example, shows him bearded and enthroned, surrounded by his apostles.

The nave of Saint Paul Outside the Walls (385 CE) also contains imperial imagery: the wall surface at the juncture between nave and apse is treated like a triumphal arch (c. 450 CE), with Christ—in an *imago clipeata* (framed portrait) at its apex—surrounded by the evangelist symbols, the twenty-four elders of the apocalypse, and images of Saint Peter and Saint Paul.

In 332 CE, to escape the disruption of intensifying tribal invasions, Constantine moved the seat of the empire to the ancient city of Byzantium on the Bosphorus, which resulted in the division of the Christian world into two empires, East and West. The Eastern Empire remained continuous from Constantine's era until the sack of Constantinople (now Istanbul) by the Ottoman Empire in 1456. Art forms became stabilized and persisted over those years as in a time capsule. The Western Empire went through a decline that took centuries to reverse. As Christianity moved from its Mediterranean base to outposts in northern Europe, the integration of diverse sources influenced artistic development.

Tribal Migration

In the age of migration a new imagery developed from the melding of northern tribal stylistic motifs with the Mediterranean structures that had become identified with Christianity. Indigenous northern styles were based upon a nonrepresentational visual vocabulary used in decorating portable secular objects. Often the size and complexity of the object reflected the status of its owner, as seen in the so-called Tara Brooch (c. 725 CE). A large ring brooch made from an assemblage of materials—its every surface, both front and back, is divided into sections teeming with complex, tightly entwined, boundary-pushing interlace. Even the slim vertical fastener is decorated, its finial a dragon's head with two bosses (button-like projections) for eyes.

The Book of Kells, a gospel manuscript—probably written and illustrated by monks on Scotland's island of Iona during the latter part of the eighth century CE, brought to the monastery in Kells, Ireland, in the late ninth century, and described in the twelfth century by Giraldus Cambrensis as "the work of angels"—reveals a similar decorative concept applied to a Christian object. A richly decorated page, in which the first words of the text are embedded in a lavishly wrought design covering the entire surface, introduces each gospel. The *Chi Rho* page (beginning the story of Christ's birth from the Book of Matthew) resembles a painted version of the Tara Brooch in which the large forms of the first Greek letters of Christ's name (*XPI*, or *chri*) have been divided into sections, crammed with interlace, and woven in to the page's surface with decorative motifs. A keen observer, however, notices human and animal forms hidden among spirals and abstract shapes; a wonderful bit of realism appears in the lower left-hand side: two cats crouch, ready to attack a pair of mice about to seize a Eucharistic wafer.

The Book of Kells also incorporates classical elements. Borrowing from the late Roman practice of preceding texts with portraits of their authors, the manuscript includes portraits of each gospel author sitting under an elaborately decorated arch. The book contains early northern attempts at creating visual narrative, such as the page depicting the arrest of Christ. Finally, this manuscript also reveals a fusion with Egyptian sources, probably related to the eremitic monastic tradition. The image of the Virgin holding the Christ child emphasizes the tender connection of the pair, as seen in images of Isis suckling Horus, rather than the rigidity of the Hodegetria (literally, "she who shows the way") frontal view, in which Virgin most often holds Jesus in her left arm and points toward him with her right hand, a pose ubiquitous in early Byzantine art.

Medieval Art, East and West

Two differing artistic traditions co-existed during the Middle Ages, corresponding to the division of the Roman Empire into East and West. Although they developed separately, there were occasional points of contact between them and they both exerted influences on the art of the following period.

Eastern

The major division in Byzantine art distinguishes works produced before the period of iconoclasm (early Byzantine art) and works produced after (middle and late Byzantine art). The emperor Justinian (527–565 CE) viewed himself as a second Constantine, and his reign is referred to as the "Golden Age" of Byzantine art. The court church of Justinian, the Hagia Sophia (537 CE, "Holy Wisdom") in Constantinople, designed by Anthemius of Tralles and Isidorus of Miletus, brilliantly merges centralized and longitudinal architectural forms and embodies the aesthetics of this first period. According to Justinian's court historian, Procopius, the vast, undulating space, its interior covered with gold mosaics and multicolored marble, seemed to radiate its own light. The dome, an engineering marvel supported on pendentives (spherical triangles) and punctuated by a ring of small windows, seemed to hover above the central space—in Procopius' words, "as if suspended from the heavens by a golden chain."

The period of iconoclasm (726–843 CE) involved a theological and cultural dispute concerning the nature of images, their veneration, and their relation to the godhead. Its resolution in the mid-ninth century resulted in a formula that remained operational until the mid-fifteenth century, when Constantinople was conquered by Islamic forces. The middle Byzantine church was built around a domed, centralized plan and was decorated with very restricted images arranged hierarchically. The highest areas were limited to images of Christ; the Virgin and child could be depicted in the apsidal area; the lower regions were limited to images relating to the liturgical feast days. This approach to decoration was prevalent not only in Constantinople, but in Greece, the Holy Land, and the Balkans.

During the latter period of Byzantine art, the image of the Virgin and child underwent an important transformation. Icons that used the older Hodegetria pose—in which the Virgin points to Christ as the way to salvation, continued to be produced—but the image of the "Madonna of Tenderness" served to express the intense emotional relationship between mother and child and exerted an important influence on images that were later developed during the Italian Renaissance.

During the Middle Ages the Eastern and Western empires were parallel universes, for the most part separate, but with numerous points of contact and interpenetrations. For example, an Ottonian (Germanic) king married a Byzantine princess in the late tenth century, which resulted in the increased use of Byzantine artistic styles and motifs. After 1096, crusaders to the Holy Land encountered many examples of Byzantine artistic production, which they brought back to the West. (Unfortunately, they also conquered and occupied Constantinople for just over fifty years, from 1204 to 1261 CE.) The city of Venice was a crossroads between the West and the East, as seen in the Church of San Marco (1071 CE) with its five Byzantine-inspired domed compartments, each covered in golden mosaics.

Western

Art and learning in northern Europe from the ninth through the twelfth centuries were practiced in monastic centers that were often supported by temporal rulers. Beginning with the reign of Charlemagne (742–814; reigned as Frankish king 768–814 and as emperor of the West 800–814), who had himself declared Holy Roman Emperor in the tradition of Constantine and Justinian, there were several so-called *renascences*, periods where the body of knowledge and the artistic styles of the classical world were consciously reinterpreted as models for contemporary practice.

The major achievement of the Western Middle Ages was the development of large architectural forms, the Romanesque pilgrimage church and the Gothic cathedral. Writing in the middle of the eleventh century, the monk Raoul Glaber described how the world began to be covered with a "white mantle of churches" after the year 1000 when, contrary to popular expectation, it had not been destroyed during the second coming. Whether or not for millennial reasons, during the eleventh century, western Europeans began to consolidate

Innovative architectural advances allowed Chartres Cathedral to be suffused with light. The significance was metaphoric: divine light modulated on Earth was emphasized by stained-glass windows depicting both sacred and secular subjects.

and expand their knowledge of construction methods. By the thirteenth century, the Western cathedral had been developed, primarily in France but also in England, Germany, and Italy.

The cathedral dedicated to the Virgin Mary at Chartres, southwest of Paris, provides an excellent example of how cathedrals (literally, bishops' seats) were encyclopedic embodiments of human knowledge. In its architecture, Chartres illustrates the most important advances of the period: how to build a tall building with a stone vault, for which the flying buttress was developed as a means of transferring the load from the interior to the exterior of the building through the logical application of the bay system of construction. This method allowed the building to be suffused with light, whose significance was metaphorical, the divine light modulated on Earth, emphasized by stained-glass windows that depict both sacred and secular subjects.

Monumental column statues—depicting nineteen of the twenty-two Old Testament figures said to be precursors of Christ—flank each of three portals, marking the passage from secular to sacred space; along with thematically coordinated high-relief sculptures set into arches over the doorways, they communicate a message of salvation through Christ while at the same time evoking the unity of human history and knowledge. Chartres was a center of learning, and such classical concepts as the *trivium* and *quadrivium* (curricula including, respectively: grammar, rhetoric, and logic; astronomy, geometry, arithmetic, and music) are also expressed on its surface, as is the passage of human time through the depiction of the signs of the zodiac and the labors of the months. Thus the building reflects the cosmos, the establishment of the Heavenly City of Jerusalem on Earth.

Renaissance and Baroque Art

Although there had been several smaller rebirths of classical culture during the Middle Ages, the ultimate one took place during the period (formally) called the Renaissance, when learned people made a concerted attempt to copy and reinterpret Greco-Roman texts and images with greater authenticity. This movement was self-defining and it was centered in Italy, although it was experienced in other geographical locals. Two important artistic developments emerged during the Renaissance: an emphasis on the human rather than on the divine, and the ability to make illusionistic depictions of the real world. Whereas in the Middle Ages the church was the major patron, the Renaissance, in concert with the emphasis on the individual, fostered the rise of the wealthy, aristocratic patron.

There is a substantial overlap between the late Gothic and the Renaissance periods: the tendency to make images that reflected actual human interactions

I live and love in God's peculiar light. • Michelangelo (1475–1564)

can be seen as early as the twelfth and thirteenth centuries. Nonetheless, the Renaissance is characterized by a conceptual shift, where, following the ancient Roman architect Vitruvius, "man" became the measure of all things, although the cosmos was still given divine authorship. The painting by Masaccio (1401–c. 1427) of the *Expulsion from Paradise* for the Brancacci Chapel, Church of Santa Maria del Carmine (Florence, 1426 CE) provides a good example of this change in consciousness. Here, the first humans are shown in a state of utter desolation and abjection—Adam covers his face, Eve lets out a wail—as they are forced to walk the face of the Earth in punishment for their disobedience. During the next hundred years the tendency to create accurate and convincing images of the human body became progressively more important; by the early sixteenth century Michelangelo (1475–1564) described his process of sculpting as "liberating" the human form that was "hiding" in the stone.

Likewise, during the fifteenth century artists sought to create pictorial illusions, conceiving the picture surface as a "window," a continuation of actual space. The ability to create illusionistic space was dependent on the mathematical discovery, by Brunelleschi (1377–1446) and Alberti (1404–1472), of single-point perspective, a method of accurately representing on a two-dimensional surface the spatial relationships of human vision, characterized by the convergence of parallel lines at a single vanishing point on the horizon. Although for many years artists had used an "empirical" perspective in which spatial relationships were approximated, mathematical single-point perspective was first employed in the early fifteenth century by artists such as Masaccio in his *Trinità* fresco (Florence, c. 1425).

Masaccio's northern contemporaries, such as Jan van Eyck (1395–1441), were less interested in mathematical construction, but these artists excelled in using atmospheric perspective (the progressive graying and loss of detail at the horizon) to communicate the sense of deep space. By the next century both methods had become standard painting procedure. Works centered around the papal chambers in the Vatican, such as Michelangelo's paintings on the Sistine Chapel ceiling (1510) or Raphael's on the walls of the Stanza della Signatura (1511), feature expansive vistas created through spatial illusionism.

The emphasis on verisimilitude that developed during the Renaissance remained a dominant artistic feature for the next four hundred years. During the Baroque period Caravaggio (1573–1610) used stark contrasts of light and dark to create intensely dramatic works, and Rembrandt (1606–1669) explored profound psychological states. Pictorial illusionism has become so normalized and naturalized that, even now, it is difficult to realize that those artistic criteria are relatively unique in human history, and that they are not the sole criteria of artistic skill and sophistication. Furthermore, a hierarchy of value developed in the post-Renaissance—Western "high art" tradition, where subjects drawn from history, myth, or the Bible were considered to be more "important" than others, such as landscapes, everyday scenes ("genre paintings"), or still life.

The Modern World

During the nineteenth century artists became interested in painting the actual without needing to imbue it with ulterior meaning. This lack of interest in ulterior meaning continued into the early twentieth century, when many artists also became interested in showing multiple perspectives, and culminated in an art that needed no external reference at all.

Nineteenth Century

Painting for its own sake was a goal of Impressionism, which began in France around 1870 and persisted for about twenty years. Like earlier nineteenth-century painters, the Impressionists were interested in depicting the specifics of the real world, but, pushing the envelope further, they attempted to make images that appeared to catch the transitory nature of perception.

The Impressionists took two basic approaches in their desire to capture the fleeting moment. The work

Mary Cassatt, *The Bath*. (1891–1892). Oil on canvas. By the 1890s Cassatt's compositions and color schemes showed a Japanese influence.

of Claude Monet (1840–1926), who was particularly interested in depicting the effects of light, exemplifies the first. In his *Impression: Sunrise* (1872), which gave its name to the movement when a journalist belittled the painting for its seeming lack of polish, or his *Sailboats at Argentueil* (1873), he used a broken brushstroke and patchily applied color to express the shimmer of light refracted in water. In the 1880s he began to paint in series, to observe the same scene at different times of day under different weather conditions, as in his many images of grain (or hay) stacks under the differing effects of sunrise, sunset, full sun, haze, rain, and snow. In the series depicting the water lilies in his garden at Giverny, on which he continued to work until his death in 1926, the desire to capture the ephemeral nature of perceived light is carried to its extreme as all referential objects dissolve into fragments of color.

The other approach, practiced by more artists, sought to depict the vagaries of "modern life," particularly the life of the modern city with its hustle and bustle of strangers in streets, cafés, and dance halls. Camille Pissarro (1830–1903) painted the boulevards of Paris seen from above, the traffic and people indicated by specks of paint. Edgar Degas (1834–1917) and Auguste Renoir (1841–1919) painted dancers caught in motion and people in cafés pausing in mid-drink. This way of seeing was particularly gendered, with women artists such as Mary Cassatt (1845–1926) and Berthe Morisot (1841–1895) concentrating on the interactions between women and children in their homes. The invention of photography in the first half of the nineteenth century influenced painters; Degas's image *Place de la Concorde: Vicomte Lepic* (1876), for instance, uses photographic compositional devices such as cropping. Degas and others were also aware of motion studies by photographers such as Eadweard Muybridge.

Japanese prints exerted another important influence on painters in both content and structure. With the opening up of Japan to the West in 1859, Western artists were introduced to the *ukiyo-e* (floating world) prints that presented images of ephemeral, daily human actions. Many painters sought to emulate the pictorial structure of Japanese woodcuts, which consisted of flattened planes and oblique entrances into the compositional space. Mary Cassatt was especially successful at capturing the effects of *japonisme* in her series of colored etchings achieved in the early 1890s, showing women going about their daily tasks, such as writing letters and bathing their children.

Early Twentieth Century

During the early twentieth century artists challenged the spatial system that had been devised during the Renaissance, seeking alternative approaches to representing three-dimensional space on a two-

Claude Monet, *Impression, Sunrise* (1873). Oil on canvas. The painting "gave" its name to the movement when a critic belittled Monet's technique as lacking in polish.

dimensional surface. The interest in showing multiple perspectives can be related to scientific developments of the early twentieth century that emphasized the reality of phenomena not readily apparent to the naked eye.

Cubist artists wanted to create a picture surface that reflected the active experience of seeing, where the eye is not static but rather composes an image by integrating myriad simultaneously perceived points of view. ("Cubism" was a pejorative term given to the movement by critics who found it puzzling and disturbing.) Pablo Picasso (1881–1973), Georges Braque (1882–1963), and Juan Gris (1887–1927) were the first to develop works that used this technique; rather than paint a recognizable image of a guitar player, for instance, the artist would depict "facets"—fragments of the guitar's strings, the player's fingers, and smoke from his cigarette—which the viewer would need to piece together in order to read the image. The first phase, known as "analytic cubism," is characterized by a greater use of faceting than in "synthetic" cubism, a slightly later phase, where the multiplicity of the facets is resolved into overlapping planes, as in Picasso's *Three Musicians* (1921).

The development of Cubism was important in that it integrated pictorial structure from non-European cultures with European modernism. In Picasso's *Les Demoiselles d'Avignon* (1906), for example, the face of the figure on the right looks very much like an African mask, with its abstracted features and multiple facets. By the early twentieth century, African art was being exhibited in European ethnological museums, where many artists responded to the abstract pictorial techniques of masks and other sculptures, as well as to their aura of mystery. Ironically, the structures were appropriated without a full understanding of the cultures from which they derived, and without consideration of the works' meanings within those cultures.

The way of seeing that developed in Cubism was influential in numerous other twentieth-century artistic movements. Artists in both Italy and Russia used related techniques to communicate the experience of physical motion. Umberto Boccioni (1882–1916) and the Futurists sought to communicate the experience of speed. Natalia Goncharova's (1881–1962) depiction of a bicyclist uses faceting to show the motion of the bicycle wheels and also the experience of the bicyclist as he sees the visual data of the world go by. Later, Goncharova and others attempted to depict moving rays of light, and other artists, such as Sonia Delaunay (1885–1979) and Robert Delaunay (1885–1941), also used faceting to communicate the simultaneity of vision, and to analyze light and its motion as well as the motion of the human eye. These latter artists began to make art that seemed increasingly more abstract, dependent less on perceived reality than on pictorial reality. Based on "pure plastic form" (the tensions that exist between colors and shapes and their placement on a pictorial surface), the work of art was conceived as sufficient to itself, needing no external reference, an extreme effect of the nineteenth-century turn away from content.

An interesting, and seemingly contradictory, extension of the development of artistic abstraction was the renewed desire to blur the boundaries between art and life. Many artists whose work was based on purely formal tensions sought to apply the same principles to the design of everyday objects. In Russia around the time of the Revolution (1917) artists such as Liubov Popova (1889–1924) wanted to make a "new art for a new age," an art that was based on principles of abstraction but that had application in design—fabrics, dishes, book covers, and stage sets. Sonia Delaunay designed stage sets, fabrics, and even the furnishing of automobiles, commenting, "One day I make a painting, the next I make a dress—there's no difference." An entire school dedicated to the universal application of design principles, the Bauhaus, was founded in Germany during the 1920s. Many artists associated with this project—its two founders Walter Gropius and Mies van der Rohe, as well as other members of the avant-garde such as Piet Mondrian—emigrated to the United States during the rise of Nazi Germany, effectively transplanting the International Style and European modernism to the United States.

Later Twentieth-Century Developments

Surrealism, which developed from Dada, was the major European art movement during the interwar years. Born in the cafés across Europe in the later years of World War I, especially the Café Voltaire in Zurich, Dada was a response to the perceived absurdity and destructiveness of the modern world, which its adherents believed called for a similarly irrational approach to art (both visual and literary). The name of the movement itself is ambiguous, possibly deriving from both the Russian word for "rocking horse" and the babbling sounds made by a baby learning to talk. Because it espoused "anti-art" Dada was not a movement per se, nonetheless works from such adherents as Marcel Duchamp became very influential in art of the later twentieth century. Duchamp was especially known for his "readymades," in which he would take a "found object," embellish it slightly or not, and then exhibit it as a work of art. Two such examples, both "made" in 1919, are *Fountain* (a urinal) and the cheap postcard-sized reproduction of Leonardo's iconic portrait of (Mona) Lisa Gherardini del Giacondo, on which he drew a moustache, a goatee, and the hand-printed title, "L.H.O.O.Q." (The letters, if read quickly in French, phonetically approximate the phrase, *elle a chaud au cul*, which Duchamp translated colloquially to infer that Mona Lisa's smile was a reflection of her considerable sexual desire.)

The Surrealists sought to build upon the irrational as the source of artistic imagery and activity, to break from the restrictions of humdrum everyday reality, and to free the mind from convention and logic. André Breton, who wrote two Surrealist "manifestos" (in 1924 and 1927) developed the technique of "automatic writing" as a means of creating a direct line to the unconscious. Breton also wrote *Surrealism and Painting*, a tract that identified artists whose art was consistent with the two primary goals of the movement: either those like Joan Miró, whose work was mostly abstract and who attempted to find a visual equivalent of automatic writing, and those like Salvador Dalí, who tapped into dream imagery but depicted it realistically so that the unexpected became palpable. Surrealists valued eroticism as a way of accessing the unconscious, and they valorized the "femme-enfant," the child-woman, who could serve as a muse to the male artist. Several such "muses"—Leonora Carrington, Lee Miller, Dorothea Tanning, and Meret Oppenheim, whose fur-lined tea-cup (*Breakfast in Fur*, 1936) became the iconic surrealist object—were artists in their own rights, who helped to keep the movement alive for decades after its first appearance. When a number of Surrealist artists fled the Nazi persecution, like Max Ernst (who had been involved with Leonora Carrington while in France but who married Peggy Guggenheim and later Dorothea Tanning), they established residency in New York, and with other émigrés contributed to the transplantation of European modernism to the New World.

Europe in New York

During the 1940s and 1950s New York City, despite its location across the Atlantic, assumed the role that had previously been identified with Paris and became the art capitol of the European art tradition. Abstract Expressionism, the most significant movement of the mid-twentieth century, grew from the Surrealist impulse to exteriorize internal states. Jackson Pollock's drip technique, in which the control of the artist's hand was subverted as he danced around a canvas placed on the floor, splattering paint, could be considered a form of automatic writing. During the fifties and sixties in Europe *art brut* ("raw art") and *arte povera* ("poor art") were prominent, both movements influenced by the anti-art aspects of Dada.

In the latter part of the century it seemed as if the debate accelerated to the point where the purpose of art was being continually redefined every few years, in such movements as Pop Art and its use of everyday imagery, or Minimalism and its total eschewal of representation. The German sculptor and performance artists Joseph Beuys (and other conceptual artists in particular) referred back to Dada, using the stuff of everyday life in their work. Furthermore, art became increasingly more self-referential and began to challenge the hegemony of Western culture and its master

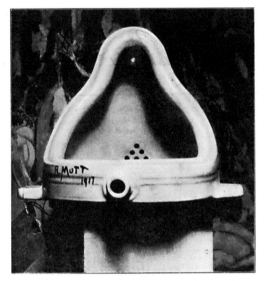

Marcel Duchamp, *Fountain* (1917). Duchamp often took a "found object," such as this urinal, and, after embellishing it or not, exhibited it as a work of art. Photograph by Alfred Stieglitz.

narratives through irony, parody, and the blurring of lines between the high and the low, in an attempt to destabilize and decentralize the artistic tradition. These traits became associated with the stance of Postmodernism, a philosophical movement expressed also through architecture and literary criticism.

At the same time, feminists began to retrieve the works of many "lost" women artists, individuals who might have had an impact in their times but who were obscured by the historical narrative. The art historian Linda Nochlin found that many of the women who were able to have artistic careers prior to the nineteenth century—such as, famously, Artemisia Gentileschi (1593–1656)—did so because their fathers were artists, which gave them access to the requisite education. This historical recovery work was very significant to women artists during the 1970s and subsequent years, and they began to engage through their art with the historical exclusion of women. Hundreds of volunteers from 1974 to 1979 worked with Judy Chicago on her installation *The Dinner Party*, to which Chicago "invited" thirty-nine significant female figures (including Hatshepsut, Hildegard von Bingen, and Sacajawea). Three 48-foot banquet tables, configured in a triangle and covered in embroidered textiles, held individually themed place settings, each organized around what Chicago described as central core images, as well as other symbols significant to each guest.

In The French Collection (1991–1997), a series of painted "story quilts," the Harlem-born painter and writer Faith Ringgold drew on iconic works and figures from European art and culture to present a narrative of "art in the making" in which "history" is either altered by (or infused with) the presence of a fictional African American female artist as a central character. Works such as *The Picnic at Giverny*, which juxtaposes full-bodied allusions to the paintings of Manet (*Dejeuner sur l'herbe*) and Monet, function as both playful and serious social commentaries.

In many world cultures art is an intrinsic form of lived experiences whereas in the European art tradition, high art and the daily environment became bifurcated. Unfortunately, despite the aforementioned attempts, during the remainder of the twentieth century, they only became more separated, and in the twenty-first century there seems to be an increasingly unbridgeable gap between artists and their audience.

Mara R. WITZLING
University of New Hampshire

Further Reading

Bowlt, J. E., & Drutt, M., Eds. (2003). *Amazons of the avant-garde: Alexandra Exter, Natalia Goncharova, Liubov Popova, Olga Rozanova, Varvara Stepanova, and Nadezhda Udaltsova*. New York: Harry F. Abrams.

Clark, T. J. (1984). *The painting of modern life: Paris in the art of Manet and his followers*. Princeton, NJ: Princeton University Press.

Edgerton, S. (1976). *The Renaissance rediscovery of linear perspective*. New York: Harper and Row.

Freedberg, S. J. (1983). *Painting in Italy, 1500–1600, pelican history of art*. (2nd ed.). Baltimore: Penguin.

Grabar, A. (1967). *The beginnings of Christian art, 200–395* (S. Gilbert & J. Emmons, Trans.). London: Thames and Hudson.

Grabar, A. (1968). *Christian iconography: A study of its origins*. Princeton, NJ: Princeton University Press.

Gray, C. (1986). *The Russian experiment in art: 1863–1922* (Rev. ed.). London: Thames and Hudson.

Harrison, C., Frascina, F., & Perry, G. (1993). *Primitivism, cubism, abstraction: The early twentieth century*. New Haven: Yale University Press.

Hartt, F. (1994). *A history of Italian Renaissance painting* (4th rev. ed.). New York: Thames and Hudson.

Henderson, G. (1987). *From Durrow to Kells: The insular gospel books, 650–800*. London: Thames and Hudson.

Jantzen, H. (1962). *High Gothic: The classical cathedral at Chartres*. Princeton, NJ: Princeton University Press.

Krautheimer, R. (1968). *Studies in early Christian, Medieval, and Renaissance art*. New York: New York University Press.

Krautheimer, R. (1986). *Early Christian and Byzantine architecture (Pelican history of art)* (4th ed.). Baltimore: Penguin.

Laing, L. (1992). *Art of the Celts*. New York: Thames and Hudson.

Mathews, T. F. (1999). *The clash of gods: A reinterpretation of Early Christian art*. Princeton: Princeton University Press.

Panofsky, E. (1969). *Renaissance and renascences in western art*. New York: Harper and Row.

Pollock, G. (1988). *Vision and difference: Femininity, feminism, and histories of art*. New York: Methuen.

Rosenblum, R. (1984). *Cubism and twentieth century art* (Rev. ed.). New York: Harry N. Abrams.

von Simpson, O. G. (1988). *The Gothic cathedral: Origins of Gothic architecture and the Medieval concept of order* (3rd ed.). Princeton, NJ: Princeton University Press.

de Sanato Swinton, E. (Ed.). (1996). *Women of the pleasure quarter: Japanese paintings and prints of the Floating World*. New York: Hudson Hills Press and the Worcerster Art Museum.

Snyder, J. (1989). *Medieval art: Painting, sculpture, architecture, 4th–14th century*. New York: Harry N. Abrams.

Tucker, P. H. (1995). *Claude Monet: Life and art*. New Haven, CT: Yale University Press.

Witzling, M. R. (1991). *Voicing our visions: Writings by women artists*. New York: Universe.

Art—Japan

Japanese art has alternated between a native style and others inspired by Chinese, Korean, and, later, Western influence. Neolithic Jōmon pottery was the earliest art; metalwork, calligraphy, and painting appeared in succeeding periods. Buddhist art and architecture dominated from 600 to 1600 CE. Japanese culture flourished after 1600 with economic prosperity, and Western contact after the mid-1800s brought new styles and international exposure.

The art of Japan demonstrates the sensitive character of the inhabitants of that East Asian archipelago over a period of more than eighteen thousand years. Among the more consistent qualities revealed through Japanese art are a love of nature, attention to detail, playfulness, a preference for natural materials, and the ability to succinctly capture the innate qualities of a subject. Japanese history is divided into periods that are named for the location of the national seat of political power.

Jōmon Culture

The oldest human artifacts of unglazed earthenware appear to date from Japan's Jōmon period (c. 10,000–300 BCE). These ceramics, mostly vessels, are typically decorated with overall patterns of incised or impressed decoration, some of them made by rolling the surface with braided cords or ropes. For this reason, the ceramics, the people, and the long Neolithic period to which they belong were given the name "Jōmon" (cord-marked). The Jōmon people, unlike most ceramics-producing cultures, were primarily hunter-gatherers. Scholars since the mid-twentieth century have debated the date for the beginning of the period, as early as 16,500 BCE by some estimates—not only about when the transition from Paleolithic to Neolithic technology took place (the dates continue to recede with new discoveries), but whether Jōmon earthenware is indeed the world's oldest ceramic type.

The stylistic characteristics of Jōmon pottery vary geographically and according to the phase from which they date. In Middle Jōmon, earthenware vessels often featured spectacularly extruded mouths, referred to as "flame-style" (*kaenshiki*) rims by Japanese archaeologists. In Final Jōmon, clay figures called *dogu* were created to be broken during rituals that may have been intended to improve fertility or to combat illness. The predominantly abstract decoration on Jōmon wares may be of religious or ritual significance.

Yayoi Culture

The beginning of the Yayoi period (300 BCE–300 CE) marks an influx into Japan of immigrants from continental Asia who brought

---

Jōmon (cord-marked) pottery (10,000–8,000 BCE) is decorated with incised or impressed patterns made by rolling the surface over braided cord or rope. Tokyo National Museum, Japan.

systematized wet rice agriculture, hierarchical societal organization, and technology for manufacturing bronze. Tools, weapons, and mirrors of bronze began to be made within a century or two after similar items arrived from China and Korea. One of the more idiosyncratic Yayoi bronze objects is a type of bell known as the *dōtaku*. These bells appear to derive from bronze bells of the Chinese Han dynasty (206 BCE–220 CE) and, made during the second half of the Yayoi period, were probably intended for ritual use. One example bears cast designs, including a representation of a grain storehouse on stilts. The similarity of this storehouse to existing Shinto shrine buildings, such as the principal halls in the shrine complexes of Ise and Izumo, may indicate that at least some aspects of the Shinto religion originated during Yayoi period. Yayoi period earthenware, simpler in form than that of the Jōmon, comprised vessels for ritual and household use. Like Jōmon ware, it was made from coils of clay, but was smoothly finished by the use of a small handwheel.

Kofun Period

The Kofun period (300–710 CE) is named for the numerous tumuli (*kofun*) constructed from around the mid-third century until after the introduction of Buddhism in Japan, around 550 CE. Buried within these tomb mounds were a variety of items that reveal close connections between Japan's aristocracy and inhabitants of the Korean Peninsula. Some items, such as gray earthenware funerary vessels, beads, and certain items of metalwork from fifth- and sixth-century Japanese and Korean tombs, can be distinguished only by specialists. Tumuli were mostly small, especially at the beginning of the period, but those built for emperors such as Nintoku (reigned 313–399) were huge, keyhole-shaped constructions surrounded by moats. Some tumuli had burial chambers lined with stone that were decorated with wall paintings. Earthenware cylinders known as *haniwa*, arranged atop and around the perimeter of some tomb mounds, were commonly surmounted with clay figures in the form of humans, animals, or even inanimate objects such as shields or buildings. The exact purpose or function of these earthenware sculptures is uncertain, but it seems likely that they were intended to support the deceased in the afterlife.

Asuka Period

The Asuka period (552–645 CE) overlaps the preceding Kofun period and marks the introduction of both Buddhism and writing from continental Asia. Because of those features, it is Japan's first fully historical period. Within three decades following the adoption of Buddhism as the state religion under the Soga clan in 587 CE, three Buddhist temples in the Nara-Osaka region were established. Although all three were completely or mostly destroyed over the centuries, works of art from them survive, mainly in the temple called Hōryū-ji (in Nara Prefecture). The most significant Buddhist sculpture of the period comprises several works by Tori Busshi (active late sixth–early seventh centuries). Tori's masterpiece is the gilt bronze *Shaka Triad* of 623, now located in the Golden Hall (Kondō) of Hōryū-ji. The three figures resemble Chinese

Dōtaku Bronze Bell. Late Yayoi period, third century CE. These bells, intended for ritual use, apparently derive from Han-dynasty (206 BCE–220 CE) China bronze bells. Musée Guimet, Paris.

Tori Busshi, *Shaka Triad of 623.* From *Selected Relics of Japanese Art, 20 Volume Set. Photographs and Collotypes by K. Ogawa.* (1899–1908). Nippon Shimbi Kyokwai: Shimbi Shoin.

Buddhist sculptures from the Northern Wei kingdom (part of China's Southern and Northern Dynasties, 220–589 CE). A bodhisattva (enlightened deity) figure in Hōryū-ji is known as the *Kudara Kannon*, which tradition says was brought to Japan from Korea's Paekche (Kudara) kingdom (18 BCE–663 CE). These sculptures, as well as the layout and architecture of buildings such as Hōryū-ji's Golden Hall and pagoda (late seventh century), reflect the strong influence of continental Buddhist models.

Nara Period

Continental models were even more influential during the Nara period (710–794 CE). Throughout the eighth century CE, the influence of Tang dynasty China (618–907 CE) was dominant in works made for the Buddhist establishment and the aristocracy. Heijō-kyō, the capital (modern Nara City), was laid out in the manner of Chang'an (modern Xi'an), the capital of the China's Tang dynasty. During the rule of Japanese emperor Shōmu (reigned 715–749 CE), a huge temple, called Tōdai-ji, was built in Nara to house a massive bronze image of the Dainichi Buddha (called Vairocana in Sanskrit). The current hall, an eighteenth-century replacement only two-thirds the size of the original, remains the largest wooden building in the world. Emperor Shōmu also ordered the establishment of regional Buddhist temples throughout Japan under the *kokubunji* system, which necessitated the production of large numbers of Buddhist statues and implements in Tang dynasty style. In contrast with Asuka period Buddhist images, Nara period sculpture featured rounder, fleshier figures imbued with a sense of elegance and movement.

As rulers of the easternmost point of the Silk Roads, eighth-century Japanese emperors had access to luxury goods from as far away as Persia. The active trade that took place is reflected in the high-quality artworks preserved in the Shōsō-in repository, established in 756 to house the possessions of Emperor Shōmu. Among the items kept there are mirrors, textiles, ceramics, lacquerware, furniture, musical instruments, glass objects, and paintings. Some of the works are of continental manufacture, while others are domestic products that show the impact of imported forms, materials, and techniques.

Heian Period

In 794 CE, Emperor Kanmu (737–806 CE) moved the capital to a new site, Heian-kyō (modern Kyoto), initiating the Heian period (794–1185). Contact with China declined after 894, when the Japanese court ceased to send embassies to the continent. In response, native art and architecture began to develop along independent lines. The buildings of the imperial palace were constructed in a hybrid Sino-Japanese form, with gardens and furnishings of native taste, while retaining certain Chinese elements to communicate weight and authority. A distinctly Japanese court culture grew up, described in great detail in Lady Murasaki Shikibu's tenth-century novel *The Tale of Genji*, and illustrated in a superb set of twelfth-century narrative hand scrolls, the *Genji monogatari emaki*. The scrolls, only a few of which survive, feature not only compelling paintings of scenes found in the novel, but outstanding calligraphy, another hallmark of visual culture of the Heian court. The illustrations, which use a complex system of perspective, placement, and color but depict human faces in a quite generalized manner, represent the beginnings of a native form of painting known as Yamato-e.

In the early part of the period, the two Esoteric Buddhist sects of Tendai (Tiantai in Chinese) and Shingon (Zhenyan in Chinese) were introduced from China. These sects emphasized secret knowledge and complex rituals, often using cosmic diagrams known as mandalas. Numerous colorful and minutely detailed mandala paintings were made during the Heian period. In the middle and latter parts of the period, the populist Pure Land (Jōdo) sect grew, and many sculptures of the Amida Buddha (Amitabha in Sanskrit) were constructed. Most notable is the sublime Amida figure by Jōchō (d. 1057) made for the Phoenix Hall (Hōōdō) at the temple called Byōdō-in. The temple was built as a personal shrine for the

Mandala of the Single-Syllable Golden Wheel. (Heian period, twelfth century.) Minutely detailed cosmic diagrams (mandalas) became popular as the Pure Land sect of Buddhism grew. Nara National Museum.

government official Fujiwara Yorimichi (990–1074) in 1052.

Kamakura Period

In 1185 CE, the Minamoto warrior clan defeated its rival, the Taira clan, and established a military government that ruled in the emperor's stead. Seeking refuge from court influence, the first shogun moved his seat of power to Kamakura, far from earlier capitals. In contrast to the refined and elegant Heian art, Kamakura period (1185–1333) works are characterized by stronger, more straightforward approaches. In Buddhist sculpture, works by Unkei (1148?–1223) and others of the Kei school of sculptors display a powerful naturalism that reflects the rise of military culture. The Jōdo monks Hōnen (1133–1212) and Shinran (1173–1263) exploited unease about the changes in society, inspiring greater numbers to place faith in the Amida Buddha. As a result, paintings of Amida descending to greet the soul of a dying believer (*raigō* paintings) and depictions of Amida's Western Paradise (Saihō Gokuraku) came to be made in large numbers using valuable materials such as silk and gold leaf. Portraiture grew in popularity, especially among the military elites and Buddhist clergy, following the same trend toward naturalism as sculpture.

Muromachi Period

Following his defeat of the Kamakura government regents in 1333, Ashikaga Takauji (1305–1358 CE) set up his own military government in the Muromachi district of Kyoto. Although much of the Muromachi period (1333–1573) was tumultuous, certain art forms did flourish. Zen temples grew in number and influence because of the support of the military class. Zen-inspired calligraphy and ink painting prospered, as did rock-and-gravel gardens (*sekitei*) such as those at the Kyoto temple named Ryōan-ji. The most famous painter of the period was Sesshō Tōyō (1420–1506), a priest whose work built upon styles of ink painting developed in China during the Song dynasty (960–1279). Sesshō traveled to China in 1469–1470, and his painting reportedly was highly admired by Chinese at the time. His most celebrated works are landscapes in ink, sometimes with light color added.

The cultural apex of the period came under the rule of Ashikaga Yoshimitsu (1358–1408), who subdued warring factions, reopened official contacts with China, and encouraged the arts. Under his patronage, the Noh drama developed, and outstanding masks and robes for the theater were created. Yoshimitsu built a personal retreat at Kitayama, which included a building called the Golden Pavilion (Kinkaku). The three-story building, famous for the gold leaf on its exterior, is an innovative combination of three architectural styles: Zen temple, warrior dwelling, and court residence. Sited in a beautiful strolling garden with a lake, the current building is a close replica of the original, which burned in 1950. Yoshimitsu's grandson, Ashikaga Yoshimasa (1435–1490), built his own retreat at Higashiyama, with its own unique building, the Silver Pavilion (Ginkaku). The two-story building, never covered in silver, was the centerpiece for Yoshimasa's aesthetic diversions, later known collectively as "Higashiyama culture" (Higashiyama *bunka*). These pastimes included Noh drama, garden design, art collecting, and tea ritual. Yoshimasa's influence continued to be felt in these areas over the succeeding centuries.

Momoyama Period

In 1573, Oda Nobunaga (1534–1582) deposed the final Ashikaga shogun and continued his quest to consolidate military and political power over all Japan. After his assassination in 1582, the same pursuit was taken up by Toyotomi Hideyoshi (1537–1598) and largely achieved; yet it was not until Tokugawa

Kongorikishi statue. (Kamakura period, fourteenth century.) This flamboyantly realistic wood statue, typical of the period, originally stood guard at the gate to Ebaradera, a temple in Sakai, near Osaka. Sackler Gallery at the Smithsonian Institution.

Thank God for tea! What would the world do without tea? How did it exist? I am glad I was not born before tea. • **Sydney Smith (1771–1845)**

was characterized by the growth of several existing schools and the establishment of others, spurred by the demand for artistically embellished sliding doors and folding screens for the interiors of elite residences and castles. Many of these works featured backgrounds of gold-leafed paper that helped reflect light in the dark interiors of large buildings. Among the most prominent painters were Hasegawa Tōhaku (1539–1610), Kaihō Yōshō (1533–1615), and Kano Eitoku (1543–1590), whose bold and striking works came to characterize the vibrant ambiance of the Momoyama period.

Under the influence of codified tea drinking, sometimes known as the tea ceremony, notable

Sesshū Tōyō, landscape (1495). Hanging scroll, ink on paper. The artist originated the *hatsuboku* (splashed ink) technique of this painting.

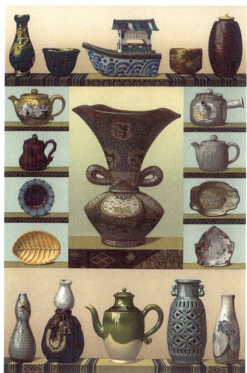

Perfume burner modeled in the form of boat (top center), with teapots, vases, tea bowls, and saké bottles once in the possession of James L. Bowes, Esq. From *Keramic [sic] art of Japan* (1875).

Ieyasu (1543–1616) that an enduring dynasty could be established and internecine warfare eliminated. Despite intermittent warfare, the Momoyama period (1573–1600) marked one of the most creative eras in the history of Japan. Active trade provided cultural stimulation, as Japanese ships sailed throughout East and Southeast Asia. European merchants and missionaries were welcomed, and many of the items they brought were incorporated into Japanese visual and material culture. Decorative motifs in applied arts such as lacquerware and textiles were particularly influenced by foreign designs. Painting

Ogata Korin, *White Plum Blossoms* (Edo period). Ink, color, and gold and silver leaf on paper. One of a pair of twofold screens. Museum of Art, Atami.

advancements were made in ceramics. In the 1570s, the low-fired, glazed ceramic later to be called Raku ware was devised, and Raku tea bowls soon achieved popularity among tea connoisseurs. The capture and inducement of continental potters to Japan during the 1592–1598 invasions of Korea resulted in the rapid advance of ceramics technology and the concurrent expansion of production throughout the country. Tea masters like Sen Rikyō (1522–1591) encouraged the creation of original and idiosyncratic wares that reflected the somber and restrained aesthetic known as *wabi* (rustic simplicity).

Edo Period

In 1603, Tokugawa Ieyasu became shogun, establishing in the city of Edo a line of hereditary military rulers who would control Japan for over 250 years (known as the Edo period, 1600/1603–1868). The beginning of Tokugawa rule overlaps with the latter Momoyama period, since Ieyasu did not completely vanquish his Toyotomi rivals until 1615. Once in control, the Tokugawa shogunate instituted a policy of national isolation and a rigid Neo-Confucian class system. Such measures curtailed individual freedoms, but also contributed to general economic prosperity and social stability. These in turn stimulated unprecedented growth in the arts, especially among the common people.

During the seventeenth century, Kyoto remained the capital of arts and culture, experiencing a renaissance of culture reminiscent of that of the Heian period. Emblematic of this renaissance was Hon'ami Kōetsu (1558–1637), a Kyoto artist who excelled in calligraphy, lacquerware, and raku tea bowls. Collaborating with the painter Tawaraya Sōtatsu (flourished early seventeenth century), founder of

Rinpa-style painting, Hon'ami created scrolls featuring classical poems inscribed against a backdrop of evocative natural designs by Tawaraya in gold and silver pigments. Toward the end of the century, Ogata Kōrin (1658–1716) brought Rinpa style to full flower in his striking compositions created by abbreviating and carefully arranging pictorial elements. Kōrin's brother, Ogata Kenzan (1663–1743), translated Rinpa into the ceramic format, devising innovative implements for use in the practice of tea.

Among warrior-class elites, the two most influential painting schools were the Kano school, based upon Chinese art traditions, and the Tosa school, descended from Heian period Yamato-e. In the eighteenth century, however, new styles of painting developed. Notable among them were the literati (Bunjinga) style, an outgrowth of Chinese scholar painting of the Ming (1368–1644) and Qing (1644–1912) dynasties, and the Maruyama-Shijō school, which incorporated elements of European naturalism into native modes of depiction. Within the merchant class, genre painting gave way to paintings and woodblock prints featuring beautiful women, actors, and travel landscapes. This style, known as *ukiyo-e* (floating world pictures), eventually became Japan's most widely known artistic style.

Modern Period

In 1854, the re-establishment of international contact began with the opening of ports that had been closed to foreign commerce for more than two centuries. European artistic ideas flowed freely into the country, and soon "painting in the Western manner" (Yōga) was firmly established. In the 1880s, with the encouragement of the American scholar Ernest Fenollosa (1853–1908), native painting practices reasserted themselves, combining into a new tradition called Nihonga (Japanese painting). Nihonga used native materials and formats, such as painting with ink and mineral pigments on paper or silk, but also incorporated certain aspects of Western traditions such as shading and perspective. During the twentieth century, distinctions between the two modes became increasingly blurred, but the separation continued to be recognized in official art circles, especially the annual national art exhibitions first held in

"Entrance to the Kasuga Shrine at Nara and Group of Consecrated Maidens," circa 1910. This shrine of the Fujiwara family was rebuilt through the centuries after its initial construction in 768 CE. New York Public Library.

Kitagawa Utamaro (c. 1753–1806), *Uzuki no hototogisu*. Utamaro was renowned for prints of beautiful women and Kabuki actors. Here, a cuckoo hovers over the women's heads.

Andō Hiroshige (1797–1858), *Meguro taikobashi yūhinooka* (Meguro drum bridge and sunset hill). Oban (half o-bosho [Japanese handmade paper] size) Nishiki-e (brocade-style) print.

1907 and later known as Nitten (Japan Exhibition). In the 1950s, artists like Yoshihara Jirō (1905–1972) began to explore concepts such as abstraction and performance art, becoming the first in Asia to present a credible challenge to the West from an equal artistic footing.

In the twenty-first century, art in Japan is as diverse as in any country in the world. A large number of Japanese artists are recognized internationally, especially in nontraditional genres such as installation art and video. In addition, the comic book / cartoon art genres of Manga and Anime have had tremendous impact on artists worldwide, especially those born after 1980.

Andrew L. MASKE
University of Kentucky

Further Reading

Addis, S. (1996). *How to look at Japanese art*. New York: Harry N. Abrams.

Addis, S. (2006). *77 dances: Japanese calligraphy by poets, monks, and scholars*. New York: Weatherhill.

Addis, S., Groemer, G., & Rimer, J. T. (2006). *Traditional Japanese arts and culture: An illustrated sourcebook*. Honolulu: University of Hawaii.

Adolphson, M., Kamens, E., & Matsumoto. S. (2007). *Heian Japan: Centers and peripheries*. Honolulu: University of Hawaii.

Calza, G. C. (2007). *Ukiyo-e*. London: Phaidon Press.

Delay, N. (1999). *The art and culture of Japan*. New York: Harry N. Abrams.

Habu, J. (2004). *Ancient Jomon of Japan*. New York: Cambridge.

Hickman, M., et al. (2002). *Japan's golden age: Momoyama*. New York: Yale.

Kato, S. (1994). *Japan: Spirit and form*. Rutland, VT: Tuttle.

Mason, P. (1993). *History of Japanese art*. New York: Harry N. Abrams.

Murase, M. (1990). *Masterpieces of Japanese screen painting*. New York: George Braziller.

Noritake, T., & Graham, P. (2009). *A history of Japanese art: From prehistory to the Taisho period*. Rutland, VT: Tuttle.

Roberts, L. P. (1976). *A dictionary of Japanese artists*. New York: Weatherhill.

Sadao, T., & Wada, S. (2003). *Discovering the arts of Japan: A historical survey*. New York: Kodansha.

Singer, R., et al. (1998). *Art in Edo Japan 1615–1868*. Washington, DC: National Gallery.

Takashima, S., et al. (1987). *Paris in Japan: The Japanese encounter with European Painting*. Tokyo: Japan Foundation.

Art—Native North America

More than five hundred cultural groups, and many more prior to Spanish colonization in the early sixteenth century, have created the body of art attributed to Native North Americans. The category is thus not cohesive, ranging from ancient petroglyphs to contemporary photographs, and from horse-effigy dance sticks to installation and performance art. In its great diversity, however, it typically incorporates and conveys a relationship to place and community.

In the twenty-first century many art historians, as well as scholars in related and interdisciplinary fields, have begun to refer to art produced by the indigenous populations of North America—from the Rio Grande to the Arctic Circle and from the Atlantic to the Pacific coasts—as "First American art." The term establishes the corpus of diverse material artifacts made by original and descendant inhabitants of these lands—and not by occupants who arrived through waves of colonial encounters beginning in the sixteenth century—as primary among the arts of the United States and Canada (where it is called "First Nations art"). Even in its great diversity, this art typically incorporates and conveys a relationship to place and community. Often a deliberate reference to identity (or intimacy with the culture) is central to its expressive intent. The wide span of this art created over space, time, and cultures attests to its vitality and conceptual continuity, from 4500 BCE Lower Mississippi Valley mound architecture to the recently opened National Museum of the American Indian, a native-designed structure housing the world's largest collection of First American art.

Ancient architectural ruins in the Southwest, sites that have now been differentiated as pre-European contact, include cultures of the Anasazi (700–1400 CE), Hohokam (550–1400 CE), and Mogollon (200–1150 CE). All these cultures created painted murals, decoratively elaborated pottery, worked shell and stone, and early textiles that tangibly evinced a technologically advanced "primitive" society perceived as a nascent civilization. The material remains of other ancient peoples, including the Adena (1100 BCE–200 CE), Hopewell (100 BCE–500 CE), and Mississippian cultures (still noted for extensive mound construction in 1000 CE) in the east and central United States, together with Norton Tradition, Old Bering Sea, Dorset, and Thule cultures in the Canadian Arctic (spanning the period 500 BCE–1000 CE), provide evidence of America's antiquity, and are today also appreciated for their aesthetic legacy.

But with contributions from more than five hundred cultural groups and many more prior to Spanish colonization, the category is by no means cohesive. First American art spans an array of media, from petroglyphs to contemporary photographs, for instance, and from horse-effigy dance sticks to installation and performance art. Critical reception to indigenous art is divided and often depends on whether the works were wrought in traditional (that is, historic and pre-contact) materials or created in modern times in contemporary modes.

First American Art: From "Curiosity" to Aesthetic

The need to designate "First American art" evolves from a long-standing debate about whether or not

Tsimshian head-on mask. (1800s.) This painted wood mask, used during the initiation rituals of the great winter ceremonies (*halait*), was collected at the mouth of the Nass River, British Columbia (Canada).

art work created by the indigenous peoples of North America can be called "art." Europeans (especially the Spanish, English, Dutch, French, and Russians) began acquiring "curiosities" made by the native inhabitants of the "New World" when they arrived on its foreign soil, and many of these objects still exist in European museums in cities such as Berlin, Helsinki, Leningrad, London, and Paris. In the nineteenth century objects made by American Indians became the focus of systematic U.S. collecting and formed the core of most urban museum collections: Indian imagery provided a potent focus of the young nation-state until France's 1883 gift of the Statue of Liberty.

Indigenous peoples often exchanged valued objects with Europeans, symbolically solidifying international relations and sometimes representing them. For instance, the first treaty between the Haudenosaunee peoples and the Dutch settlers in their region was recorded in the Two-Row Wampum Belt in 1613. The pattern of purple wampum beads sewn in two strips against a background of white beads signifies the path of two vessels, an indigenous canoe and a European ship, as they travel the river of life together, parallel but never touching. The three underlying white stripes symbolize peace, friendship, and respect. Another iconic example in Native American art history is the late eighteenth-century Mandan or Lakota pictographic bison robe attributed to the collection acquired by the Lewis and Clark Expedition (1804–1806). On battle robes such as this one, made from tanned buffalo hide decorated with deerskin fringe, bird and porcupine quills, and native plant materials, indigenous artists used brown, orange, and green pigments to paint scenes using a complex iconography that detailed their exploits in war. The Lewis and Clark robe, now at the Peabody Museum of Archaeology and Ethnology at Harvard, provides an early example of Plains biographical art and serves as a symbol of the diplomacy and political relations that helped form the United States.

The observations that the German artist Albrecht Dürer recorded in his 1520 travel journal about an exhibit in Brussels of Aztec jewelry, clothing, weaponry, and armor—"nothing . . . rejoiced my heart so much as these things, for I saw amongst them wonderful works of art"—marks a historic moment in the European appreciation of the potential value of objects from the Americas (Dürer 1520). (Hernan Cortés had sent the Aztec treasures as tribute to Charles V, Spanish king and Holy Roman Emperor, who put them on display throughout Europe.) Such exposure increased as these objects were housed in national museums beginning in the eighteenth century. Representation of Native Americans began to pervade the wider visual media beginning in the sixteenth century, sometimes as illustrative material accompanying traveling exhibitions about indigenous peoples, but by the nineteenth century Indians became pictorial subjects in their own right (in the paintings of George Catlin, for example) or were portrayed as "natural" elements within other genres like landscape painting (in the work of Albert Bierstadt and George Caleb Bingham).

The cultural evolutionism of nineteenth-century theorists such as Lewis Henry Morgan provided the stimulus for large-scale collecting in America. Patterned after their natural history counterparts, exhibitions resulting from nineteenth-century archaeological and ethnological exploration were displayed in museums as "remnants of a waning race" organized by the culture–area approach, a classification of peoples by geographic and environmental criteria that often still informs even art museum exhibitions. In those displays and the curatorial descriptions that accompanied them, Pueblo ruins were likened to European prototypes as an "ancient Pompeii," "Greek theatre," or "Roman forum" (as, for example, in William H. Jackson's *Reconstruction of Pueblo Bonito, Chaco Canyon*). By the twentieth century Pueblo architecture and other native influences inspired diverse architects to develop specifically American forms. Mary Colter used Hopi, Zuni, and Navajo elements in the tourist-oriented buildings she designed to rim the Grand Canyon; Vincent Scully, the renowned art historian, wrote (and taught) extensively about native influences in American architecture; and Frank Lloyd Wright incorporated native influences in form as well as in decorative elements that he himself designed, such as the friezes of Native American chieftains found on a the lintels of a house in Milwaukee.

World fairs and industrial expositions, notably the U.S. Centennial Exhibition (Philadelphia, 1876) and the World's Pre-Columbian Exhibition (Chicago, 1893), were important venues for the representation of America's native peoples and their arts (although both were pictured as technological inferiors). Euro-American intellectuals gained access to native peoples not only through visual and textual representations, but also through intimate association with them. Aby Warburg, a central figure in modern art history specializing in the Italian Renaissance, was impressed by the religious practices of the Hopi Indians he visited and photographed. Warburg, who considered his encounter with the Hopi as a journey to the origins of human imagery, collected a number of carved and painted wooden katchinas and dance wands in the 1890s. For other Euro-American collectors, too, ritual objects have been particularly desirable (despite the consternation of the natives to whom such objects remain living beings). Western European fine artists have continued to use non-Western images and objects to explore philosophical ideas and to challenge and subvert their own cultural conventions.

The aesthetic concern with Primitivism, a handmaiden of Modernism in which Native American art figured importantly, was prominent from the 1890s through World War II; its influence is still felt in current non-native representations of Native American art. The Aesthetic and Arts and Crafts movements also stimulated a wider interest in—and the collection of—Native American objects in the late nineteenth and early twentieth centuries.

Beginning in the twentieth century, studies of Native American art (notably the elaborate carvings and richly costumed performances of the Northwest Coast's stratified societies, many of which were explored in the seminal work of anthropologist Franz Boas and his students) helped to turn academic attention away from evolutionary concerns to the formal properties of objects and their cultural contexts. In fashioning a particularly American fine-art tradition, namely Abstract Expressionism, New York avant-garde artists, chief among them Jackson Pollack and Barnett Newman, drew on Native American art between the two world wars and rejected European academic traditions. By espousing a universal concept of art in which visual qualities were valued independent of historical and cultural specificity, these artists (and critics such as Clement Greenberg) demonstrated the value of native cultures to a modern American heritage on the eve of global conflict at mid-century. Canada and Australia, sister postcolonial nation-states, have also utilized the aesthetic value of indigenous productions in their national identities.

The Museum of Modern Art's 1941 exhibit "Indian Art of the United States" and especially the later "'Primitivism' in Twentieth Century Art: Affinity of the Tribal and the Modern" (1984) were watershed events in the representation and classification of Native American objects, provoking academic debate that has lasted into the twenty-first century. In the twentieth century, American museums were distinguished from their European counterparts by their emphasis on modern or contemporary and primitive art over classical forms, with Native American art figuring prominently in several national and international traveling exhibitions (especially the one that commemorated the U.S. Bicentennial). In Europe prior to World War II, the surrealists favored Native American art as a way of subverting established canons and establishing new syntheses of perception and representation in opposition to modernist trends.

Thus by the mid-twentieth century a concentrated articulation of aesthetic value for these objects emerged in concert with an increasing number of named artists and private collectors; an expansive market, wide museum exhibition, and art historical surveys characterized the last quarter of that century. In the Western art tradition work must be inscribed into a canon that assesses its quality and defines its criteria, and Native American work was just beginning to be "written" as a tradition. By the late twentieth century Native American art became a recognized field with the full complement of institutional networks, including academic specialization. Controversy over classification still centered on how to appreciate "traditional" work that seemed to morph out of an altered social landscape by incorporating European materials and designs (such as the flourishing "souvenirs" of Native American art from the Northeast in the eighteenth and nineteenth centuries, or post-reservation Plains beadwork). Debates arose over how to distinguish between an ethnological artifact and an aesthetic object—natural history and art history paradigms, respectively.

In 2003 the Smithsonian's National Museum of the American Indian opened a three-year-long exhibition culled from the Charles and Valerie Diker collection and called "First American Art." The exhibit departed from the traditional, historically influenced approach of displaying and analyzing native works according to tribe or region; instead it attempted to define a First American art paradigm. Because the Dikers were drawn to the work they collected by its beauty rather than by an interest in a specific "category" of work, the native and non-native artists, curators, and anthropologists involved in the planning the exhibit sought a way to present the collection based on a First American Art aesthetic. They isolated and explored the following seven qualities inherent to, or elicited from, the work of Native Americans, and structured the exhibit around ways to explore them: *integrity* (to tribal identity, values, and ideals, despite the incorporation of new materials and techniques); *emotion* (in response to ideas and materials combined); *movement* (literally kinetic, or symbolic through pattern and design); *idea* (being part of a larger system of knowledge and philosophy, or being the idea itself); *composition* (the physical and spiritual combination of technique and materials); *intimacy* (the relationship of the maker and the user to the art); and *vocabulary* (the ability to express and encode the culture in materials, technique, and iconography). While such components may arguably be assigned to apply to world art (the material objects created by all cultures, whether they are to be deemed art or craft) the effort was an important step in a world-historical way—an opportunity to model not just exhibitions of Native

A rare Yokut Sun Dance basket woven with alternating rows of diamond patterns and human figures joining hands. Dover Pictorial Archives.

American art, but the field of study itself, so that art can help to explain the functioning and beliefs of a given culture.

Present-Day Identity and Artists

Difficulty or a lack of interest in identifying the maker of an object, combined with the problem of determining the maker's reputation for quality work, contributed to anonymity throughout the history of Native American artistic creations. Due to the frequently remote locations of origin, the fact that objects were often traded among indigenous groups and European merchants before arriving in private or public institutions, and the social nature of production in many traditional arts, individual makers and even tribal attributions could not always be made. Further, until the twentieth century, as a result of forced assimilation policies and compulsory off-reservation education, linguistic differences also separated objects from their original contexts and meanings in non-native eyes. Hence, the recognition of individual artists was an important twentieth-century development because it contributed to the value of the work in the art world, and yet many unnamed native artists still produce a vast array of aesthetic material without such recognition.

Among the notable practitioners of traditional native arts before the twentieth century who did not remain anonymous is the Washoe artist Dat So La Lee (Louisa Keyser) who died in 1925 yet gave name and face to the otherwise perceived "utilitarian" (and hence derided) aesthetic practice of basketry. Until very recently, these traditional art forms and others (for example, Navajo weaving) continued to be represented by non-natives as objects and practices of a presumed "past" way of life, not the aesthetic expression of surviving and thriving contemporary peoples who are giving continuing meaning to their lives. New forms have arisen from these precursors, such as haute couture clothing utilizing Northwest Coast crest art (Dorothy Grant and Robert Davidson, Haida) and the fine-art tapestries of Ramona Sakiestewa, Hopi.

Pablita Velarde, *Basketmaking* (1940). Casein paint on board. The Bandelier National Monument in New Mexico, dedicated to preserving the ancient Pueblo site, commissioned this painting under the Works Progress Administration (WPA).

Pueblo pottery and Northwest Coast carving continue to flourish today, some having undergone revivals through stimulation by traders, dealers, and native artists, and often using museum collections as prototypes. The Hopi-Tewa potter Nampeyo, active from the 1880s to her death in 1942, was the first Indian artist recognized by name in the art world in her lifetime. Her descendants, including Dextra Quotskuyva and many others, continue to make distinctive hand-coiled and ground-fired pottery of local materials interpreted in new ways. Robert Davidson, Haida, works to expand the carving tradition recognized in the nineteenth century and practiced by his forebear Tahaygen (Charles Edenshaw).

Training in contemporary media and studio art for native persons was first undertaken in Santa Fe's School of Indian Art, founded in the interwar years (and often called the Dorothea Dunn school after one of its most prominent teachers); it became the Institute of American Indian Arts in 1962. Renowned and award-winning students include Pablita Velarde (1918–2006), Santa Clara Pueblo, a watercolorist who later turned to using pigments she derived from minerals and rock, and which she ground herself; Allan Houser (1914–1994), Chiricahua Apache, a sculptor of bronze, marble, and stone whose vision to create a family compound near Santa Fe culminated in sculpture gardens and studios that are now open to the public by appointment; Fritz Scholder (1937–2005), Luiseño, a prolific and controversial expressionist painter who used distortion, vivid color, and explosive brushstrokes to explore publicly held stereotypes of Native American; and Gerald McMaster (b. 1953), Plains Cree, who in 1995 curated an exhibition of First Nations Canadian artists at the prestigious Venice Biennale.

Formal training now occurs in departments at major universities and art schools across the United States and Canada, launching a new generation of artists eager to articulate the significance of their art. These artists typically work in contemporary or nontraditional media but often combine elements of both; they create provocative works that challenge the boundaries of conventional representations in traditional work as well as the romanticism reproduced in them (the densely packed compositions of Jane Ash Poitras, Cree/Chipewyan, provide an example).

Recent scholarship in both anthropology and art history, by non-natives and natives alike, has begun to break the steel-like frame of criteria used to evaluate "primitve," "traditional," and "contemporary" media. New studies also explore the cultural significance of media (for instance, clay, grasses, hide, or wood) from the practitioners' perspectives, and look at how language and storytelling, as "indigenous national histories," construct not only the object's value but also the activity or process of making art. Native voices have been reclaimed and given prominence in a new articulation of value, as the enumeration of seven aesthetic principles articulated by the "First American Art" exhibit at the Smithsonian attests. Manipulating a variety of media, including that of their ancestors, these artists challenge the very basis of aesthetic appreciation in the Western fine-art world. Their art and the articulation of its meaning is now being inscribed into the art-historical discourse. This marks a new moment in both the philosophy and the history of art. Gender, of course, is an integral dimension of this transformation, since native women have long been recognized as artists and creators of material forms that embody and help to reproduce local systems of knowledge. In this global environment, Native North American, First Nations, or First American art reveals how hybrid forms based on the knowledge of indigenous contexts relate to a wider world and thus actively realize beauty and meaning in rich and varied ways.

This achievement may yet be the greatest influence of this art in world history.

Lea S. McCHESNEY
Independent scholar, Rochester, New York

Further Reading

Berlo, J. C. (Ed.). (1992). *The early years of Native American art history: The politics of scholarship and collecting.* Seattle: University of Washington Press and Vancouver: UBC Press.

Berlo, J. C., & Phillips, R. B. (1998). *Native North American art.* Oxford, U.K.: Oxford University Press.

Bernstein, B., & McMaster, G. (Eds.). (2003). *First American art: The Charles and Valerie Diker collection of American Indian art.* Washington, D.C. and New York: Smithsonian Institution/National Museum of the American Indian.

Boas, F. (1955). *Primitive art.* New York: Dover Publications.

Brasser, T. J. (1976). *Bo'jou, Neejee! Profiles of Canadian Indian art.* Ottawa, Canada: National Museum of Man.

Breeze, C. (1990). *Pueblo deco.* New York: Rizzoli International Publications.

Brody, J. J. (1977). *Indian painters and white patrons.* Albuquerque: University of New Mexico Press.

Coe, R. T. (1977). *Sacred circles: Two thousand years of North American Indian art.* Kansas City, KS: Nelson Gallery of Art and Atkins Museum of Fine Arts.

Coe, R.T. (1986). *Lost and found traditions: Native American Art, 1965–1985.* Seattle: University of Washington Press.

Coe, R. T. (2003). *The responsive eye: Ralph T. Coe and the collecting of American Indian art.* New York: The Metropolitan Museum and New Haven: Yale University Press.

Connelly, F. S. (1995). *The sleep of reason: Primitivism in modern European art and aesthetics, 1725–1907.* University Park, PA: Pennsylvania State University Press.

Douglas, F. H., & D'Harnoncourt, R. (1941). *Indian art in the United States.* New York: Museum of Modern Art.

Dürer, A. (27 August 1520). On Viewing Aztec Gold. Retrieved May 2, 2010, from http://nationalhumanitiescenter.org/pds/amerbegin/contact/text2/durerjournal.pdf

Fane, D., Jacknis, I., & Breen, L. M. (1991). *Objects of myth and memory: American Indian art at the Brooklyn Museum.*

New York: The Brooklyn Museum (in association with the University of Washington Press).

Feder, N. (1971). *American Indian art.* New York: Harry N. Abrams.

Feest, C. F. (1984). From North America. In W. Rubin, Ed., "Primitivism" in twentieth century art: Affinity of the tribal and the modern (pp. 84–97). Boston: Little, Brown.

Feest, C. (1980). *Native arts of North America.* Oxford, U.K.: Oxford University Press.

Flam, J., & Deutch, M. (Eds.). (2003). *Primitivism and twentieth-century art: A documentary history.* Berkeley: University of California Press.

Gritton, J. L. (2000). *The institute of American Indian arts: Modernism and U.S. Indian policy.* Albuquerque: University of New Mexico Press.

Guidi, B. C., & Mann, N. (Eds.). (1998). *Photographs at the frontier: Aby Warburg in America 1895–1896.* London: Merrell Holberton Publishers.

Haberland, W. (1965). *The art of North America.* New York: Crown Publishers.

Jonaitis, A. (Ed.). (1995). *A wealth of thought: Franz Boas on Native American art.* Seattle: University of Washington Press.

Jonaitis, A. (1991). *Chiefly feasts: The enduring Kwakiutl potlatch.* Seattle: University of Washington Press.

Leuthold, S. (1998). *Indigenous aesthetics: Native art, media, identity.* Austin: University of Texas Press.

Lippard, L. R. (1992). *Partial recall: Photographs of Native North Americans.* New York: The New Press.

McChesney, L. S. (2003). *The American Indian art world and the (re-)production of the primitive: Hopi pottery and potters.* Ann Arbor, MI: University Microfilms.

McLaughlin, C. 2003. *Arts of diplomacy: Lewis and Clark's Indian collection.* Cambridge, MA: Peabody Museum, Harvard, and Seattle, WA: University of Washington Press.

Maurer, E. M. (1977). *The Native American heritage: A survey of North American Indian art.* Chicago: The Art Institute of Chicago.

Morgan, L. H. (1965). *Houses and house-life of the American aborigines.* Chicago: The University of Chicago Press.

Mullin, M. H. (1995). The Patronage of difference: Making Indian art 'art', not ethnology. In G. E. Marcus & F. R. Myers (Eds.), *The Traffic in culture.* Berkeley: University of California Press.

Napier, A. D. (1992). *Foreign Bodies: Performance, art, and symbolic anthropology.* Berkeley: University of California Press.

Patterson, A. (1994). *Hopi pottery symbols.* Boulder, CO: Johnson Books.

Paolozzi, E. (1985). *Lost magic kingdoms and six paper moons from Nahuatl: An exhibition at the Museum of Mankind.* London: British Museum Publications Ltd.

Phillips, R. B. (1998). *Trading identities: The souvenir in Native North American art from the Northeast, 1700–1900.* Seattle: University of Washington Press and Montreal: McGill-Queen's University Press.

Rhodes, C. (1994). *Primitivism and modern art.* London: Thames and Hudson.

Rushing, W. J. III. (1995). *Native American art and the New York avant-garde: A history of cultural primitivism.* Austin: University of Texas Press.

Rushing, W. J. III (Ed.). (1999). *Native American art in the twentieth century.* New York: Routledge.

Sloan, J., & LaFarge, O.. (1931). *Introduction to American Indian art.* New York: The Exposition of Indian Tribal Arts, Inc.

Treuttner, W. H. (1979). *The natural man observed: A study of Catlin's Indian gallery.* Washington, DC: Smithsonian Institution Press.

Wade, Edwin L. (Ed.). (1986). *The arts of the North American Indian: Native traditions in evolution.* New York: Hudson Hills Press.

Art—Paleolithic

In light of recent archaeological discoveries in Africa, scholars in a growing number of disciplines are reviving interest in Paleolithic (Old Stone Age / foraging era) art, opening up debate on fundamental world history questions that involve the origins of human art making; the physical, mental, social, and cultural conditions that made it possible; and the fact that creating art has endured and become increasingly integral to our existence.

Humans have practiced the visual arts in whatever part of the globe they came to inhabit. Within the context of world history the earliest manifestation of these arts in the Paleolithic (foraging) era merits attention. The basic questions of when and how the visual arts had come into being raised considerable interest among students of art history, archaeology, and anthropology in the decades surrounding 1900. But for most of the twentieth century discussion about the earliest art forms was relegated to the margins of academic concern, due in part to the highly speculative character of the various theories that proposed to account for them. Today questions concerning Paleolithic art have become topical again, although speculation remains. One important impetus to rejuvenating the field are the archaeological discoveries that have recently been made in Africa. These discoveries prompt us to completely reconsider early artistic behavior in terms of both time and place. Various new theories attempting to explain the emergence of art making add excitement to the field. This article introduces some of the latest developments in Paleolithic art studies.

The Beginning of Aesthetics and Meaning

The Paleolithic era, or Old Stone Age, starts when humans begin making stone tools, some 2.5 million years ago. The art historian David Summers has provocatively suggested that art history, too, starts at this moment. Whatever art is, he theorizes, it refers to something that is made—it is an instance of what he calls "facture." Rudimentary as the earliest stone tools from East Africa may be, they do present the first material evidence of the human capacity to transform a medium, in this case to shape a stone by working it with another. By employing the qualifying term *art*, however, we usually imply additional characteristics, most frequently either "aesthetics" or "meaning," and quite often both. "Aesthetics" requires that an object have a captivating appearance for it to be called art. Visual artistic behavior then refers to such activities as modifying human bodies and objects so as to give them heightened visual interest by means of shape, color, or line. When emphasizing "meaning," we require an art object to have referential content (which may in itself be captivating). Artistic behavior then refers to such activities as drawing, painting, sculpting, or otherwise creating visual stimuli that evoke perceptual and/or semantic referents—a bird, a deity, the concept of ten, and so on—in a human beholder. Clearly the boundaries between these two analytical sets of activities are often hard, if not impossible, to establish, as when modifying the human body's appearance implies both aesthetic effects and signals social status, or when a visual representation of a deity is made to look as handsome, or as fearsome, as possible.

From around 1.4 million years ago onward, early humans started to produce a new type of stone tool, the so-called hand ax. By 500,000 to 400,000 years ago, some of these pear-shaped artifacts displayed a striking symmetry, both en face and in profile. Although the imposed symmetry allowed the object to sit comfortably in the hand, some scholars argue that the symmetrical design went beyond utilitarian requirements and introduced an aesthetic element. In addition, the material from which these exquisitely crafted objects were made seems to have been carefully chosen, partly for its visual effect (often glistening stone, exceptionally with a fossil in the middle of the finished product). Although we will never be sure of the impact these objects had on comtemporary viewers, the symmetrical hand axes may have been the first material evidence of the human tendency to create objects that command attention though their visual qualities.

These hand axes, however, were already disappearing from the archaeological record when "anatomically modern humans" arose in Africa some 200,000 years ago. The creation and use of art is especially associated with this new species, *Homo sapiens*. Nonetheless, until very recently research suggested that we had to wait until some 30,000 years ago before modern humans became involved with "art and personal ornamentation" after arriving in Europe. New evidence continues to revise this picture considerably.

Finds from the Blombos Cave

Recent finds from Blombos Cave, a coastal site at the southernmost strip of the African continent, are central to present-day discussions on early artistic behavior. Excavations led by Christopher Henshilwood have yielded, among other things, a piece of flattened ochre showing cross-hatched marks that appear to be framed by incised lines. When the finding was announced in late 2001—the engraved Blombos piece dated to about 75,000 years ago—archaeologists considered it the earliest unquestionable example of a human-made geometric pattern known so far. Its discovery led to considerable attention in the popular press. Newspaper headings hailed the Blombos ochre as "the world's oldest art object," and it was claimed that because of this find "art history doubles"—an assertion referring to figurative cave paintings of Chauvet in southern France, estimated to be some 32,000 years old. Meanwhile in 2009, findings were published about additional engraved pieces of ochre from Blombos, the oldest dating to some 100,000 years ago.

We do not know whether the geometric patterns from Blombos were created to please the eye. Scholars observe, however, that in order to make sense of their visual environment, humans long ago evolved to become sensitive to such features as straight lines and repetitive patterns. Purified versions of such geometric features would then hyper-stimulate the brain and increase the pleasure that follows the detection of visual regularity. The brain's innate response to visual patterning might then shed light on why humans started creating geometric designs, once the prerequisite motor and mental capacities had developed.

Some scholars, however, see the geometric patterns from Blombos predominantly in terms of symbolism, as a form of an intentional visual referencing that would represent a major step in human cognitive evolution, especially if the relationship between signifier and signified is established on a conventional or arbitrary basis (that is, when it is "purely symbolic"). Although what the designs might refer to remains unclear, this symbolism would demonstrate that the Blombos people were capable of "abstract thought," and that they were able to store, as well as retrieve, information outside the brain. The mental capacities involved are in themselves often held to presuppose the existence of syntactical language, not so much because it is similarly symbolic but rather because language would be required to establish link between the engraving and its stipulated meaning.

Adherents of a symbolic reading of the Blombos ochre also draw attention to another find in the cave: some forty deliberately perforated estuarine shells (*Nassarius kraussianus*) that show signs of having been strung and worn as beads. Archaeologists, inspired by studies in ethnography, almost universally regard such beads as symbolic and emphasize their social role in signifying individual and collective identities. Beads may signal the wearer's age, kin group, marital status, and so on, thus visually marking and accentuating social differentiations.

When the discovery of the Blombos shells was first announced in 2004, it was considered as spectacular as that of the ochre, in that generally the perforated shells, likewise dated to 75,000 years ago, were held to have almost doubled the age for human bead production. This led to claims that the Blombos beads were too anomalous to allow significant conclusions to be drawn about human behavior during the time period concerned. Meanwhile, deliberately perforated shells, some of which are ochered, have been discovered in a cave in Taforalt, Morocco, and they have been firmly dated to some 82,000 years ago. Excavations in the cave continue with findings of shell beads that are 86,000 years old. A few other perforated shells from northern Africa and adjacent parts may even be older. Interestingly, all these beads are made from *Nassarius* shell, as are the Blombos beads from southern Africa, and they were found up to 200 kilometers (about 124 miles) from the sea, implying transport and probably exchange or trade.

Although archaeologists consider beads to be symbolic, in describing their probable use in necklaces they do use terms like "ornament" or "decoration," implying that the wearing of beads also had an aesthetic effect. Indeed, the shells used as beads in Paleolithic contexts exhibit visual qualities such as bright color and luminosity. A repetitive pattern emerges when similar-sized beads are strung together; alternation of color might add to the pattern as well. Aesthetic and symbolic functions do not rule each other out, and may in fact be mutually strengthening.

Individuals who managed to secure particular types of shell and were dexterous enough to make them into beads by means of perforation—a feat not easily accomplished by present-day experimenters—may have worn these precious possessions themselves, as a form of visual display demonstrating self-awareness. They might also have presented them to others, for example in the context of courtship; beads could as well have been instrumental in creating and maintaining intergroup contacts. If worldwide practices today are anything to go by, the wearing of shells or other pendants might also have early acquired a protective function, or served as a talisman to bring good luck.

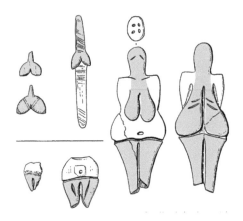

The anthropomorphic symbolism in a Venus figurine suggests a cryptogram combining female breasts with a male penis and testicles. Archeologists are uncertain about the function of these figures, whether as fertility symbols or early forms of pornography.

As do some older perforated shells, four of the Blombos beads show traces of red ochre, a possible result of deliberate coloring or perhaps due to the shells having been worn on ochered bodies. Ochre is found in large quantities at African archaeological sites associated with anatomically modern humans, although its first use predates the arrival of *Homo sapiens* by at least tens of thousands of years. Some pieces of ochre have clearly been rubbed against surfaces. Research suggests that ochre might have been used for preparing hides, for medicinal reasons, or as an adhesive. Many archaeologists make a more popular "symbolic" interpretation, however, assuming that ochre was applied especially to human bodies in ritual contexts. Although this interpretation is

Carving of a running lion in ivory, excavated from Pavlov (Czech Republic), a site that reveals the hunting and tool-making skills of its Upper Paleolithic–period inhabitants.

mainly based on contested parallels with present-day hunter-gatherers, ochre is likely to have had some "significance" for early modern humans; its use in burials, for example, is attested from 100,000 years ago onward.

Iconic Representation

The application of ochre to surfaces would at some point also result in geometric and figurative images. Figurative imagery brings us to a subject that some call "iconic representation": the two- or three-dimensional rendering of humans and other animals, or, to be more precise, the representation of things resembling those in the external (or imaginary) world(s)—fauna especially, but also flora, topographical features, built environments, and other human-made objects.

Specialists seem to agree that producing and perceiving three-dimensional figurative images takes less exacting cognitive ability than creating and making sense of two-dimensional iconic depictions. To understand such phenomena, consider what we presently know about the first human creation of figurative or iconic images in the round: as yet no unambiguous evidence exists that early modern humans in Africa produced three-dimensional figurative imagery, although the few indications we do have give some credence to the speculation that they might have done so using such perishable, nonrecovered, but more easily modified media such as mud or vegetal materials including wood. Similarly for this period, we lack information on any ephemeral forms of modifying the body's appearance, involving, say, flowers, feathers, and plaited fibers (but also hairdressing), or about such possible practices as drawing in, and perhaps with, sand.

Two controversial modified stone objects can serve as examples of early iconic representation, both dating, in fact, to before the arrival of the anatomically modern humans we presently conceive. One is an object discovered near the Moroccan town of Tan Tan, found in layers that are provisionally dated to between 500,000 and 300,000 years ago. The so-called Tan Tan figurine is a small stone whose natural shape resembles that of a human being. Some of the object's natural grooves, which are in part responsible for its anthropomorphic appearance (e.g., a groove separating the "legs"), seem to have been accentuated artificially in what is interpreted as an attempt to enhance the human semblance. Interestingly, red pigment appears to have been applied to the object's surface. The second, the "Berekhat Ram figurine" found in present-day Israel in an archaeological context dated to 233,000 years ago, presents a similar but even more contentious case of semi- or proto-sculptural activity.

Exceptional and controversial as these objects may be, they indicate that hominids have long been capable of discerning human features in natural objects. The oldest specimen to-date is a naturally weathered pebble resembling a hominid face that was found at a three-million-year-old occupation site in Makapansgat in South Africa, probably having been brought there from a nearby riverbed. Given humans' evolved sensitivity to the visual appearance of the human body, particularly when choosing a mate, it is not all that surprising that their increasing capability to modify materials eventually led to the further elaboration of objects bearing a natural resemblance to human features. The late arrival in hominid evolution of this type of behavior, however, should warn us not to think too lightly of the combined capacities involved.

Natural objects suggesting the shapes and outlines of animals, such as cave walls, appear to have held a similar appeal. Apart from European cave paintings, we may rely for evidence here on a 2006 report about a large piece of rock found in a cave in the Tsodilo Hills in Botswana that resembles the body and head of a python. The surface of the rock shows hundreds of artificial indentations that might have been applied to evoke a snake's scales. The indentations appear to have been made by stone tools excavated in the cave, and which are provisionally dated to more than 70,000 years ago.

"Out of Africa"

Somewhere between perhaps 80,000 and 60,000 years ago, modern humans left Africa to colonize the rest of the world (where they would gradually replace earlier humans, such as *Homo neanderthalensis* in Europe and descendants of *Homo erectus* in Asia). Following a coastal trajectory, groups of humans are likely to have migrated along the present-day Arabian peninsula via India to Southeast Asia and on to Australia, a continent that in all likelihood had not yet been populated by hominids. Other migrants, at some point turning north, would colonize Eurasia, following river courses at first.

In Australia, where modern humans arrived perhaps some 50,000 ago, shell beads in all likelihood continued to be worn, with the oldest finds so far including perforated shells that are dated to more than 30,000 years ago. From around this time we also have burials containing human bones covered with ochre. Red ochre was used as well for what is claimed to be the oldest evidence for rock painting in the world today: an piece of rock painted with ochre, found in Kimberley, in northwestern Australia, a region famous for its rock paintings, and dated to around 40,000 years ago.

Is this indeed the first evidence we have of humans applying paint to rock? If so, could this mean such activity developed only after modern humans had left Africa? Africa's oldest paintings yet discovered were found in a cave in Namibia, where images of animals appear on slabs of rock. The paintings are traditionally dated to approximately 28,000 years ago. Recent scholarship suggests, however, that the images may in effect be some 60,000 years old. If so, this increases the possibility that Africa is the birthplace of two-dimensional figurative imagery. This would suggest in turn that the ability to produce such imagery might have been part of the neurocognitive (although not necessarily behavioral) repertoire of modern humans moving out of Africa.

For the oldest indisputable examples of three-dimensional imagery discovered so far we must turn to western Eurasia. Recent excavations of the earliest levels at the site of Kostenki, on the river Don in present-day Russia, suggest that modern humans first arrived in this part of the world at least 45,000 years ago. The excavations have yielded shell beads and a worked piece of mammoth ivory that may represent a human head. Less ambiguous are recent finds from Vogelherd in southwestern Germany, including a small ivory figure of a woolly mammoth and an animal interpreted as a lion. The figures date to between 38,000 and 32,000 years ago. From roughly the same period are the figures that were discovered a few years back in Hohle Fels cave, also in southwestern Germany. Here archaeologists dug up three small ivory carvings: the oldest known representation of a bird, the head of an animal resembling a horse, and a sculpture interpreted as therianthropic (combining feline and human traits), which is compared to the roughly contemporaneous, but much larger figure known as the "Lion Human" from Hohlenstein Stadel, found in 1939.

Until very recently, the so-called Venus figurines from Upper Paleolithic Europe, typically representing corpulent or obese women, were thought to be a somewhat more recent phenomenon, with the most famous example, found in Willendorf in 1908, being dated to about 25,000 years ago; this limestone figure, fitting in the palm of a hand, is covered with red ochre. In 2009, however, archaeologists announced the finding of an ivory figure of a headless woman, with large breasts and buttocks, that was made at least 35,000 years ago and that might in fact be several millennia older. This figure, from the oldest level of Hohle Fels Cave, is considered the earliest inconstestible representation of a human body known to date. The function and meaning of the "Venus figurines" remains unknown, with speculations ranging from fertility symbols to early forms of pornography.

Like their relatives who migrated to Australia, the newly arrived modern humans in Europe not only made shell beads (as well as other beads and pendants) but their activities included engraving and painting images on rock. Depictions of animals and geometric designs found in Chauvet Cave in southern France, the earliest of which are assumed to be some 32,000 years old (which makes them roughly twice as old as the famous examples of Lascaux and Altamira), attest to this, as do other findings. Until the early years of the twenty-first century, Europe was in fact considered the cradle of human artistic behavior, with scholars employing such expressions as "creative explosion" for what was regarded as the sudden advent of bead making, painting, and sculpture in this region some 30,000 years ago.

Farther afield, in the site at Mal'ta, to the west of Lake Baikal in Siberia, archaeologists found ivory sculptures depicting the human form and birds, which are estimated to be some 23,000 years old. The majority of the anthropomorphic figures seem to represent women, some wearing clothing. Most of the avian sculptures depict birds in flight (they are interpreted as swans, geese, and ducks). Like some of the human figures, they are perforated. By analogy with nineteenth- and twentieth-century Siberian hunter-gatherer practices, the perforated sculptures have been interpreted as "spirit helpers" that were attached to a shaman's costume.

Interpreting Paleolithic Art

Other Paleolithic art forms, too, are today interpreted in the context of shamanism, with special reference to David Lewis-Williams' intriguing theory on the beginnings of human image making. The research published in his *The Mind in the Cave: Consciousness and the Origins of Art* (2002) suggests that the images characteristic of Paleolithic art, namely animals and geometric designs, find their origin in hallucinations or "altered states of consciousness," especially as experienced by "shamans" in a state of trance (induced by ritual, sensory deprivation, or psychotropic drugs), and thus that the first human images were created to "fix" shamans' hallucinatory experiences.

In proposing his theory, Lewis-Williams draws on shamanistic practices found today in hunter-gatherer societies all over the world. He argues that present-day humans have basically the same brains as their Paleolithic ancestors tens of thousands of years ago. Now when we perceive the world it is ultimately the brain that generates the images we experience. The brain may in fact produce images even in the absence of external visual stimuli, as in mental visualization and perhaps more vividly in dreams or other altered states of consciousness (but also, for example, when

This mammoth, one of the world's earliest ceramic figurines, was also found at Pavlov (Czech Republic).

one slightly pushes the eyeball, resulting in the visual experience of various geometric or abstract shapes in different colors, something experienced more intensely by people suffering from migraine).

Research also suggests that images, specifically of animals, which were generated and experienced by the brain in trance-like conditions, would have been interpreted as pertaining to phenomena existing on another plane, as glimpses or visions of beings that populated "alternative realities." Indeed, Lewis-Williams argues that the modern human brain is not only able to self-generate images, but it is also able to remember these and to share and discuss them with others through both verbal language and the visual images that serve as records of what shamans powerfully experienced when sojourning in "other realms."

Shamanistic rituals can involve not only experiencing spirits in the form of animals, but the shaman's transformation into such a spirit being. This might shed light on the occurrence of therianthropic images in Paleolithic art. Some researchers object to such a theory, however, saying that not all artifacts interpreted as therianthropic represent actual mixtures of humans and other animals: the so-called Lion Human of Hohlenstein Stadel, for example, might as well be a depiction of a bear standing upright. Furthermore, some of these images, which are said to be actually quite rare, may in fact render a human in disguise, pretending to be an animal in the context of the hunt. But scholars also argue that the scientific literature on hallucination is less supportive of Lewis-Williams' neuropsychological theory than suggested.

R. Dale Guthrie, a specialist in Arctic biology, presents an alternative account of Upper Paleolithic art but does not, however, address the preconditions or origins of human image making. Guthrie, focusing on Ice Age Europe, proposes that the images of animals on cave walls, but also on portable objects, result from their creators' fascination with the local wildlife. Countering the prevailing "magico-religious paradigm" in prehistoric art research, Guthrie posits that many images might in fact have been made by male adolescents who were inspired by what he calls "testosterone moments," such as the excitement of the

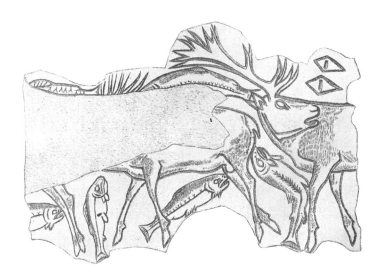

This illustration of a drawing incised on a cave wall in southern France shows salmon and huge-antlered stags embellished with line patterns and cross-hatching.

hunt or the confrontation with large predators. This profane perspective on Paleolithic art making is also deployed to elucidate the sexual imagery frequently found in cave paintings, rock engravings, and other artistic expressions. Featuring mainly women and female sexual organs, this prehistoric "graffiti" could present young men's sexual fantasies or experiences. Guthrie's views share elements with the interpretation developed by John Onians, who bases his analysis on recent neuroscientific findings.

Paleolithic art has always been and continues to be a fascinating field of competing interpretative theories. One currently debated topic concerns the question of whether or not early art forms had an "adaptive function," meaning whether or not artistic behavior contributed to the survival and reproduction of those who practiced it. Could it be that, once having come into existence, the tendency to create visual art was able to spread because it turned out to confer some evolutionary advantage on individuals or groups so inclined? Among the proponents of an adaptionist perspective on art, a distinction may be made between those who favor an explanation of art's role in the competition among individuals (specifically for mates, in which case art would serve as a way of showing off one's skill and creativity) and those who argue for the social benefits of art's presence, such as its effects on group solidarity, cooperation, and the intergenerational transmission of knowledge (for example, by making messages more memorable). Scholars who deny that visual art may be assigned an adaptive value suggest that it evolved as a byproduct of capacities and tendencies that in themselves are probably adaptive, such as the ability to create and manipulate tools and the positive innate responses to certain colors, lines, shapes, and subject matters that better helped humans to survive and reproduce.

The Future of Paleolithic Art Studies

After decades of relative neglect, Paleolithic art and the concomitant issue of the origins of art are today hotly debated by specialists from an ever-growing range of disciplines, including archaeology, art history, and anthropology, as well as evolutionary biology and neuroscience. While new archaeological discoveries are being published at an increasing rate, this interdisciplinary group of scholars is bringing new conceptual tools, interpretative frameworks, and research methods to bear on a fundamental set of

Where the spirit does not work with the hand there is no art. • **Leonardo da Vinci**

questions in world history: when and where did human beings begin making and using visual art, what conditions made this behavior possible (physical, mental, social, cultural), why has this artistic behavior been retained in human history, and how has art increasingly become integral to our existence?

Wilfried VAN DAMME

Leiden University and *Ghent University*

See also Art—World Art Studies; Art—World History and Art

Further Reading

Anikovich, M.V. et al. (2007). Early upper Paleolithic in Eastern Europe and implications for the dispersal of modern humans, *Science, 315*(5819), 223–226.

Bahn, P. G. & Vertut, J. (2001). *Journey through the Ice Age*. Los Angeles: University of California Press.

Balme, J. & Morse, K. (2006). Shell beads and social behaviour in Pleistocene Australia, *Antiquity, 80*, 799–811.

Bednarik, R. G. (2003). A figurine from the African Acheulian. *Current Anthropology, 44*(3), 405–413.

Bouzouggar, A. et al. (2007). 82,000-year-old beads from North Africa and the implications for the origins of modern human behavior. *Proceedings of the National Academy of Sciences of the United States of America, 104*, 9964–9969.

Clottes, J. (2003). *Return to Chauvet Cave: Excavating the birthplace of art*. London: Thames and Hudson.

Conard, N. J. (2003). Palaeolithic ivory sculptures from southwestern Germany and the origins of figurative art. *Nature, 426*(6965), 830–832.

Conard, N. J. et al. (2007). Einmalige Funde durch die Nachgrabung am Vogelherd bei Niederstotzingen-Stetten ob Lontal, Kreis Heidelheim, Archäologische Ausgrabungen in Baden-Württemberg 2006, J. Briel (Ed.). pp. 20–24. Stuttgart: Theiss.

Conard, N. J. (2009). A female figurine from the basal Aurignacian of Hohle Fels Cave in southwestern Germany. *Nature 459*(7244), 248–252.

Dart, R. A. (1974). The waterworn pebble of many faces from Makapansgat. *South African Journal of Science, 70*(6), 167–169.

d'Errico, F., Henshilwood, C. S., & Nilssen, P. (2005). *Nassarius kraussianus* shell beads from Blombos Cave: Evidence for symbolic behavior in the Middle Stone Age. *Journal of Human Evolution, 48*(1), 3–24.

Dissanayake, E. (2008). The arts after Darwin: does art have an origin and adaptive function? In K. Zijlmans and W. van Damme (Eds.), *World art studies: Exploring Concepts and Approaches* (pp. 241–263). Amsterdam: Valiz.

Guthrie, R. D. (2005). *The nature of Paleolithic art*. Chicago: University of Chicago Press.

Henshilwood, C. S. et al. (2002). Emergence of modern human behaviour: Middle Stone Age engravings from South Africa. *Science, 295*(5558), 1278–1280.

Henshilwood, C. S., d'Errico, F., & Watts, I. (2009). Engraved ochres from the Middle Stone Age levels at Blombos Cave, South Africa. *Journal of Human Evolution, 57*(1), 27–47.

Hodgson, D. (2006a). Understanding the origins of paleoart: The neurovisual resonance theory and brain functioning. *PaleoAnthropology 2006*, 54–67.

Hodgson, D. (2006b). Altered states of consciousness and palaeoart: An alternative neurovisual explanation. *Cambridge Archaeological Journal, 16*(1), 27–37.

Lewis-Williams, D. (2002). *The mind in the cave: Consciousness and the origins of art*. London: Thames and Hudson.

McBrearthy, S. & Brooks, A. S. (2000). The revolution that wasn't: A new interpretation of the origin of modern human behavior. *Journal of Human Evolution, 39*(5): 453–563.

Mithen, S. (2003). Handaxes: The first aesthetic artifacts. In E. Voland and K. Grammer (Eds.), *Evolutionary Aesthetics* (pp. 261–275). Berlin: Springer.

Morwood, M. J. (2002). *Visions of the past: The archaeology of Australian Aboriginal art*. London: Allen and Unwin.

Onians, J. (2008). Neuroarthistory: Making more sense of art. In K. Zijlmans and W. van Damme (Eds.), *World Art Studies: Exploring concepts and approaches* (pp. 265–286). Amsterdam: Valiz.

Schlesier, K. H. (2001). More on the "Venus" figurines. *Current Anthropology, 42*(3), 410–412.

Summers, D. (2003). *Real spaces: World art history and the rise of Western modernism*. London: Phaidon.

White, R. (2003). *Prehistoric art: The symbolic journey of humankind*. New York: Harry N. Abrams.

Art—Pre-Columbian Central and South America

The arts of Central and South America created prior to the arrival of Europeans in the 1500s represent the development of many sophisticated civilizations, some of which still exist. Although countless changes occurred after the European conquest, many indigenous philosophies, cultures, and customs did not vanish; rather, people of the Americas found ways to combine aspects of old and new, especially in their art and architecture.

Before the late fifteenth- early sixteenth-century European conquest of Central and South America, indigenous peoples—such as the Inca, Maya, Mixtec, Aztec/Mexica, and Zapotec—had developed art and architecture with distinctive characteristics. Many artifacts exist to inform world historians and researchers studying those civilizations, and scholars continue to excavate, analyze, and publicize the remains of ostensibly vanished cultures. Native Americans and mestizos (those of mixed Native American and European ancestry) continue to spur discussion and exploration of pre-Columbian cultures, and to revive an indigenous past that formerly was suppressed or hidden during the colonial era.

Pre-Columbian Art: Overview

Although artistic traditions in the Americas continued long after the arrival of Europeans, the end of the pre-Columbian period in the Caribbean is marked by 1492, the year in which Christopher Columbus came to the Antilles. In the highlands of Mexico, pre-Columbian art is generally dated prior to 1521, the year in which the conquistador Hernán Cortés and his allies conquered the Aztec/Mexica capital Tenochtitlán. Francisco Pizarro's 1533 conquest of the Inca capital Cuzco, Peru, ends the pre-Columbian creation of art in South America.

The exchange of art and ideas occurred across vast distances and influenced widely disbursed groups in the Americas; sometimes art materials were brought from afar to satisfy philosophical, spiritual, political, and aesthetic needs. Much extant pre-Columbian art is made of durable stone, metal, stucco, or clay, but the people of the Americas created goods for home and trade using materials as varied as amaranth seeds, animal hide, bark paper, bone, cotton, feathers (especially the quetzal's), gold, greenstone, jade, mineral and vegetal paint, pearls, shells, silver, turquoise, wood, wool, and yucca. Public and semipublic monuments communicated messages asserting the legitimacy of the right to rule; they commemorated conquests of polities and foes, celebrated the histories and awe-inducing qualities of gods, and informed successive generations about historical and mythological events. Thus, art in the ancient Americas transmitted much more than ideas about beauty.

Although the Americas comprised various ethnic groups and city-states, they shared similar beliefs (pan-American bird-feline-lizard religion; rain or lightning gods), cultural practices (patronage and trade; sacred architecture; art used in rituals and ceremonies), and motifs (preference for abstraction; substantial use of red pigments; accordion-style record books). Historians once accounted for these similarities in Mesoamerica by theorizing that the Olmec (c. 1500–550 BCE) established norms that successors followed, but today they believe cultures such as the Zapotec may be nearly as ancient. As for South

American indigenous peoples, scholars believe they maintained the customs, aesthetics, and culture of the Chavín (c. 800–200 BCE) of the Andes. Recurrent themes also abound in pre-Columbian South American art and architecture: food and agriculture; gods and rulers; sacrificial rituals; sexuality and fertility; and symbols of wealth and status.

Most surviving pre-Columbian art emphasizes contour line, pattern, and hieratic scale (the depiction of more important figures as larger than others in the scene). Artists, apparently suffering from *horror vacui* (literally, the fear of empty spaces), filled the entire composition with images, glyphs, or repeated motifs. They preferred composite perspective for figures, a style comparable to Egyptian art in which arms and legs appear in profile while the torso is frontal. Pre-Columbian art rarely, if at all, used perspectival systems to create illusions of the realistic world humans inhabited. These practices were the product of aesthetics, not a lack of technique: oral histories, documents, and material evidence indicate that pre-Columbian artists were extensively trained.

This survey takes a geographical approach to the settlements of the pre-Columbian period, starting in ancient Mesoamerica with the Olmec and ending in the Andean cultures of South America.

Mesoamerica: Pyramids, Ceramics, and Ball Courts

Ancient Mesoamerica, the region that encompassed present-day central Mexico, Guatemala, and Honduras, included numerous settlements and cities populated by various indigenous people who shared specific religious and aesthetic philosophies—and who documented sociocultural structures and practices in their art.

Olmec

Once called the "mother culture" of Mesoamerica, the Olmec settled along the Gulf of Mexico in the areas now known as Vera Cruz and Tabasco as early as 1500 BCE and continuing through 550 BCE. Data accumulated since the late 1990s, however, suggest that other groups, such as the Zapotecs of southwest Mexico, may have origins stretching back that far. The Olmec were not homogenous or static while

Panorama of Monte Albán from the South Platform, 2006. Photo by Matt Saunders.

they flourished; archaeologists have found Olmec art several hundred kilometers from their gulf-coast centers.

The Olmec developed a complex calendrical system and demonstrated an interest in writing. Glyphs found at La Venta and on the Cascajal Block (a writing tablet–sized slab dating to the first millennium BCE and discovered in Veracruz), may be the earliest example of writing in North and South America. Archaeological evidence in sites at San Lorenzo (flourished 1200–900 BCE) and La Venta (900–400 BCE)—including clay and stone architecture, monumental and small-scale sculptures, bas-reliefs, and decorative ceramics—suggests a sophisticated, well-developed civilization with an interest in agriculture, aquatic and amphibious life-forms, leadership traditions, and status. Ceramics and small stone carvings, exchanged along extensive economic trade routes from about 1150 to 900 BCE, likely influenced artwork in the Mexican highlands, where large Olmec-style petroglyphs and pictographs have been found in caves. From about 900 to 550 BCE, the Olmec traded carved jade, usually in the forms of celts (chisels) or axes. Artists incised anthropomorphic and animal features—most notably of snarling, jaguar-like creatures, reflecting the belief that jaguar deities could assume human form—into jade, later rubbing red-brown cinnabar (mercury sulfide) into the lines. (The poisonous cinnabar signified a kind of untouchable sanctity to the works.) Frowning, puffy-faced, carved figures—some referred to as the "were-baby" or "jaguar-were-baby"—pervade Olmec art. Scholars suggest the were-baby was symbolic in the transmission of power from one ruler to another, or served as a representation of the origin of power in the Olmec tradition.

The Olmec transported huge pieces of basalt some 96 kilometers from the Tuxtla Mountains to build a portion of the 30-meter-high Great Pyramid in La Venta. (The structure, estimated to have taken 18,000 men about a million man-hours to construct, has been noted for its similarities, including its north-south axial orientation, to the great Egyptian pyramids. The best-known examples of Olmec sculpture, sacrificial offerings in the form of colossal heads, likely represented individual rulers; while they all exhibit fleshy faces, almond-shaped eyes, and down-turned mouths, each face is different. The Olmec sacrificed items, such as statuary configurations and

A monumental head of Dzahui, the Rain God, "guarded" by frogs. Late Postclassic. Teotitlan del Camino, Oaxaca. Photo by Danielle L. Pierce.

mosaic floors, by burying or somehow hiding them from public view after completion (again, a striking similarity to the Egyptians). The pre-Columbian art scholar Mary Ellen Miller has called this type of offering *hidden architecture*.

The Olmec built ball courts and played the Mesoamerican ballgame, a political-religious, culture-defining ritual of pre-Columbian societies, especially the Maya, that persisted until the time of the conquest. On a slope-walled, I-shaped court, heavily padded players used their arms, hips, shoulders, and torso—but not hands—to hit an approximately 4-kilogram rubber ball through small raised goals. Small ceramics depicting ball players and spectators have been found in southwestern Mexico. Some scholars suggest that the ball represented celestial bodies held aloft by the players' skill.

Characteristics distinctive to Olmec—the colossal head, the use of red pigment as a means of expression, jaguar or feather headgear, and deity masks—influenced later cultural groups well beyond the third century CE.

Maya

The Maya, scattered like the Olmec, were located in southern Mexico, Belize, El Salvador, Guatemala, and Honduras; their stratified society engaged in farming, hunting, masonry, and trade. Distinctively Maya centers emerged circa 300 BCE and endured until the time of the conquest. Some Maya edifices, such as the Temple of the Cross and Temple XIX at Palenque, have deteriorated significantly, while other artifacts remain subsumed by jungle or buried beneath earth.

The Maya kept their historical documents in codices (accordion-style record books). They did, however, maintain an oral history tradition in such collections as the Popol Vuh, written down in the sixteenth-century by a Maya noble; it details the adventures of Hero Twins who attempt to defeat the gods of the underworld and resurrect their father. Many Mayan ceramics depict scenes from the Popol Vuh: the renowned Blom Plate, for instance, illustrates the twins using blowguns to shoot a boastful macaw that wrongly claims to have created the sun and moon.

Gods, sacrificial victims, and rulers appear repeatedly in Mayan art. Deities comprised of body parts from more than one animal are shown with humanoid hands, legs, and heads. Sacrificial victims are usually depicted as nude or semi-nude, to the Maya a condition of shame. The Maya practiced ancestor worship, burying the dead with the tools of their professions, cremating or interring the remains of royalty, and, later, building temples and tombs to honor them. Stelae honoring current and departed rulers included dates and symbols of their accomplishments.

The Maya continued to refine the 260-day ritual calendar, establishing the "long count" of days since the beginning of time, which they believed to be 3114 BCE. Twentieth-century scholars who discovered that glyphs appearing in Mayan iconography were often numeric notations from this calendrical system were able to discredit the prevailing view of the Maya as peaceful philosopher-kings. Evidence is

In this mural at Teotihuacán the puma's claws are drawn with characteristic, cartoon-like exaggeration. Photo by Danielle L. Pierce.

in the art: Mayan glyphs, frescoes, relief carvings, and wall panels suggest that bloody conflicts and sacrifices existed throughout known Mayan history—and that political posturing, war, and human sacrifice, in addition to agricultural and environmental factors, may have contributed to the decline of populous Mayan settlements circa 800–900 CE. The Maya lived in less populated, more decentralized settlements at the time of the Spanish conquest.

Zapotec

The Zapotec civilization, which established its earliest settlements in Oaxaca, Guerrero, and Puebla, may have existed somewhat concurrently with the Olmec, although for a longer period. At the time of the conquest, Zapotecs engaged in trade across central Mexico but did not dominate the region like Mixtecs or Mexica.

The Zapotecs maintained a pantheon of gods, a 260-day ritual calendar, a priest-scribe class, and a belief in a universal life force called *pè*. The visage of Cocijo, their god of lightning, appears on many complex ceramic pieces from Oaxaca. Scholars suggest that the Zapotecs' militaristic society created arts and temple architecture to connote power and status and to revere ancestors, especially previous rulers. (From about 200 to 1000 CE the Zapotecs built large mounds and structures over older structures, as did the Maya.) Relief carvings in the city of Monte Albán (built 300–200 BCE and declined 200 CE) depicted named, sacrificed captives in varying levels of mutilation. In Tomb 7 at Monte Albán, archaeologists discovered collars with golden beads shaped to resemble jaguar teeth and turtle carapaces, personal adornments (including labret plugs, i.e., decorative status items that enter below the lower lip inside the mouth and project outward away from the face), ceramic urns, and incense burners.

Teotihuacán

Teotihuacán, established during the beginning of the first century CE about 48 kilometers from present-day Mexico City, flourished from 350 to 600 as one of the world's largest cities (population c. 200,000). Residents worshipped the Rain God and the Feather God (Quetzacoatl), recognizably antecedent to gods of later Mesoamericans. The city's ceremonial center burned in the eighth century; thereafter Teotihuacán declined but remained a pilgrimage center until the conquest. The Mexica, who then predominated and gave the city its name, believed the site to be the place where gods created the sun and the moon. (Teotihuacán means "The City [gathering place] of the Gods.")

The Avenue of the Dead forms a 5-kilometer north-south axis through the city beginning in front of the Pyramid of the Moon. Multiple, symmetrically arranged residences, temples, and open courts flank the road, which then passes, on the left, the dual stairway of the Pyramid of the Sun. Continuing south, in the heart of the city, the avenue leads to the Cuidadela (Citadel), a vast sunken plaza whose focal point is a six-platform step pyramid, the Temple of the Feathered Serpent. The temple structure exhibits a hallmark of Teotihuacán *talud-tablero* style: each sloping base (*talud*) supports a vertical entablature that is surrounded by a frame and filled with sculptural decoration.

Pyramid of the Moon in Teotihuacán, where the Mexica believed the gods created the sun and the moon. Photo by Danielle L. Pierce.

Teotihuacán murals exhibit easy-to-understand, cartoon-like line drawings in which elements of color and style can be read symbolically. The jade green nose adornment, headdress feathers, and beads of the Great Goddess of Tetitla (Teotihuacán) denote spiritual wealth and the sustenance it provides. The repeated C curls and lines attached to her hands represent abundance and flowing water.

Archeological evidence of human and animal artifacts buried with precious jade figurines, adornments, and obsidian suggest that the Teotihuacános engaged in sacrificial practices; evidence of sacrificial rituals appears in Teotihuacán.art. A fragment of a mural called *Maguey Bloodletting Ritual* (600–750 CE, Cleveland Museum of Art) shows a priest piercing his hand on the spine of a maguey plant—a source of food and fiber (for fabric, rope, and paper), as well as a sacramental drink. The priest then scatters his blood on seeded, rectangular plots of earth.

Mixtec

The Mixtec settled between 1500 and 750 BCE in Oaxaca, Guerrero, and Puebla, where they became powerful circa 900 CE. Mixtec culture continued to develop somewhat concurrently beside the Mexica, who conquered several Mixtec city-states during the 1400s and early 1500s, exacting tribute from the conquered villages. The Mixtec used alliances created through marriage to determine the inheritance of titles and the right of rule. Spaniards later came to rely on this elite ruling class to aid in conversion and cultural changes.

Scholars have labeled extant codices, jewelry, and ceramics as Mixteca-Puebla, a style that emphasized the planar qualities of a figure and object by outlining and filling the image with flat, consistent earth tones and eschewing realistic representation for economical stylization.

Aztec/Mexica

At the time of the conquests, Nahuatl-speaking peoples who called themselves Mexica, not Aztec, were the dominant power and culture in Mesoamerica. (The name "Aztec" only became popular when scholars in the nineteenth century adopted it as a way to distance "modern" Mexicans from pre-conquest Mexicans.) The Mexica controlled a vast empire spanning central Mexico from the gulf to the Pacific, an accomplishment achieved through military campaigns, marriage alliances, an education system for elite males, and control of trade networks.

The Mexica developed communities as early as 950 CE in central Mexico; they built portions of their capitol Tenochtitlán, where Mexico City stands now, as early as the twelfth century, constructing it on islands in Lake Texcoco that were built up from debris. One renowned Mexica myth, now part of modern Mexican national identity, describes the peoples' origins on an "island of whiteness" (Aztlán). The hummingbird god Huitzilopochtli directed them to leave Aztlan and travel until they saw an eagle, perched on a prickly pear cactus, gobbling a snake—and there to build their new home. After Mexico won independence from Spain in the late 1880s, leaders evoked images of the Mexica past to inspire the future: Mexico's coat of arms depicted an eagle clutching a snake in its beak, and symbols from Mexica carvings began to appear on postage stamps. In the 1920s, when Mexico's education minister invited artists including Diego Rivera and José Clemente Orozco to paint murals on public buildings to commemorate those who fought in the revolution, many painters drew upon Mexica mythology and symbols. For Rivera, the Earth goddess Coatlicue (Huitzilopochtli's mother) was an especially iconic image.

Scribes recorded details of Mexica history, religion, and culture in codices—the pre-Columbianist Elizabeth Boone calls them "containers of knowledge"—by using glyphs that represented components of words, ideas, names, and dates and by arranging them in "scenes" with symbolic, interpretative clues. Very few of these books exist today. The Mexica king Itzcoatl became notorious (in part) for rewriting or destroying these historical chronicles when he came to the throne in 1428. After installing the first bishop in Tenochtitlán in 1528, Spaniards also embarked on a campaign to destroy indigenous records.

The main temple of the Mexica Empire, the Templo Mayor, held dual shrines, one dedicated to Huitzilopochtli and the other to the rain god Tlaloc. Excavations revealed a cave and offerings below the pyramid, as well as artworks depicting Mexica origin myths. The Coyolxauhqui disk, for example, illustrates the dismemberment of Huitzilopochtli's traitorous sister, who attempted to kill their mother, Coatlicue ("she of the serpent skirt"), after learning of their mother's pregnancy.

The Mexica first fell to Hernán Cortes in 1519 and suffered a final defeat in 1521. On 22 October 1522, Holy Roman Emperor Charles I (V) declared Cortés Governor and Captain General of New Spain. Over the next several years, Spanish forces subdued much of the rest of Mexico and established it as a colony.

South America: Textiles before Ceramics

Ancient peoples of the Peruvian Andes developed textile technology before ceramic technology. Woven items dating from the ninth to the sixth centuries BCE found in Guitarrero Cave are the oldest artifacts from the continent, and archaeologists discovered mummies wearing intricate textile designs from as early as 5,000 BCE at Huaca Prieta. The high grasslands of the Andes—the habitat of llamas, alpacas, vicuñas, and guanacos (all a rich source of wool)—made the creation of textiles in South America a flourishing art form. Textiles designed by artists for private use reflected a measure of ethnic, political, and social status. Textiles in Andean public life assumed the significance equal to ceramics in Mesoamerican ritual sacrifices and bronze in Chinese ancestor worship—and yet relatively few textiles, at least compared to in number to their durable clay and metal counterparts, exist in the archaeological record.

Early South American Origins

In the central Andes of South America (present-day Peru and Bolivia) civilizations developed, as they did in Mesoamerica, with rich and varied artistic traditions, but in the midst of a more dramatic geography—dry desert between the Pacific and the snow-capped peaks, highland grasses (home to the Andean camelids), and steep slopes that descended on the east to the rainforest of the Amazon Basin. The earliest ceremonial mounds and plazas on the coast date to the third millennium BCE, the same period as the earliest pyramids in Egypt. Multi-room stone structures in the highlands featured sunken fire pits that were used to burn ritual offerings. During the second millennium BCE, prior to the settlement of Chavín de Huantár, coastal peoples became more dependent on agriculture, and thus began to build canal and irrigation systems. A distinct style of architecture emerged as populations moved inland: large, U-shaped ceremonial structures, with sunken, circular spaces, were oriented toward the mountains, the rising sun, and the source of the water they needed to grow food.

Coyolxauhqui Stone, Mexica (Aztec). Photo by Danielle L. Pierce.

Chavín

The people who populated Chavín de Huantár (c. 900–200 BCE), a settlement located on a trade route through the mountains that connected the Pacific Coast and the Amazon Basin, were influential in South America for centuries. The Chavín incorporated influences from earlier surrounding peoples, appropriating the U-shaped buildings of the coastal regions and the recessed spaces of South American highland structures to create a uniquely Chavín aesthetic.

Archaeologists have found golden objects, ceramics, and textiles produced by the Chavín far north and west of the mountain pass, an indication of their complex trade network. Artisans produced gold and gold alloy sheet-metal adornments, headgear, pectorals (chest pieces worn by elite men), and ceramic stirrup-spout vessels. The abstract style of Chavín art deals with recurrent motifs and subject matter, especially religion and spiritual transcendence.

Nazca

The residents of Nazca (Nasca), Peru, established their settlement as early as 600 BCE. The adobe pyramid—altered hills made to resemble large structures—burials mounds, plazas, and funerary offerings at Cahuachie are associated with the Nazca.

Chavín textiles and ceramics influenced Nazca weaving and pottery, but the Nazca are best known for transforming the living surface of the Earth to create monumental artworks, called geoglyphs, on the

Pampa de Nazca. The Nazca dug contour lines in the dark gravel of the plains to form gigantic images—a hummingbird, a killer whale, and a monkey, for example—and then they edged the underlying lighter soil they'd exposed with sea and river stones, shells, and ceramics full of corn beer in what scholars believe were fertility or water rituals. Some have posited that the people of Nazca could not have made the geoglyphs themselves—that the makers and intended audience were space aliens. Scholars do agree, however, that early humans were capable of creating such large imagery (and that such endeavors could take place without conscription or slavery). Pre-Columbian art produced only for the eyes of gods is not unusual: the Olmec offered hidden architecture below buildings and under special spaces; the Mexica gave offerings in the layers of the great Templo Mayor.

Moche

The Moche, whose origins are not fully understood, resided in a desert valley in the Andes (north of Chavín de Huantar) from the first century CE to the eighth century; the capital, Cerro Blanco, was located close to an ancient trade route connecting the coast and the edge of the highlands.

Allusions to agricultural and commercial pursuits appear in many Moche artworks. The burial site of the Lord of Sipán, discovered north of the Moche Valley, included a gold and silver collar made from beads representing the peanut (an important source of protein and fat), as well as silver-and-gold-gilded ear spools, masks, textiles, and ceramics. Excavation of the burial site suggests that the Moche were a stratified, militaristic society with a many skilled artisans.

The enormous adobe pyramid at Cerro Blanco, a royal residence known as the Pyramid of the Sun, was made using sun-dried mud bricks, some of which retain the distinctive marks identifying the communities that made them. A second pyramid, the Pyramid of the Moon, was built on a hill, probably as a ritual or ceremonial space. The repetitive building of pyramids in Central and South America suggests a possible early connection between the two cultures, although the building of such structures could have been independent of each other.

The Moche mass-produced molded ceramics and created one-of-a-kind pieces that were both functional and decorative; such objects displayed naturalism and convincing detail. Scholars believe that vessels portraying rulers were used in rituals and later buried with elites. *Moche Lord with a Feline* (Art Institute of Chicago) is a square vessel on top of which sits a lord, wearing an elaborate headdress with coordinating ear spools, who pets the head of the cat (or jaguar cub) lying next to him. Behind the figure the ceramicist attached a stirrup spout—an upside-down, U-shaped, hollow handle with a single spout protruding from the top—a feature probably appropriated from the Chavín.

Other vessels convey scenes from daily life and sacrificial practices. Some depict food (e.g., corn and beans), deities, flora and fauna, birds, and ocean creatures. Many display sexual imagery, such as prisoners of war with exposed genitalia, or dancing skeletons with erect penises; still others show scenes in which numerous lively figures engage in numerous forms of sexual activity. (Replicas of these so-called Moche sex pots, ubiquitous in marketplaces that target tourists, and are also the subject of considerable anthropological discussion.) Although not much is known about Moche spirituality, several Moche ceramics depict a warrior priest holding a ritual cup, presumably filled with blood or other sacrificial libations.

The arrival of El Niño in the Moche Valley circa 600 CE started the decline of the civilization, and, eventually, the Moche abandoned Cerro Blanco. After the conquest a local river was redirected to flood the site and make it easier to pillage precious objects.

Inca

The Inca developed circa 1100 and by the sixteenth century grew to rule the empire of Tiwantinsuyo, laying stones over the ancient paths that ran from Ecuador to southern Chile. (In the early 1500s its territory rivaled China's in size.) The capital, Cuzco, included ritual routes called *ceque*, lines radiating out from the Qorikancha (Coricancha, or the Temple of the Sun), the city center.

Several versions of the Incas' origin stories are known and referenced in colonial paintings of ancient ancestors. One tells that the Inca believed the incestuous brother/sister husband/wife pair, Manco Capac and Mama Ocllo, received a prophecy about a new homeland in which a golden staff could miraculously penetrate the soil. Eventually they found that place, defeated the people who lived there, and took control of what was to become the center of their empire.

Political systems of the Inca, which required subjects to make tax payments in the form of food, labor, or textiles, and to exchange equal amounts of work among households, fostered advances in textile arts and architecture, two distinctive features of Andean civilizations. Andean textiles are among the most technically complex cloths ever made, some containing five hundred threads per square inch. Making textiles consumed a major part of the human resources of Andean society, whose dyers, weavers, and embroiderers employed and invented nearly every technique known over the centuries. Some cloths, dually appreciated for their beauty and labor intensiveness, were woven, unwoven, and rewoven to achieve special effects. Cotton, grown in Peru as early as 3000 BCE, was the most commonly used plant fiber. The earliest cloths were made without looms, and the techniques of knotting, winding, twining, braiding, and looping continued after the invention of the loom in the early second century BCE. Possessing finely woven cloth conveyed wealth and status; textiles, considered offerings worthy of the gods, were often draped around gold statues. (The conquistadors, of course, kept their sights on the gold). Incan textiles were primarily woven by *aclla*, or female weavers who were under the jurisdiction of state religion. Special administrators called the *quipumacayu* probably tracked such items, in addition to histories, census data, and tribute, with record-keeping systems using *quipus*, knotted and colored cord.

Although the Inca domesticated llamas, these animals could not bear the weight of the monumental stones used in construction. Thus human labor was necessary for two types of architectural construction: cyclopean masonry and pirca (pirka) masonry. Cyclopean masonry involved the mortarless configuration of load-bearing walls that were able to withstand destruction from earthquakes endemic to the region. Pirca was a load-bearing approach that used mud mortar. Some Incan buildings were constructed of pirca walls with a cyclopean masonry façade. A geometric style emphasized basic shapes and lines instead of complex or crowded iconography. Thus Incan builders created other stonework of refinement and durability, such as roads and bridges to link the empire, terraces for growing crops, and irrigation systems essential for supporting a highland population increasingly dependent on agriculture.

When the Europeans arrived, Incan rulership was in dispute. King Huayna Capac died unexpectedly without selecting an heir, leaving his two sons to fight for control of the empire. In 1532 the victorious son Atahualpa fell hostage to Francisco Pizarro, his band of men, and, likely, his Native American allies. After receiving a room full of gold as ransom, Pizarro and his men strangled Atahualpa, appropriating the Incan Empire for the Spanish crown, and took Cuzco in 1533.

Aftermath of the Conquest

Exploitive policies of European conquerors (and ravages of disease they carried, to which indigenous peoples were not immune) caused a sharp decline in native populations in Central and South America. Colonizers suppressed local beliefs and practices, tore down temples, and built churches. Religious conversion fell to Franciscan, Dominican, and Augustinian missionaries, many of whom were appalled by the conquerors' treatment of their subjects.

To some extent, indigenous symbolism was absorbed in Christian iconography, especially in the form of crosses installed in church atriums, where converts gathered to be educated. Missionaries recruited native sculptors to carve these stone crosses, and although the images were likely copied from

> *As for your pope of whom you speak, he must be mad to speak of giving away countries that do not belong to him.* • **Atahualpa, on hearing that in 1493 Pope Alexander VI had awarded parts of Peru to Spanish monarchs**

illustrated books the missionaries supplied, elements of pre-Hispanic sculpture pervaded. One such sixteenth-century cross (in the Basilica of Guadalupe in Mexico City), carved with dense low-relief images such as Christ's crown of thorns, suggests an ancient Mesoamerican symbol, the World Tree (or Tree of Life), with its stark form and rich surface symbols; the image of blood sacrifice correlates to indigenous beliefs of the Teotihuacán culture, for example, but the newly converted artists who carved it might not yet have experienced the spiritual resonance.

The customs and arts of many indigenous peoples, rather than disappear, mixed with those of their conquerors or survived intact among smaller groups (only to be revived as research in pre-Columbian art piques). While adopting Spanish cultural ideas and practices, the Maya preserved their traditions and language throughout the colonial era, and continue to reside in Chiapas, Mexico, as well as in Belize, Guatemala, and Honduras. Today Zapotecs are concentrated in many southwestern Mexican regions where their ancestors lived. Mixtecos in the twenty-first century are engaged in a revival of their language and pre-Columbian thought and culture, while blockbuster museum exhibits in all things "Aztec" have brought a more nuanced approach to the Mexica. Still-practicing weavers and other textile artists, whose craft has been handed down through centuries, provide a source of pride and world recognition today, as well as a storehouse of information for historians.

Danielle L. PIERCE
University of North Texas

Further Reading

Balkansky, A. K. et al. (2000, Winter). Archaeological survey in the Mixteca Alta of Oaxaca, Mexico. *Journal of Field Archaeology, 27*(4), 365–389.

Boone, E. (2000). *Stories in red and black: Pictorial histories of the Aztec and Mixtec.* Austin: University of Texas Press.

Cortes, H. (2001). *Letters from Mexico.* A. Padgen (Ed. & Trans.). New Haven, CT: Yale University Press.

Jansen, M. R. G. N. & Pérez Jiménez, G. A. (2000). *La dinastía de Añute: Historia, literatura e ideología de un reino mixteco.* Leiden, The Netherlands: Research School of Asian, African and Amerindian Studies (CNWS), Universiteit Leiden.

Kowalski, J. & Kristan-Graham, C. (Eds.). (2007). *Twin Tollans: Chichén Iztá, Tula, and the Epiclassic to early postclassic Mesoamerican world.* Washington, DC: Dumbarton Oaks.

Lockhart, J., (Ed.). (2004). *We people here: Nahuatl accounts of the conquest of Mexico.* Eugene, OR: Wipf & Stock Publishers.

Marcus, J. (1978, October). Archaeology and religion: A comparison of the Zapotec and Maya. *World Archaeology: Archaeology and Religion, 10*(2), 172–191.

Miller, M. (2001). *The art of Mesoamerica: From Olmec to Aztec.* London: Thames & Hudson.

Miller, M. & Martin, S. (2004). *Courtly art of the ancient Maya.* London: Thames & Hudson.

Pasztory, E. (1998). *Aztec art.* Norman: University of Oklahoma Press.

Xeres, F. et al. ([1872] 2005). *Reports on the discovery of Peru.* C. Markham (Ed. & Trans.). Boston: Elibron Classics, Adamant Media Corporation.

Spores, R. (1967). *The Mixtec kings and their people.* Norman: University of Oklahoma Press.

Stone-Miller, R. (2002). *Art of the Andes: From Chavin to Inca.* London and New York: Thames & Hundson.

Stuart, D. & Stuart, G. (2008). *Palenque: Eternal city of the Maya.* London: Thames & Hudson.

Terraciano, K. (2001). *The Mixtecs of colonial Oaxaca: Ñudzahui history, sixteenth through eighteenth centuries.* Stanford: Stanford University Press.

Townsend, R. F. (Ed.). (1992). *The ancient Americas: Art from sacred landscapes.* Chicago: Art Institute of Chicago.

Unknown as transcribed by Ximenez, F. *Popol Vuh: The sacred book of the Maya: The great classic of Central American spirituality.* A. Christenson (Ed. & Trans.). Norman: University of Oklahoma Press.

Vega, G. (2006). *The royal commentaries of the Incas and general history of Peru, abridged.* H. Livermore (Trans.). & K. Spalding (Ed.). Indianapolis: Harold Hackett Publishing Company.

Whittington, E. M. (Ed.). (2001). *The sport of life and death: The Mesoamerican ballgame.* London: Thames & Hudson.

Art—Russia

Religious icon painting prevailed in Russia until the European Baroque style surfaced in Moscow in the seventeenth century. With Peter the Great (reigned 1682–1725) came radical change and Russia's ascendance as a European power. From then on Russian artists were both inspired to emulate their Western counterparts and provoked to assert their Russian identity. Contemporary Russian artists continue to experience this dynamic tension in the international art world.

Russian art is far less well known than Russian literature or music, but it has a rich history—both as part of and set apart from European tradition.

Early Russian Religious Art: 1000–1700

The Russian acceptance of Christianity from Orthodox Constantinople around 988 BCE determined the distinctive forms of Russian religious art—churches with cupolas, which later evolved into "onion" domes, and images of Christ, the Virgin Mary, and the saints. Icons, mosaics, and frescoes were windows to heaven, depicting holy persons in their transfigured state, beyond the boundaries of the natural world. Generally icons were unsigned, painted by a collective of artists as an act of worship. Such sacred art, protected from radical innovation by theology, dominated Russian culture for centuries.

Russian icon painters were no doubt inspired by the legendary *Virgin of Vladimir*, a tempera painting brought from Constantinople to Kiev in the twelfth century. It was moved later to the new capital of

Unknown, *Virgin of Vladimir*. Egg tempera on wood. An inspiration to Russian icon painters for its human appeal, the painting was brought from Constantinople to Kiev in the twelfth century.

Vladimir, then to Moscow in 1365, and, because it was reputed to protect those who lived in the city where it was displayed, it remains one of Russia's most revered holy images. More humanized than

ART—RUSSIA · 113

Andrei Rublev, *Old Testament Trinity* (c. 1420s). Tempera on wood. The painting depicts three Angels who visited Abraham at the Oak of Mamre; by omitting other figures involved in the biblical narrative, Rublev emphasizes the triune nature of God.

many icons of the Byzantine era, the Mother and Child are shown touching cheeks and gazing tenderly at each other. Russia's most famous icon painter was Andrei Rublev (c. 1360–1430). In his remarkable tempera panel called *Old Testament Trinity* (*Three Angels Visiting Abraham*, c. 1420s?), the angels are harmoniously composed so that their figures form a circle echoed in the shape of their halos.

The Mongol invasion (1237–1240) and occupation, which lasted until 1480, limited Russia's contacts with Western culture without radically influencing its Christian art, although Oriental influences can be detected in applied and decorative art. From the 1470s through the 1490s Italian architects constructed many buildings in Moscow's Kremlin, but the secular art of the Renaissance made little impact. No realistic likeness survives even of Ivan the Terrible (Ivan IV, reigned 1533–1584), although he and other Russian rulers appear in idealized form in religious art.

The seventeenth century is known as an age of transition in Russian culture. Influences entered from Ukraine, annexed to Russia in the 1650s, and from Belarus, both of which, as part of Poland, had experienced Catholic Baroque culture. The ornate style of the later seventeenth century is sometimes known as Moscow Baroque. Some Western European artists and craftsmen entered the czars' service, working in the Kremlin studios, where they contributed to the production of the first stylized portraits of Russian rulers and nobles. The icon *The Tree of the Muscovite State* (1668) by the Moscow artist Simon Ushakov (1626–1686) contains a small portrait of Czar Alexis I (reigned 1645–1676). Ushakov incorporated elements of Western perspective and lighting effects into this and other icons. Alexis's daughter Sophia (1657–1704) was perhaps the first Russian woman to have her portrait painted; generally the segregation of upper-class women from male society created strong resistance to female portraiture.

Eighteenth-Century Cultural Revolution

The modernizing czar Peter the Great (Peter I, reigned 1682–1725) brought radical changes to Russia and made the country a major European power. The showcase for Peter's cultural reforms was his new capital and "window on the West," Saint Petersburg, founded in 1703. Virtually all of Peter's chief artists and architects were foreigners. The Frenchman Louis Caravaque and the German Gottfried Tannhauer painted portraits and battle scenes and helped to train a new generation of Russian secular artists, including the former icon painter Ivan Nikitin (c. 1680–1742?).

Nikitin himself became an iconic figure for a time. His bold and creative approach, which reputedly surpassed his foreign counterparts' unfeeling treatment of Russian subject matter, was especially evident in the expression of grief and loss in the deathbed portrait of Peter attributed to Nikitn, who in fact left behind only two signed canvases. Contemporary Russian art historians are now free to acknowledge and study the original foreign paintings (and their full impact) inspired by Peter's patronage. Although Peter hired the Italian sculptor Carlo Rastrelli (1675?–1744), most famous for his controversial equestrian statue of the czar, Orthodox suspicion of "graven images" retarded the development of a Russian school of sculpture. After Peter's death his daughter Catherine thwarted the planned bronzing and prominent placement of the statue in front of the palace because of its Baroque qualities, but the work was eventually lauded for its likeness to Peter and for conveying character evocative of the epoch.

Peter's reign marked the beginning of an "era of apprenticeship," when Russia mastered the conventions of Western art under the sponsorship of the imperial court and aristocracy. High art rarely penetrated into the peasant village, where culture retained traditional features. But the barrier between the Westernized upper classes and the peasantry was not impenetrable. Folk art assimilated Baroque and Classical decorations, while educated Russians collected *lubok* woodprints (popular prints often circulated as broadsides) and read folktales.

In 1757 the empress Elizabeth Petrovna (reigned 1741–1761) founded the Academy of Arts in Saint Petersburg. With a curriculum rooted in the study of classical history and classical models, it remained the unchallenged center for training Russian artists, architects, and sculptors until the mid-nineteenth century. Successful graduates were sent to France or Italy for further training. In 1764 Catherine the Great (Catherine II, reigned 1762–1796) issued the academy's charter of imperial patronage. Catherine was an avid collector, buying numerous paintings by old masters and works of applied art. One of the academy's first Russian professors of

Dmitry Levitsky, *Catherine the Great in the Temple of Justice* (1780s). Levitsky's portraits earned him the title "Russia's Gainsborough." Collection of the Hermitage Museum.

painting was Anton Losenko (1737–1773), whose *Vladimir and Rogneda* (1770) was the first work on a theme from Russian history. The many portraits by Dmitry Levitsky (1735–1822), another academy associate known as "Russia's Gainsborough," include the allegorical *Catherine II in the Temple of Justice* (1780s), seven canvases from the 1770s depicting Catherine's favorite students at the Smolny Institute for Noble Girls (a school she founded in 1764 to nurture and cultivate loyal subjects), and a number of "society portraits" that created an image of the aristocracy Levitsy's patrons hoped to emulate. The range of Russian subject matter was still limited, however. Aristocratic patrons preferred Italian and classical vistas to scenes of

The Baroque qualities of Carlo Rastrelli's bronze bust of Peter the Great were eventually praised for evoking the spirit of the man and his era. Collection of the Hermitage Museum.

Ilya Repin, *Barge Haulers on the Volga* (1873). Oil on canvas. A young blond man, symbol of Russia's new generation, rises among the exhausted peasants.

the Russian countryside or town. Serf artists trained in Western idioms were more likely to produce Russian scenes, such as *Portrait of an Unknown Woman in Russian Dress* (1784) by Ivan Argunov.

From Romanticism to Realism: 1800–1880

Napoleon's burning of Moscow in 1812 and the march on Paris by Alexander I (reigned 1801–1825) in 1814 aroused patriotic feelings about Russian culture; German Romantic ideas about national "spirit" (*geist*) further stimulated a search for Russian themes, as did the slogan of "Orthodoxy, Autocracy, and Nationality" propagated by Nicholas I (reigned 1825–1855). The portrait of Alexander Pushkin (1827) by Orest Kiprensky (1782–1836), which depicted Russia's national poet inspired by his muse, celebrated the literary life, while portraits of serfs at "home" on the land, produced in the 1830s by their noble master (and painting teacher) Aleksi Venetsianov, seemed simultaneously to support Russia's existing ideology and set the stage for the Realist movement to come. Still, many artists with royal patronage studied and painted classical scenes in Europe; *The Last Days of Pompeii* by Karl Briullov (1799–1852) was the first such Russian painting to receive international acclaim. Some of these academic painters could incorporate a Russian nationalistic message into works done abroad, as did Alexander Ivanov (1806–1858); his biblical scene, *The Appearance of Christ to the People* (1837–1857), prefigured what Ivanov believed to be the Russians' destiny as God's chosen people.

The middle of the century saw a significant shift in Russian painting as younger artists forsook many of the approved themes of the royal academy. A decisive event came in 1863 when a group of fourteen students walked out of the Academy of Arts, turned their backs on its royal patronage, and began to paint realistic scenes of everyday Russian life that were often infused with strong overtones of social protest. (Just two years earlier Alexander II (reigned 1855–1881) had freed 22.5 million serfs from private ownership, and the general feeling of emancipation that ensued allowed artists to approach painting as a vehicle for social criticism.) Under the leadership of Ivan Kramskoi (1837–1887), the group established the Society for Traveling (Itinerant) Art Exhibitions to show their independent works in towns and cities away from the capital. Soon dubbed the Wanderers (*Peredvizhniki*), they continued to express the critical progressive spirit of the age of reform under Alexander II, appealing both to disaffected intellectuals and the rising Russian bourgeoisie. In fact it was wealthy new industrialists, such as the Moscow-based Pavel Tretiakov (1832–1898) who bought their paintings, thus creating the first art market in Russia and breaking artists' dependence on royal and aristocratic patronage.

The strong social commentary in their work and its exclusively Russian content appealed to both liberal political thinkers and Russian nationalists. Perhaps the most famous of these paintings from the age of reform is *Barge Haulers on the Volga* (1870–1873, also known as *The Volga Boatmen*) by Ilya Repin (1844–1930). The painting, with its line of peasants exhausted from brutal work—all of them ragged and aged except for the young blond man rising up in their midst—embodied the suffering of the Russian people while it conveyed the hopes for a generation of youth awakening to the need for change and reform. Other Wanderers' paintings, such as *Easter Procession* (1861) by Vasily Perov (1833–1882), criticized the cruelty or corruption of both the religious and political establishment. But there was another side to the Wanderers' work. Their ultrarealistic paintings had a strong nationalistic appeal, as in the quintessentially Russian landscapes of Isaak Levitan (1860–1900) and the more chauvinistic, sweeping historical panoramas of Vasily Surikov (1848–1916). Surikov's *General Suvorov Crossing the Alps* (1900) depicts a scene from the Napoleonic wars, while his *Yermak's Conquest of Siberia* (1895), with musket-wielding Cossacks slaughtering arrow-shooting natives, more directly relates to Russia's imperialistic expansion. In fact, by the end of the century, the Wanderers and their realistic style were no longer critical of the czarist order and had been appropriated as a national school of painting.

The Birth of Modern Russian Art

The radical impulse in Russian art, both stylistically and politically, would come from a very different direction. Again the artistic stimulus originated in Europe and the patronage from Russia's new bourgeoisie. Prominent among such benefactors was the merchant-industrialist Saava Mamontov (1841–1918) whose artists' colony on his estate north of Moscow became a cradle for modern Russian art. Among those who gathered there in the 1880s and 1890s were Vasily Polenov (1844–1927), a pioneer of Russian *plein air* painting; Konstantin Korovin (1861–1939), "Russia's first Impressionist"; and Mikhail Vrubel, whose

Mikhail Vrubel, *Demon Seated* (1890). Oil on canvas. Vrubel's fragmented brushwork prefigures Cubism.

Vladimir Tatlin, *Monument to the Third International* (1919–1920). Had the monument actually been built—this model is one-tenth the size of the proposed structure—it would have surpassed the Eiffel Tower as an architectural symbol of modernity.

fragmented brushwork in *Demon Seated* (1890) prefigured Cubism while his play of light on water in works such as *Swan Princess* resembled Impressionism.

Vrubel was the most obvious connection between these late-nineteenth-century innovators and the more radically modern avant-garde that arose in the years before World War I, but this blossoming of the new had an organizational headquarters in the Saint Petersburg–based World of Art group (Mir iskusstva), which incorporated figures from the performing arts such as the ballet impresario Sergey Diaghilev. Set and costume designs for Ballets Russes, which took Europe by storm after its opening in 1909, drew heavily on those inspired by World of Art aesthetics, and thus established a precedent for the close association of visual and performing arts in the Russian avant-garde of the 1910s and 1920s.

World of Art's dissemination of works by Cezanne, Gauguin, van Gogh, and others, as well as purchases of modern Western art by entrepreneur collectors, paved the way for Russia's own prominence in the avant-garde. In the first two decades of the twentieth century as new art movements swept Europe, Russian artists, often after a spell in Paris or Berlin, made their own original contributions. Pavel Kuznetsov (1879–1968), for example, promoted Symbolism with his tempera painting *Blue Fountain* (1905), in which shadowy figures hover near a fountain—symbolic of life—set against a backdrop of green-blue foliage. The Russian avant-garde was showcased in a series of radically stylized exhibitions such as Blue Rose (1907), Knave of Diamonds (1910), Donkey's Tail (1912), and Target (1913). Typically, as in other moments of Russian history, the strong connections with Europe in the early twentieth century provoked assertions of Russian identity.

Mikhail Larionov (1881–1964) and Natalia Goncharova (1881–1962) declared that Western art had nothing to teach Russia. These and other artists found inspiration for their neo-Primitivist works in peasant villages, among city low life, and in icons, *lubok* prints, signboards, and painted toys. The most innovative was Kazimir Malevich (1878–1935), who painted his way through Impressionism, Primitivism, and Cubo-Futurism, the latter being a fusion of French Cubism and Italian Futurism. (His *Knifegrinder* of 1912 is an example of how Cubo-Futurism's systematic and tubular geometric patterns, as well as the diagonal tilt of those forms in the picture plane, give the illusion of three dimensions.) In what Malevich called an attempt to free art from the "ballast" of objectivity he founded Suprematism, a style heralded by the exhibition of his seminal *Black Square*, the "zero of form," at the "0.10" exhibition in 1915. It signified a landmark in the evolution of Western Art—from reproduction of natural forms to pure abstraction—but other Russians were also in the forefront of experiments with abstraction. In Germany, Wassily Kandinsky (1866–1944) was independently pursuing his own experiments in the reduction of figurative elements and expressiveness of colors and shapes (*Improvisations*, 1910–1920). In fact, seldom in world art has their been such an explosion of innovation as in the last few years of czarism in Russia. The artistic radicals were not politically active, but they fully shared the Bolsheviks eagerness to sweep out the old in favor of the new.

Russian Revolution and Soviet Art: 1917–1953

After the Bolshevik coup of October 1917, avant-garde artists rushed to assume the artistic leadership of revolutionary Russia. Some artists who would later leave the Soviet Union to become major figures in modern art in the West, notably Kandinsky and Marc Chagall, eagerly served the new revolutionary government. From 1917 well into the 1920s a gamut of artistic credos and styles coexisted, as the Bolsheviks had no blueprint for the arts but welcomed all who served the cause. Lenin was no avant-gardist and opposed radical appeals to eliminate all "bourgeois" art, but he was glad to have the enthusiastic efforts of avant-garde artists in creating "agit-prop" art—posters, political cartoons, billboards, and designs for mass parades and political celebrations, all of which fused abstract and figurative design.

The project that best represents this brief, passionate embrace of political and artistic radicalism is the *Monument to the Third International* (1919–1920) by Vladimir Tatlin, a leading member of the Constructivists. This group of artists believed that "fine art" was dead: artistic endeavors should employ modern, real-life materials—and preferably have real-life applications—in building, furniture design, clothing, theater sets, and costumes. Tatlin's "monument," never existing except in sketches and as a model one-tenth the scale of its intended size, was to have been a building of futuristic design: a 1,300-foot-high spiral tower of steel and glass with revolving parts that would span the Moscow River, house the headquarters of the international Communist Party (Comintern)—and surpass the existing architectural symbol of modernity, the Eiffel Tower.

Given the technology of the time and the poverty of war-torn Russia, it was totally impractical—a dream project for a future that never was.

Other real-life Constructivist projects did materialize in the new society. Women artists had been prominent in the early stages of the Russian avant-garde and some of them, such as Varvara Stepanova (1894–1958) and Liubov Popova (1889–1924), became leaders in futuristic fashion design for the new society. The application of photography to graphic design and poster art was more directly useful to the new regime; innovators like Alexander Rodchenko (1891–1856) and El Lissitsky (1890–1941) were successful pioneers in the art of photomontage.

But the avant-garde ascendancy was short-lived. By the late 1920s it was increasingly being accused of "inaccessibility," its "decadent" Western features contrasted with the "progressive" Realist art of the first workers' state. With the consolidation of the one-party state under Joseph Stalin and the completion of the first phases of industrialization and collectivization, a monolithic artistic establishment emerged. In 1934, Socialist Realism was launched at the first Congress of Soviet Writers. Andrei Zhdanov (1896–1948) summoned writers and artists to depict "reality in its revolutionary development" and to provide "a glimpse of tomorrow." Socialist Realist works were supposed to inspire by embodying qualities of popular accessibility, Party spirit, ideological content, and "typicality." (In the 1950s Soviet Socialist Realism would influence the state of "revolutionary" art in the People's Republic of China under Mao Zedong.) Among the best early exponents of Soviet Socialist Realism were Alexander Samokhvalov (1894–1971), who used sport and physical culture as metaphors for progress, and Alexander Deineka (1899–1969), who produced bold monumental paintings on labor themes. Another classic of Socialist Realism was *Collective Farm Festival* (1937) by Sergei Gerasimov (1885–1964), whose "glimpse of tomorrow" reveals happy, healthy workers presiding over tables groaning with festive fare. In sculpture the colossal *Worker and Collective Farm Woman* (1937) by Vera Mukhina (1889–1953), which pairs a male factory worker and

Sergei Gerasimov, *Collective Farm Festival* (1937). The painting exemplifies the Socialist Realism movement and its revolutionary message.

a female farm laborer holding aloft a hammer and sickle, the tools of their respective trades, became an icon of the USSR. During World War II Russian art remained Socialist Realist in style—modernism was still prohibited—but changed to become nationalist in content as artists depicted heroic war heroes and struggling partisans.

From the Thaw to the Fall—and Beyond

With Stalin's death in 1953 and Nikita Khrushchev's de-Stalinization came a thaw in the arts; artists were allowed more scope for private themes and individual expression, but the government's focus was still on positive portrayals of "real" Soviet life. Khrushchev himself famously denounced abstract art. In the 1960s and 1970s some artists tested the boundaries of official art by expanding the subject matter of Realism or by experimenting with modernist styles. The authorities quickly closed independent exhibitions, most blatantly by bulldozing an open-air art show in 1974. Many artists left the USSR for the West, while others, though disaffected with Socialist Realism, turned their backs on the West. Ilya Glazunov (b. 1930), for example, explored the pre-Revolutionary, Orthodox past in *Eternal Russia* (1988), a panoramic "group portrait" of iconic figures, both sacred and secular, who shaped one hundred centuries of Russian history.

In the era of glasnost and perestroika nonconformist artists such as Eric Bulatov (b. 1933), Ilya Kabakov (b. 1933), and Anatoly Zverev (b. 1931) were able to operate more openly, mocking the socialist artistic and political system with conceptual and installation art as well as painting and graphics. Since the fall of the USSR in 1991, pluralism has been the watchword of the "second avant-garde," embracing irreverent pastiches of Socialist Realism and Soviet symbols, religious themes, abstraction, grotesquerie, nostalgia, eroticism and kitsch, pop art, and video and installation art—all the banned styles and subjects from the Soviet years.

The late 1990s and early 2000s have seen the virtual elimination of censorship, the opening of commercial outlets for sales and exhibitions, a buoyant market for Russian art, both in Russia and abroad, and a flood of Russian publications on previously neglected topics such as the pre-Revolutionary avant-garde and religious painting. Russian artists actively engage in the international art world but still in dynamic tension with their Russian heritage, both recent and traditional.

Lindsey HUGHES

Deceased, formerly of the School of Slavonic and East European Studies

Further Reading

Billington, J. H. (1966). *The icon and the axe*. London: Weidenfeld & Nicolson.

Bird, A. (1987). *A history of Russian painting*. Oxford, U.K.: Phaidon.

Bonnell, V. E. (1997). *Iconography of power: Soviet political posters under Lenin and Stalin*. Berkeley: University of California Press.

Bowlt, J. & Drutt, M. (Eds.). (1999). *Amazons of the avant-garde*. London: Royal Academy of Arts.

Cracraft, J. (1997). *The Petrine revolution in Russian imagery*. Chicago: Chicago University Press.

Cullerne Bown, M. (1998). *Socialist realist painting*. New Haven, CT: Yale University Press.

Figes, O. (2002). *Natasha's dance. A cultural history of Russia*. Harmondsworth, U.K.: Penguin Books.

Gray, C. (1996). *The Russian experiment in art 1863–1922*. London: Thames and Hudson.

Grierson, R. (Ed.). (1992). *Gates of mystery: The art of holy Russia*. Fort Worth, TX: InterCultura.

Hamilton, G. H. (1983). *The art and architecture of Russia*. Harmondsworth, U.K.: Penguin Books.

Kirichenko, E. (1991). *The Russian style*. London: Laurence King.

Lincoln, W. B. (1998). *Between heaven and hell: The story of a thousand years of artistic life in Russia*. New York: Viking.

Lodder, C. (1983). *Russian constructivism*. New Haven, CT: Yale University Press.

Milner, J. (1987). *Russian Revolutionary Art* London: Bloomsbury Books.

Milner, J. (1993). *A dictionary of Russian and Soviet artists*. Woodbridge, U.K.: Antique Collectors' Club.

Petrov, V. (Ed.). (1991). *The World of Art movement in early 20th-century Russia*. Leningrad, Russia: Aurora.

Petrova, Y. (2003). *Origins of the Russian avant-garde*. St. Petersburg, Russia: Palace Editions.

Sarabianov, D.. V. (1990). *Russian art: From neoclassicism to avant-garde*. London: Thames and Hudson.

Valkenier, E. (1989). *Russian realist art. The state and society: The Peredvizhniki and their tradition*. New York: Columbia University Press.

Valkenier, E. (1990). *Ilya Repin and the world of Russian art*. New York: Columbia University Press.

White, G. (Ed) (1998). *Forbidden art: The postwar Russian avant-garde*. Los Angeles: Curatorial Assistance.

White, S. (1988). *The Bolshevik poster*. New Haven, CT: Yale University Press.

Art—South Asia

Unlike other cultures with a high degree of technological skill, the second–millennium BCE Indus-Sarasvati civilization in South Asia has left no evidence of monumental sculpture and architecture. Such large-scale grandeur, however, would later characterize the area—from great Buddhist stupas to the Taj Mahal. Architecture and painting embodied religious influences throughout history, especially Hindu and Islamic, and today exhibit contemporary secular expressions as well.

The cultural beliefs, ideas, and practices that find visual expression in the art of South Asia—which includes the present-day nations of India, Pakistan, Afghanistan, Bangladesh, Nepal, and Sri Lanka—have had a formative influence on the rest of Asia and continue to provide important paradigms of being and becoming in modern world culture.

Sculpture

The beginnings of South Asian sculpture may be found in the early Indus-Sarasvati civilization (present-day northwestern India and eastern Pakistan) of the second millennium BCE. The mature phase of this civilization (2500–1700 BCE) carries evidence of a high level of technical knowledge and skill but, curiously, a lack of monumental sculpture or large structures such as temples or palaces. From its ruins, archaeologists have recovered small figurines in stone or cast bronze or copper, as well as terracotta animals and female figurines, the last presumed to be cultic objects. Archaeologists have also found a large number of steatite seals with impressions of bovine unicorns, buffaloes, bulls, tigers, rhinoceros, and other composite animal figures, as well as some enigmatic human forms, surmised to have had either commercial or ritual uses (or both).

Mauryan Sculpture, c. 324–c. 200 BCE

Little material evidence has been found between the Indus-Sarasvati period and the imperial Mauryan remains of the third century BCE. The reasons for this absence are unclear, but perhaps attributable to the use of perishable construction materials and prohibitions against material representations or portrayals of deities and/or their alternatives. Vedic ritual culture is presumed to have established itself around 1500 BCE, followed by the contemplative esotericism of the Upanishads around 800 BCE and the birth of Buddhism and Jainism in the sixth century BCE.

In 326 BCE, the incursion of Alexander of Macedon (Alexander the Great) into the northwest border of the South Asian subcontinent, as part of his conquest in 330 BCE of the extensive Persian Achaemenid Empire of Darius III, created a political vacuum that was swiftly filled by the first Mauryan king, Candragupta (reigned c. 321–297 BCE). Candragupta's imperial ambitions were styled after Darius and Alexander, and scholars attribute his successor Asoka (reigned c. 273–232 BCE) with the Persian practice of building stone monuments, as well as with incorporating Achaemenid and Hellenistic motifs and devices in structures. In 265 BCE Asoka embraced Buddhism and proceeded to mark numerous prominent pilgrimage routes and Buddhist centers through his vast empire with tall polished stone pillars inscribed with edicts expounding the Buddhist law. Though this practice and the literary style of the inscribed proclamations

121

are reminiscent of an Achaemenid method used to establish the law of the emperor, they also extend to an ancient indigenous Vedic tradition, the cosmic pillar. Achaemenid and Hellenistic decorative motifs, such as rosettes, palmettes, spirals, and reel-and-bead patterns appear on these pillars and on other structural remains from Asoka's time, attesting to the cosmopolitan nature of his court and its culture.

Other monuments attributed to Asoka's patronage include Buddhist stupas (relic-mounds) and rock-cut caves, both of which became important settings for sculpture for a thousand or more years. Asokan monuments were created in sandstone and finished to a high polish, a technique that was lost to South Asia after Mauryan times.

A number of massive, frontal stone sculptures depicting male and female figures also remain from Mauryan times. These are representations of *yakshas* and *yakshinis*, supernatural elementals that had been popular in propitiatory worship for protection, fertility, or wealth. These beings and the gods of the Vedic pantheon became assimilated into early Buddhism and soon reappeared iconically as Buddhist threshold deities, protectors of devotees, bestowers of auspiciousness, and servants of the Buddha.

Sculpture during the Shunga Dynasty, c. 185–73 BCE

The Mauryan dynasty lasted for barely fifty years after the death of Asoka and was followed by the Brahminical Shunga dynasty in northern South Asia. Buddhist lay patronage, however, had developed a strong foundation, and monastic monuments continued to flourish during the second century BCE. Typical examples of the sculpture of this period are found among the remains of the stupa of Bharhut. The circular stone railing (*vedika*) enclosing the stupa has carved roundels on its horizontal and vertical components, often elaborated into ornate lotuses. Some of these roundels have carvings of human heads or animals at their center and some are filled in with narrative scenes from the life of the Buddha or episodes from tales of his past lives. At this stage, Buddha's figure is never depicted; instead we see symbols such as the Bodhi tree (under which the Buddha attained enlightenment), the Wheel of the Law, or a stupa, according to narrative context. The relief carving is shallow and frontal and harks back to a tradition in wood. On the vertical entrance-posts of the *vedika* are chiseled large figures of *yakshas* and *yakshinis*, standing on animal or dwarf mounts.

This post-Mauryan Buddhist relief tradition reached its full maturity around the first century BCE, as evidenced in the gateways (*torana*) of the Great Stupa at Sanchi. This stupa, at the center of a monastic complex, was established by Asoka and further enlarged during Shunga times. Around 100 BCE, during the reign of the Satavahanas, four great gateways were erected at the cardinal entrances to this stupa. The horizontal and vertical elements of these gateways carry carvings thematically similar to those at Bharhut. These carvings demonstrate much greater technical assurance, however; the narrative arrangements, particularly on the extended horizontal architraves, show a refined clarity of form, a varied mobility of posture, and a judicious use of devices to enhance sense of depth where necessary. Large and powerful figures of elephants, lions, or dwarfs are carved out deeply on the vertical pillars and seem to support the upper portions. But perhaps the most perfect realizations on these gates are the *shalabhanjikas*, fertility symbols in the form of voluptuous women posed seductively, the rhythmic swing of their forms clinging to fruiting tree branches. The perfect combination of ecstatic sensuousness and contemplative repose in these figures became one of the aesthetic ideals of South Asian sculpture, seeking fulfillment in different forms through history.

Sculpture during the Kushan Dynasty, 78–200 CE

Around the beginning of the Christian era, the Kushan dynasty, originating in the borderlands of Central Asia and China, established itself as the imperial power in northern South Asia. The most famous king of this dynasty was Kanishka (reigned 78–101 CE). Around this time the first figural depictions of the Buddha

make their appearance, almost simultaneously in the northwest province of Gandhara and the Gangetic metropolis of Mathura. Reasons for this iconic appearance are unknown, but may be related to doctrinal shifts in Buddhism from the more austere Theravada Buddhism toward the devotionalism of Mahayana Buddhism. Both the Gandhara and Mathura Buddha images express a consistent iconography, though they are stylistically divergent. The Gandhara Buddha is modeled after a Greco-Roman Apollonian prototype, while the Mathura figure derives from indigenous *yaksha* traditions. In both cases, the Buddha is draped in monastic robes, has a halo behind his head and a whorl of hair between the eyebrows (*urna*), and is shown with a cranial protuberance (*ushnisha*) symbolizing transcendental knowledge. He is either seated in meditation or standing erect with his right hand raised in a gesture of bestowing fearlessness.

Whereas predominant naturalism marks the features and costuming of the Gandhara figure, simplified rounded features, see-through draping, monumentality, and physical tension projecting power distinguish the Mathura image. Bodhisattva figures in the characteristic styles of Gandhara and Mathura also appeared at this time, wearing regal accoutrements and, in the case of named and worshipped bodhisattvas, carrying their distinctive attributes. The Kushan period also yields the earliest Brahmanical images in stone, representing the three major cults of Hindu worship—those devoted to Siva, Vishnu, and the Mother Goddess, particularly in her form as Durga, the destroyer of evil. Other prominent Brahmanical deities represented include Surya and Skanda.

Sculpture under the Guptas, (c. 320–c. 500)

During the fourth century, a new Hindu imperial dynasty established itself in northern South Asia, whose reign, patronage, and courtly culture are credited with the development of the classical style in South Asian art. This was the Gupta dynasty, whose most famous king was Candra Gupta II (reigned 375–415 CE). During this period, the major center for the production of Buddha images in the east shifted from Mathura to Sarnath. Idealized soft modeling and self-absorbed, tranquil features characterize the style of this period, which replaced the Kushan Buddhas. Standardized and compacted iconic elements and a vocabulary of distinctive hand gestures (mudras), meant to mark special occasions, accompanies these images. Others figures in the Buddhist pantheon undergo a similar elaboration and stylistic change, and the Buddha and several bodhisattvas also appear in bronze casts.

During this period relief sculptures draw upon a proliferation of Hindu deities, organized spatially in integrated contexts of ritual worship. Initially, these works were sited in niches inside cave-temples, but the stand-alone Hindu temple in stone also evolved at this time and henceforth became the setting for sculpture. Because the Guptas were followers of Vishnu, images of this deity and his incarnations (avatars), were frequently represented, and an increased emphasis on goddesses and other female images is apparent in the works.

A developed Saivite iconography, depicting mythical episodes connected with Siva and his consort, Parvati, also found expression at sites of cultic worship. Saivite cultic placement consigns the abstract phallic icon of Siva (the lingam) to the sanctum, faced from the entrance of the temple by Siva's mount, the bull Nandi, and surrounded along a clockwise circumambulatory path by niches carrying other gods and goddesses and scenes showing the pastimes of Siva.

By the end of the fifth century, all these figures evolved into an aesthetic that shared the monumental repose of the Gupta Buddha but integrated it with a power of massiveness and restrained ecstatic delight. Contemporaneously, in the Deccan (central India), a related but more voluptuous aesthetic developed in Buddhist and Hindu figural expression, under the patronage of the powerful Vakatakas, related by marriage to the Guptas. Examples of the full fruition of the Vakataka Buddhist style are visible at the cave excavations at Ajanta in southern central India, while the early excavations at nearby Ellora or at the island of Elephanta, dateable to the early sixth century,

The stone carving of the god Vishnu adorns the interior wall of a Hindu temple in India.

show examples of Deccan Saivite sculpture of this period at its ripeness.

Developments in Sculpture, Sixth to Twelfth Centuries

Though the stand-alone Hindu stone temple first appeared in South Asia under the Guptas, it evolved into maturity in the sixth century under the Western Calukya dynasty (543–757; c. 975–c. 1189) in the southern Deccan, and through the seventh century in southern India under the Pallavas (c. 550–728 CE).

Sculpture during this period continued to develop local variants of the Gupta iconography and style, but in these southern centers so did a marked tendency toward a greater plastic dynamism in the figures. A fine example of this may be observed in a panel from seventh-century Pallava Mamallapuram depicting Durga battling the buffalo demon. Here the dramatic interest and the portrayal of power in motion replaces the iconic stillness and massiveness of Gupta deities. Subsequent sculpture in southern India continues to develop in fluidity, reaching perhaps the zenith of integrating stillness and movement in the tenth-century image of the dancing Siva, Nataraja, which was developed in South India under Cola patronage.

From the tenth to the twelfth century, South Asian sculptors evolved such a consummate skill and facility in carving that sculpture during this period spills out of the measured enclosure of niches and dominates the temple surface. The temple as an integral whole projects the impression of the mighty, immobile, cosmic Mount Meru, which contains the multitudinous, varied activity of the world at its base. The sculpted forms of deities and celestial denizens stand or interact in various fluid postures, expressing the ecstatic repose of transcendental action. In the case of the temples at Orissa and Khajuraho in eastern and central India, respectively, a strong erotic element also found expression, indicating the prominent presence of Tantric cults. This high achievement of the successful marriage of static soaring temple forms and teeming mobile surfaces marked the final creative outburst of the South Asian tradition in sculpture.

Buddhism disappeared from India by the thirteenth century and gradual Islamic dominance of northern South Asia from the twelfth century inhibited the production of large-scale Hindu temple complexes. The Vijayanagara kingdom of the south and other pockets that offered resistance to Muslim conquest managed to continue the tradition until the sixteenth and seventeenth century, but with a progressive diminution of creativity.

Islamic architecture brought a new visual language of domes, arches, and minarets to the South

Asian building environment and found expression in mosques, tombs, and forts. Marrying Afghan and Turkish styles with the Indic skill in stone carving, it left its most prominent marks in the cities of north central India and to some extent in the Deccan region, from the twelfth to the nineteenth century. Eschewing figurative sculpture due to religious prohibition, this architecture nevertheless gives us the most exquisite carved, inlaid, and latticed surfaces with calligraphy, foliate patters, and intricate geometric designs.

Under Mughal rule (1526–1857 CE), Islamic architecture reached its greatest heights in the sixteenth and seventeenth centuries. The gates, halls, pavilions, mosques, and tombs commissioned by the third Mughal emperor, Akbar (1543–1605), at Agra and Fatehpur Skiri can be seen as precursors to the legendary beauty of the Taj Mahal, built by Shah Jehan (1592–1666) in Agra as a tomb for one of his wives, Mumtaz. Placed at the far end of a garden, the Taj's soaring dome and minarets in white marble, combined with the majestic simplicity of its design and the perfection of its proportions, evoke a supernatural archetype. Close up, its massive white marble surface reveals colorful borders with flowers, leaves, and Qur'anic calligraphy inlaid using a *pietra dura* (relief mosaic with semiprecious stones) technique.

After 1857, most of South Asia was brought under the British crown as a colony of Great Britain. The colonial period, leading up to the division and political independence of India and Pakistan in 1947, was known for its imperial Victorian architecture, particularly in the major colonial centers of Calcutta (Kolkata), Bombay (Mumbai), Madras, and Delhi. Following independence, both India and Pakistan have entered into the mainstream of a global modernity, where international functional concerns mix with national and regional identity issues in fashioning a contemporary South Asian architecture.

Painting

The earliest remaining examples of painting in South Asia are Buddhist cave murals such as those in the monasteries at Ajanta. Here, two phases of painting, corresponding to two phases of excavation, may be distinguished, the earlier being from the first century BCE and the later from the fifth century CE. The themes depict stories and scenes, mainly from the life of the Buddha. The murals are made with mineral colors on a specially plastered surface and, particularly in the later phase, are characterized by hieratic scaling (more important figures are bigger), Buddha and bodhisattvas shown in formal poses and with stylized physiognomy, and others depicted more realistically. Elements of three-dimensional modeling and perspective are mixed in with two-dimensional "flat" figuring, to introduce a semblance of realism in representations where narrative interest clearly takes precedence over natural illusion.

Early Manuscripts

In painting, following Ajanta of the Vakataka period, few other fragmentary murals in cave or temple settings remain. The earliest surviving manuscript paintings are eleventh-century illustrated Buddhist and Jaina palm-leaf manuscripts of religious texts. These texts were venerated as sacred objects and offered as religious donations by patrons.

Extant eleventh- and twelfth-century Buddhist palm-leaf manuscripts come largely from regions in eastern India and often have generic scenes from the life of the Buddha painted on the inner surfaces of the wooden boards that bind the palm leaves; such scenes also serve as dividing elements between segments of text. The images are iconic and seldom directly related to the text. Hieratic scaling and static figural postures executed using a rhythmic outline and filled in with flat opaque mineral colors characterize the painting style.

The Jaina manuscripts were mostly produced in the Gujarat region of western India. By the last quarter of the fourteenth century, paper had become the preferred medium for Jaina manuscripts, and a rectangular form more suited to larger illustrations gradually replaced the elongated palm-leaf format. Jaina manuscripts make use of a restricted and bold color scheme and rhythmically outlined, flattened figures,

The Hindu Shore Temple at Mahabalipuram, India, displays many features of South Asian monumental sculpture and ornamentation. Photo by Klaus Klostermaier.

as in the Buddhist tradition. There is no attempt to depict spatial depth. A characteristic of the figures is their invariable presentation in profile with the eye on the invisible side of the face protruded into visibility.

The oldest extant illustrated Hindu manuscripts date to the second half of the fifteenth century and follow the conventions of Jaina painting. Hindu myths and epics had by this time become standardized and pervasive in popular South Asian culture, and episodic representations of these themes found expression in these illustrations. From the early sixteenth century, a bold shift appears in this tradition, prioritizing the image over the text. The by-then standard rectangular form of the page was mostly occupied by the pictorial representation, with an abbreviated textual description in the upper margin and the extended text on the obverse of the page. This tradition made its appearance in Rajasthan and the western Gangetic kingdoms of northern India and is presumed to have originated in royal and other wealthy patronage. The contemporaneous rising popularity of medieval Vaishnavism (worship of Vishnu), with its use of an erotic symbology to describe the mystical pastimes of Krishna (Vishnu's most famous incarnation) must have played its part in fueling this production. The incorporation of a Vaishnav mystical context into literary and courtly amorous narratives characterizes this painting tradition and initiated a thematic stream that continued through the history of South Asian painting. Though these paintings attempt to convey spatial depth, they are essentially flat, with stylized figures shown in static profile, making hieratic gestures in starkly simplified color planes. This painterly aesthetic, commonly known as the "Rajput style," remained a viable South Asian idiom of painting throughout subsequent centuries, resurfacing in various times and places.

Mughal Painting, 1526–1857

The sixteenth century also witnessed the hegemonic rule of the Mughals in northern South Asia, resulting in a new school of painting, unsurprisingly and commonly known as Mughal painting. The initiation of this school occurred in the mid-sixteenth century during the rule of the second Mughal emperor, Humayun (reigned 1530–1540 and 1555–1556). Humayan brought two master painters from the court of Tabriz—Abdus Samad and Mir Sayyid Ali—to found his atelier at Delhi in 1555. Within a year, Humayun died and was succeeded by his son, Akbar (reigned 1556–1605). Akbar had an abiding passion for the arts of painting and storytelling and quickly built up his father's atelier to illustrate a large number of Persian and Hindu secular and religious texts. Akbar's earliest commission was the illustration of the *Tutinama* (Tales of the Parrot). A large number of artists recruited from existing South Asian painting traditions worked under the direction of the Persian masters, resulting in a hybrid style and aesthetic which, by the time of Akbar's second commission, had developed a distinctive identity. Mixed perspective, structured visibility of interiors, and natural elements such as mountains and trees are taken from Persian prototypes; hieratic patterning, bold coloring, and narrative arrangements are reminiscent of indigenous traditions; uniquely new with the early Mughal painting style were a patterned variety of coloring, a judicious introduction of three-dimensional modeling, and a crowded swirl of highly individualized figure-types laid out in a space divided by forms from nature (such as trees or rocks) to give an added sense of depth.

From the mid-sixteenth century, the influence of Renaissance naturalism, introduced into Akbar's court by Jesuits, began to gain prominence in the works produced in his atelier. Space and volume were defined by light and shade. Aerial perspective was introduced, as were atmospheric effects to depict spatial recession.

These techniques continued to gain prominence in paintings from the courts of Akbar's successors. The Mughal atelier remained as prolific under Akbar's son, Jahangir (reigned 1605–1627), though the thematic interest shifted from dynamic narrative episodes to carefully attentive portraiture, scenes of psychological interest, and detailed though stylized studies of flowers and animals. A number of superb allegorical portraits of the emperor come to us from this court. Though the Mughal atelier continued during the reign of Jahangir's son and successor, Shah Jahan (reigned 1628–1658), it seemed to have lost its vitality and inventiveness. The paintings of this period are marked by a courtly stiffness and formalism and lack the boldness of color or composition of either Rajput paintings or earlier Mughal work. The Mughal atelier largely dispersed during the reign of the Islamic puritan Aurangzeb (reigned 1658–1707), son and successor of Shah Jahan.

Seventeenth- and Eighteenth-Century Developments

In the Deccan kingdoms of central India, small Islamic states had established themselves since the fourteenth century and developed independent cultural traditions. Among these, the most important were the kingdoms of Golconda and Bijapur, which remained independent until late in the Aurangzeb's reign. With cultural roots in Persia and Turkey, these kingdoms developed their own painting traditions, known as the Deccani style, marked by a rich coloration dominated by lavender, gold, and green, a jeweler's eye for decorative pattern, and mystical or fantastic stylizations.

From Akbar's time, a number of the Rajput courts came under the suzerainty of the Mughals, developing close courtly liaisons. Mughal stylistic influences began appearing in the paintings of a number of these courts. In the late seventeenth century, after the dispersal of artists from Aurangzeb's court, further assimilation of Mughal thematic and stylistic idioms continued in the Hindu Rajput states. Here, the earlier predominance of Hindu religious themes was complemented by formalized portraiture of the maharaja seen in court or in gardens or terraces with attendants, or in equestrian or hunting scenes. But these scenes, and some Mughal stylistic elements, were mostly incorporated into flat decorative "Rajput" compositions in courts of this period, such as those of Kota and Mewar. The Bikaner paintings of the same period, on the other hand, show a much closer affinity to the naturalism of Mughal style combined with the decorative patterning and mystical palette of the Deccan courts.

The Mughal court saw a brief and brilliant revival during the reign of Aurangzeb's grandson, Muhammad Shah (reigned 1719–1748). The idealized moody romanticism of the paintings produced under him, thematically focused on courtly love and characterized by naturalistic atmospheric effects, carried over once more to inspire two of the finest and most charismatic schools of late Rajput and Pahari painting respectively, those of Kishangarh and Kangra.

In the mid-eighteenth century, a fruitful collaboration between Raja Savant Singh (reigned 1748–1764) of the Rajput state of Kishangarh and the two master artists of his court, Bhavani Das and Nihal Chand, both originally from Delhi, led to the formation of a unique and distinctive style of painting. Extending the moody romanticism of the late Mughal court, Kishangarh painting of this period produced a large corpus of highly stylized depictions of its patron raja and the object of the raja's affection, the court singer Bani Thani, with the two portrayed as Krishna and Krishna's beloved Radha, respectively.

A similar effect, using different means and developing a different and more refined aesthetic, also appeared around the mid-eighteenth century in the hill states of Guler, Jasrota, and Kangra, and is attributed to the efforts of two artist brothers, Manaku and Nainsukh (1710–1778), and their students. Nainsukh's work in the court of Raja Balwant Singh of Jasrota (1724–1763) in particular can be said to originate the highly prized late Kangra School. The thematic mainstay of this school, like the school in Kishangarh, drew upon the dalliances of Radha and Krishna. Here the late Mughal romantic figures and style are transformed by a dream-laden, tranquil, naturalistic backdrop into a languorous intimate amorous moment in the secret wood, where time stands still and the divine couple, stylized using an aesthetic of balanced refinement, savor eternal delight in time-born bodies.

From the mid-eighteenth century, the British presence in South Asia exerted a powerful influence on courtly taste, moving it toward photorealism. The advent of photography itself contributed in no small measure to this change. Indigenous artists trained in earlier courtly styles now adapted their work to imitate the camera. Whereas some of these artists continued serving native patrons, particularly through portraiture, the British employed several artists to record scenes of South Asian life, its landscapes, and its flora and fauna. The work of these artists forms a body known as the Company School.

Twentieth and Twenty-First Centuries

At the beginning of the twentieth century, as part of a nationalistic rethinking of identity, the Calcutta artist Rabindranath Tagore and his students

The world speaks to me in colours, and my soul answers in music. • **Rabindranath Tagore (1861–1941)**

deliberately moved away from Western-influenced styles. Known today as the Bengal School, these artists fashioned a distinctive style affiliated with an international antimaterialist movement and Pan-Asianism by integrating elements of Rajput, Mughal, Japanese, and Pre-Raphaelite style. From the second quarter of the twentieth century, international Modernism began increasingly to influence South Asian art, opening up a variety of creative adaptations. Today, the contemporary art scene in South Asia is among the most vibrant and prolific in the world, with increasing numbers of artists making bold forays into individualized modes of expression suited to the social, cultural, and local contexts of the subcontinent.

Debashish BANERJI
University of California, Los Angeles

Further Reading

Archer, W. G. (1973). *Indian paintings from the Punjab hills: A survey and history of Pahari miniature painting.* London: Sotheby Parke Bernet.

Bajpai, K. D. (1997). *Five phases of Indian art.* Jodhpur: Rajasthan-Vidya Prakashan.

Banerjee, A. C. (1983). *Aspects of Rajput state and society.* New Delhi: Rajesh Publication.

Beach, M. C. (1992). *The New Cambridge history of India: Mughal and Rajput painting.* Cambridge, U.K.: Cambridge University Press.

Brown, P. (1981). *Indian painting under the Mughals, a.d. 1550 to a.d. 1750.* Oxford, U.K.: Clarendon Press.

Coomaraswamy, A. K. (1916). *Rajput painting: Being an account of the Hindu paintings of Rajasthan and the Punjab Himalayas from the sixteenth to the nineteenth century, described in their relation to contemporary though, with texts and translations.* London: Humphrey Milford.

Coomaraswamy, A. K. (1927). *History of Indian and Indonesian art.* New York: E. Weyhe.

Craven, R. C., Jr. (1997). *Indian art: A concise history* (Rev. ed.). London: Thames & Hudson.

Craven, R. C., Jr. (Ed.). (1990). *Ramayana: Pahari paintings.* Bombay: Marg Publications.

Desai, V. N. Painting and politics in seventeenth-century North India, Mewar, Bikaner and the Mughal court. *Art Journal,* 49(4), 370–378.

Gascoigne, B. (1971). *The great Moghals.* New York: Columbia University Press.

Goswamy, B. N., & Fischer, E. (1992). *Pahari masters: Court painters of northern India.* Zurich, Switzerland: Artibus Asiae.

Harle, J. C. (1974). *Gupta sculpture.* Oxford, U.K.: Clarendon Press.

Huntington, S. L. (1985). *The art of ancient India: Buddhist, Hindu, Jain.* New York: Weatherhill.

Kramrisch, S. (1933). *Indian sculpture.* New York: Oxford University Press.

Mitter, P. (1994). *Art and nationalism in colonial India, 1850-1922: Occidental orientations.* Cambridge, U.K.: Cambridge University Press.

Randhawa, M. S., & Bhambri, S. D. (1981). *Basholi paintings of the Rasamanjari.* New Delhi: Abhinav Publications.

Randhawa, M. S., & Galbraith, J. K. (1968). *Indian painting: The scene, themes, and legends.* Boston: Houghton Mifflin.

Randhawa, M. S., & Randhawa, D. S. (1980). *Kishangarh painting.* Bombay: Vakils, Feffer & Simons.

Rowland, B., Jr. (1970). *The art and architecture of India: Buddhist, Hindu, Jain.* Harmondsworth, U.K.: Penguin.

Rowland, B., Jr. (1963). *Evolution of the Buddha image.* New York: Asia Society.

Saraswati, S. K. (1975). *A survey of Indian sculpture.* Calcutta: Munshiram Manoharlal.

Topsfield, A. (1984). *An introduction to Indian court painting.* London: Victoria and Albert Museum.

Welch, S. C. (1977). *Imperial Mughal painting.* New York: George Braziller.

Welch. S. C. (1984). *India: Art and culture, 1300–1900.* New York: The Metropolitan Museum of Art.

Welch, S. C., & Beach, M. C. (1976). *Gods, thrones, and peacocks: Northern Indian painting from two traditions, fifteenth to nineteenth centuries.* New York: Asia House Gallery.

Williams, J. G. (1982). *The art of Gupta India: Empire and province.* Princeton, NJ: Princeton University Press.

Zebrowski, M. (1983). *Deccani painting.* Berkeley and Los Angeles: University of California Press.

Art—Southeast Asia

From highly decorated pottery and small bronze utilitarian objects to the great stupa of Borobudur in Java, Indonesia, and the monumental temple complex at Cambodia's Angkor Wat, Southeast Asia's astonishing array of art and architecture was the product of innovation, invention, and transformation of cross-cultural influence, especially Hinduism and Buddhism.

Southeast Asia has some of the most distinctive and impressive art traditions in the world. From earliest times into the present the countries in mainland and insular Southeast Asia have been centers of artistic innovation and the recipients and transformers of artistic influences from outside. The names *Indochina* and *Indonesia* point to some of the outside influences but they mask a deeper sense of cultural layering, innovation, and invention.

The Earliest Art

Some of the earliest pottery and bronze artifacts in the world have been discovered in small rural villages in northern Thailand. Starting about 3600 BCE, fine decorated pottery was made at sites such as Ban Chiang and Non Nok Tha. The oldest examples from Ban Chiang are a grayish pottery decorated with incised designs, followed in about 1000 BCE by striking beige-colored pots with fine geometric shapes and restrained painted decoration in red ochre pigment. The final phase, lasting until about 250 BCE, includes elaborately shaped vessels with a profusion of painted linear decoration usually forming complex swirls.

The Bronze Age in Southeast Asia began about 2000 BCE with utilitarian implements found at Non Nok Tha. The discovery of these artifacts indicates that Southeast Asia, one of the first areas in the world in which people mastered the art of shaping bronze. Large-scale use of bronze in Southeast Asia occurred much later, however, from about 500 BCE to about 350 BCE. Some magnificent large-scale works distributed over a vast area of mainland and insular Southeast Asia date from that period. This Dong Son culture, so named after the first site unearthed in northern Vietnam, produced, among other objects, decorated socketed axes, elaborate bronze flasks, and, most famously, more than two hundred impressive metal drums. The drums are decorated with linear designs typically including a sun and star pattern at the center of the tympanum, around which images of circling birds and geometric ornaments appear in concentric rings. Some examples include three-dimensional frogs situated at the edge of the tympanum. Along the sides long narrow boats with plumed passengers are aligned as if in a procession. The symbolism of heavenly bodies and water suggests the drums had a religious significance, but they may have been used in warfare or in burial or ceremonial rituals.

Bronzes have been found as far as Lake Sentani in West Papua, Indonesia. This wide distribution, combined with the great diversity of styles throughout the Indonesian archipelago, indicates that trade in these artifacts, as well as Roman coins and early Indian items, took place prior to the formal entry of Buddhist and Hindu art from India in the ninth century CE. Powerful rulers most likely commanded the production, export, and import of valuable and elaborate artifacts.

Indian Influences

The earliest contacts between western Southeast Asia, Sri Lanka, and India were most likely in the form of trade carried forth by merchants originating in both India and the islands of Southeast Asia. The Chinese were also part of this early commerce and, traveling as Buddhist and Hindu pilgrims, may have played an important role in diffusing these religious beliefs. It is uncertain precisely when this trade began but the earliest Indian and Chinese accounts vaguely refer to Indianized sites in Funan in the third century in Cambodia, and the Srivijaya dynasty centering on Palembang in South Sumatra. Large quantities of (Chinese) Tang dynasty (618–907 CE) ceramics date the Sumatran sites to about the seventh to the ninth centuries. It appears that no invasion or colonization from India ever occurred. Southeast Asian rulers transformed social and religious concepts into practical models for their own society.

Indonesia

Metropolitan Buddhist and Hindu art from India became prevalent beginning about 800 in the Dieng plateau of central Java with a series of elaborate stone religious buildings. The earliest, built under the Sailendra rulers (778–864), are Buddhist and include the most impressive monument of ancient Indonesia, the great stupa of Borobudur.

A stupa, intended to be a monument to the Buddha, is often a giant reliquary containing some part of the body of the Buddha within its structure. It also functions as a cosmic model, incorporating the cardinal directions and the idea of the rotation of the universe around an axis. The sculpture on a stupa takes the viewer through the stages of enlightenment, beginning at the level of the everyday world, moving through the story of the life of the Buddha, and then beyond into the realms of nirvana. The stupa at Borobudur does all of this, but in a new design and on a massive scale. Built of approximately 57,000 cubic meters of stone, it has been called the largest unified work of art in the world.

Stairways lead up to the rectangular lower levels of the monument. At each tier one turns left and walks past subtly carved relief panels depicting the life of the Buddha amplified with details drawn from daily life in ninth-century Java. There are carvings of large outrigger sailing vessels and court ladies all done in a style derived from fifth-century Indian traditions but modified in a uniquely Indonesian way. Figures have a rounded sensuality with delicate features and gestures. As one goes higher in the monument there are more images of seated Buddhas, until at the highest rectangular levels there are niches with three-dimensional seated Buddha figures in them. At the upper levels rectangular tiers give way to circular tiers, and relief sculptures are replaced by open bell-shaped stupa forms. Free-standing Buddha images can be seen inside through the openwork of these smaller stupas. The pinnacle of the monument is a solid dome-shaped stupa that marks the center and axis of Borobudur.

Buddhist and Hindu dynasties competed and succeeded each other on the basis of trade and political intrigue rather than religion. In fact, religious dynastic labels are based upon the emphasis they placed upon a single religion rather than the exclusion of the other, and religious sites and statues often blend both Hindu and Buddhist concepts and iconography. The finest Hindu monument in Indonesia, reputedly constructed in 856 by King Ratu Baka, is Prambanan (also called the Lara Jonggrang complex). It consists of three tall temples, each dedicated to one of the three major Hindu deities. The largest and central *candi* (pronounced "chandi"), or temple, is dedicated to Siva. Flanking it are smaller temples dedicated to Vishnu and Brahma. The high temple symbolizes the sacred mountain where Siva lives with his consort Parvati. Although obviously derived from Indian sources, the architecture of the temple complex is not a direct copy but a reinterpretation. As at Borobudur, which is located nearby, the sculpture offers subtle variations based upon Indian sources but with gentler poses and facial expressions. The reliefs on the temples illustrate the two greatest Hindu epics, the *Ramayana* and *Mahabarata*. An interesting detail in one relief shows a building rendered in linear perspective—more than five hundred years earlier than that technique was codified in Italy. Smaller temples face the three major temples. These are dedicated to the mounts of the three deities; Nandi, the bull whom Siva rides, Garuda, the bird that Vishnu rides, and Angsa, the goose for Brahma.

As Islam began its move into Indonesia in the thirteenth century, the Hindu-Buddhist rulers move eastward on the island of Java, establishing the Singasari (1272–1293) and Majapahit (1293–1520) dynasties. There they continued to create great temples such as Candi Singasari and Candi Panataran. Eventually Islam became the dominant religion on Java, and the Hindu-Buddhist rulers moved onto the island of Bali. Despite the conversion to Islam, Hindu epics still play a vital role in the court and everyday culture in Java and elsewhere in contemporary Indonesia. Most famous are the shadow puppet (*wayang kulit*) performances and masked dances accompanied by a gamelan orchestra and singing of the Hindu epic, the *Ramayana*. Bali today is the only Hindu area outside of India and Indian diaspora communities.

On Bali art and religion merge seamlessly, and in some way or another nearly everybody engages in the production of art, music, and dance. The island is dotted with temples, shrines, and palaces. The large active volcano Gunung Agung is sacred to the inhabitants, and rituals performed in its main temple, Pura Besakih, are performed to maintain the order of the universe. Like Prambanan, Besakih is dedicated to the three major Hindu deities, but the architecture is quite different. A massive stone stairway leads up the slope of the mountain, and on the terraces above there are thatched wooden buildings somewhat resembling pagodas that represent Mount Meru, the mountain of the gods at the center of the universe in Hindu cosmology.

Cambodia

In Cambodia, the Khmer Empire, which began its rise in the seventh century and was at its peak in the ninth through twelfth centuries, fashioned equally

This cave carving is typical of many found in the Angkor Wat temple complex in Cambodia.

impressive arts that combined Hindu and Buddhist influences. One of the most remarkable world monuments is Angkor Wat. Begun around 1113 by the ruler Suryavarman II (d. c. 1150) and completed around 1250, Angkor Wat is a veritable city of art. It includes a giant stone temple complex surrounded by moats with bridges and sculpted buildings and towers. (The site is set amidst large rectangular artificial lakes that provide water for the planting season.) The lotus-bud-shaped redented towers are a distinctive feature of the architectural style, itself a unique Khmer blend of Hindu and Buddhist elements. Relief sculptures, integrated with the architecture, also use a Khmer style portraying a range of subjects from the Hindu epics, to battles, to delicate dancing maidens. The faces are delicately carved with squarish chins and rather thick, broad lips that sometimes have bow-shaped mustaches. The eyebrows flow across the ridge above the nose, also forming the double curve of an archer's bow; hair is rendered in even-lined patterns. The figures as a whole have a subtle meditative look. Many of the reliefs that depict action scenes use a great number of figures to create kinesthetic patterns throughout compositions of rhythmically repeating curves.

Although smaller than Angkor Wat, nearby Angkor Thom is also remarkable. The main structure, called the Bayon, has high towers at the periphery of the main buildings. The sides of the towers have giant faces carved on them that are thought to represent the ruler Jayavarman VII (c. 1120–c. 1215), the monarch who commanded the construction of the site. The serenely stylized portraits blur the distinction between rulers and gods, suggesting that Jayavarman VII is a *devaraja,* a king who has the attributes of a god.

Burma (Myanmar)

The great Buddhist movements of Burma (Myanmar) originated in 1056 under King Anawratha in the fertile Irawaddy River basin extending to the Salween River delta. From its beginnings, Buddhism in Burma incorporated an indigenous belief in spirits called Nats (originally meaning "lords") that had dominion over a group or object. At first these spirits were impersonal and local—the Nat of a tree or a hillside, for instance), but eventually a panoply of thirty-six "national" Nats, each a distinct personage with a life history, became the subject of much Burmese art; Buddha, in fact, is considered the thirty-seventh Nat. Hence Buddhist temples are as much Nat-houses as they are dedicated to Buddhism. The earliest large-scale Buddhist site is the city of Pagan. This city, a tremendously impressive collection of hundreds of temples, shows the evolution of their architectural tradition from Indian sources to a distinctive Burmese style.

Perhaps the most impressive monument is the giant Schwe Dagon stupa in the city of Rangoon (Yangon). Construction began in the fourteenth century under the ruler Binnya U; the resulting 22-meter-high monument was then modified many times during the next

Nguyen Phan Chanh, *Re Lua* (1960). Nguyen Phan Chanh, one of Vietnam's most celebrated artists, paints on silk with colors that evoke the countryside.

four hundred years. After an earthquake it underwent reconstruction from 1763 to 1776 to reach its present height of 99.4 meters. The white, bell-shaped form of the stucco and brick monument closely resembles prototypes in Sri Lanka, particularly at the fifth-century site of Annuradhapura. Numerous shrines resembling Chinese pagodas and an array of Buddhist sculpture surround it.

Thailand

After contact with the Burmese kingdom of Pagan, the tribal peoples of Thailand adopted Buddhism. The cities of Chiengmai in the north and Ayuthia in the south became early centers for the spread of the new religion. From its beginnings, the southern part of Thailand was dominated by Cambodian Khmer civilization. But in 1287, when the Mongols invaded

Pagan, three powerful Thai chiefdoms combined to form the kingdom of Sukhodaya and spread Buddhism to all parts of Thailand. The cannons of Therevada Buddhism prevalent in Thailand fixed the sculpture style, making it difficult to chronicle changes over time but also making it easy to identify Thai Buddhist imagery: slender forms and tall spire-like head protuberances.

When the capital of Thailand was moved to Bangkok in 1767, numerous buildings were constructed as very ornate versions of wooden architecture in other parts of Southeast Asia, particularly Burma. The Temple of the Emerald Buddha in the royal palace compound is typical with its steep roofs with dragon finials at the gables. The gables emerge in sections from within each other as they do in Burma and other parts of Southeast Asia.

Chinese and Indian Influences in Vietnam

Chinese influence predominated during their occupation of Vietnam during the second century BCE to the tenth century, and rose again in the thirteenth and fourteenth century, especially regarding the symbolism of the dragon in folklore and myth, and as a decorative motif in art. (For Vietnamese peasants, dragons represented a four-fold deity—clouds, rain, thunder, and lightning); for rulers, dragons became, as they did in China, a symbol of authority and power.) Dragon imagery is found in sculpture, painting, and architecture, and the Chinese influence is remarkable in the brick tiles (dating to about the tenth century) at the Co Loa citadel near present-day Hanoi.

Influenced by early Hindu civilization, the loose federation of states that comprised the kingdom of Champa, whose population comprised several ethnic groups, flourished in the south and central part of Vietnam in an area then called Annam. Much of its contentious history, from its founding in the second century CE to the time it was absorbed almost entirely by the Vietnamese, can characterized as a period of struggle against the Chinese (depending on the Chinese dynasty in power), a greater sense of freedom with the independence of the Vietnamese in the tenth century, and to a lesser extent its relationship with Java. The brick temples of the Champa, much influenced by Hindu elements of design, consisted of tall tower structures with flame-like arches over the doorways; the exterior walls are decorated with bas-relief columns adorned with carvings of flowers and leaves. Sandstone lintels and ornamental corner pieces are carved with the figures of gods and animals sacred to the Hindu. Cham sculpture is especially distinctive; and yet similar in some ways to the Khmer aesthetic, with very square faces, very thick broad lips and exaggerated bow-shaped eyebrows that at times extend across the forehead as a rope-like ridge. Halos typically had foliage that resembled a mass of worms. While these figures are indeed imposing, polished figures from later periods convey austerity and unearthly calm.

Tribal Arts

In the remote parts of Southeast Asia, the highlands of mainland Southeast Asia and distant islands of Indonesia, many tribal groups either resisted or missed the larger metropolitan influences coming from the west and north. Some extraordinary and unique art traditions from these locales have only recently caught the attention of the outside world. In the highlands of mainland Southeast Asia ethnic groups such as the Hmong, the Ahka, and the Yao produce intricate embroidered and dyed costumes and spectacular jewelry, particularly in silver.

Indonesia is particularly rich in these cultures. On the island of Nias, off the west coast of Sumatra, the inhabitants build large and impressive houses. One royal palace is 20 meters high, supported underneath by over 100 gigantic pillars. There are also elaborate megalithic monuments in the villages that memorialize the dead and commemorate sumptuous feasts that raise the status of the rulers. In Nias, and many other parts of tribal Southeast Asia such as Sumba, islands in South Malukku, and among the Batak peoples of Sumatra and the Toraja peoples of Sulawesi, elaborate gold jewelry celebrates status and is rich in symbolic value.

The Toraja people on the island of Sulawesi are also known for their fine architecture, but their highest artistic achievement centers on their funeral rites. To memorialize a high-ranking chief an enormous banquet is prepared as hundreds of people sing and dance in their finest attire and jewelry. Special houses are constructed for the guests and to serve the ceremonial purposes of the funeral. Life-sized wooden effigies called *tautau* are placed in grottos as testimonials to the fame of the ancestors.

Modern Art

Time-honored arts still flourish throughout Southeast Asia. Fine textiles, jewelry, traditional weaponry, and architecture can still be found in great abundance. As in cultures around the world, however, long-established ways of life and their accompanying artistic traditions are changing and to some extant vanishing under contemporary economic, religious, political, and technological influences. In much of Southeast Asia newer forms of contemporary art are being created that express the individual ideas of the artists and contemporary social and political conditions. Today, not only Southeast Asia's traditional art, but also the art created by its contemporary artists, particularly those from the Philippines, Indonesia, and Malaysia, can be now seen in the museums and galleries of New York, London, and Paris.

Jerome FELDMAN
Hawaii Pacific University

Further Reading

Barbier, J. P., & Newton, D. (1988). *Islands and ancestors*. New York: Metropolitan Museum of Art.

Bellwood, P. (1979). *Man's conquest of the Pacific: the prehistory of Southeast Asia and Oceania*. New York: Oxford University Press.

Bellwood, P. (1997). *Prehistory of the Indo-Malaysian archipelago*. Honolulu: University of Hawaii Press.

Bernet Kempers, A. J. (1959). *Ancient Indonesian art*. Amsterdam: Tropenmuseum.

Bulbeck, D. F., & Barnard, N. (2000). *Ancient Chinese and Southeast Asian Bronze Age cultures*. Taipei, Taiwan: Southern Materials Center.

Cœdès, G. (1968) *The Indianized States of Southeast Asia,* Honolulu: University of Hawaii Press.

Coe, M. (2003) *Angkor and the Khmer Civilizations,* New York: Thames and Hudson

Feldman, J. (1994). *Arc of the ancestors*. Los Angeles: Fowler Museum.

Fontein, J. (1990). *The sculpture of Indonesia*. New York, Harry N. Abrams.

Grosslier, B. P. (1962). *The art of Indochina*. New York: Crown.

Holt, C. (1967). *Art in Indonesia*. Ithaca, NY: Cornell University Press.

Higham, C. (1996). *The Bronze Age of Southeast Asia*. Cambridge, U.K.: Cambridge University Press.

Jessup, H. (1990). *Court arts of Indonesia*. New York: Harry N. Abrams.

Jessup, H. (2004) *Art and Architecture of Cambodia,* New York: Thames and Hudson.

Kandahjaya, H. (1995). *The master key for reading Borobudur symbolism*. Bandung, Indonesia: Yayasan Penerbit Karaniya.

Miksik, J. (1990). *Borobudur: Golden tales of the Buddha*. Boston: Shambhala.

Rawson, P. (1967). *The art of Southeast Asia*. New York: Thames and Hudson.

Soebadio, H. (1992). *Art of Indonesia: from the collections of the national museum of the Republic of Indonesia*. New York: Vendome Press.

Somers Heidhues, M. (2000). *Southeast Asia: A concise history,* New York: Thames and Hudson.

Taylor, P., & Aragon, L. (1991). *Beyond the Java Sea*. Washington, DC: Smithsonian Institution.

Wagner, F. (1959). *The art of Indonesia*. New York: Crown.

White, J. C. (1982). *Ban Chiang: Discovery of a lost Bronze Age*. Philadelphia: University of Pennsylvania Press.

Art—West Asia

West Asia has a long and complex artistic tradition, beginning in the Neolithic era, during which indigenous forms of visual expression have been subjected again and again to new influences from both East and West. The spread of Hellenic culture in Ionia and the influx of Islam and the crusades, for example—appears in a number of media, from splendid mosques and mosaics and from knotted carpets to arts of the book.

In early times the main centers of artistic development in West Asia were focused in the cities of Mesopotamia, Anatolia, and the west Mediterranean littoral. The Persian and Helleno-Roman empires, including Byzantium, that ruled various parts of West Asia from around 550 BCE until 650 CE and beyond introduced artistic traditions with a broader range and wider geographical span. Finally, after the seventh century CE, Islamic art gradually became the dominant visual culture in West Asia, although other traditions continued as well.

Earliest Artifacts

Among the earliest forms of art surviving from West Asia are those from Neolithic settlements and from Mesopotamia. Çatal Höyük on the south central Anatolian plain was settled from around 6500 to 5650 BCE, and excavations there have uncovered architecture, sculpture, beautifully decorated pottery, wall paintings, and the remains of what appears to have been a vibrant weaving tradition. The Ubaid culture of Mesopotamia, which flourished after 4300 BCE, appears to have provided a foundation for the later art of the Sumerians.

Due largely to twentieth-century excavations and scholarship, we now know of the artistic accomplishments of the great city-states of Mesopotamia, beginning with the Sumerian city of Kish, whose earliest inscriptions can be dated to around 2600 BCE, followed in later Sumerian times by Lagash, seat of the Sumerian ruler Gudea around 2050 BCE, and Ur, whose excavation has yielded remarkable royal and priestly objects, as well as a giant ziggurat constructed around 2100 BCE. In 2334 BCE the Akkadian king Sargon built a new empire, with Nineveh as its political and cultural capital, before falling to a Sumerian resurgence. One of the most remarkable artifacts from the period, a famous copper head of a Ninevah man, was stolen during April 2003 looting of the Iraq Museum in Baghdad. (Ironically, it is possible that the head had been symbolically mutilated during antiquity, much in the same way as contemporary Iraqis mutilated statues of Saddam Hussein; when the object was discovered its ears and the inlays that filled its eye sockets appeared to have been deliberately removed.) Among the thousands of other works pilfered was an iconic 91-centimeter-high carved alabaster libation vase (circa 3500–3000 BCE) from Uruk and the carved marble female head of the same period and sacred region. The museum lootings prompted much reflection (and some excellent journalism) about the concept of historical consciousness and identity. Zainrab Bahrani, in his article "Iraq's Cultural Heritage: Monuments, History, and Loss," wrote in some detail about the stolen Uruk vase—one of the earliest examples of narrative art—noting as well the Mesopotamian anxiety about the safety of their monuments, texts, and works of art during times of war (an anxiety about the loss of both memory and identity, he interprets). Three days after he drafted the article, on 11 June 2003, three individuals in a battered car returned the Uruk vase to the museum.

Subsequently the Babylonian civilization flourished; under its greatest ruler, the lawgiver Hammurabi (d. 1750 BCE), sculptors created notable monuments. Babylonian dominance bowed in turn to the Assyrians, under whom artistic production reached new heights; their palace city of Khorsabad (c. 701 BCE) and later their reconstruction of Babylon, whose celebrated Ishtar gate (c. 575 BCE) is now located in Pergamon Museum in Berlin, were major centers of artistic activity in all media. Assyrian relief sculptures from Nineveh and Nimrud are now dispersed among museums worldwide.

In Anatolia, numerous civilizations with distinctive artistic traditions flourished in the two millennia before the common era. Among them were the Hittites, whose capital of Hattusas has yielded up remarkable stone and metal objects, the best of which are in the Museum of Anatolian Civilizations in Ankara. Urartians, Lydians, and Phrygians, among others, left their mark on the history of material culture in Anatolia, creating fortified cities with masonry walls and furnishing their courts with beautiful objects and well-crafted stone buildings.

The Persian Artistic Tradition

The Achaemenid Persian Empire (550–330 BCE), followed by Alexander of Macedon (Alexander the Great, 356–323 BCE) and the Seleucids (312–64 BCE), the Arsacids, (247 BCE–224 CE), and the Sasanids (224/228–651 CE), created a continuing artistic tradition that in some ways can be traced in an unbroken line from the works produced in such great early centers as Persepolis, Susa, and Bisitun down to the art of the present day. The palace of Darius I at Persepolis (c. 500 BCE), with its huge, fluted columns and dramatic reliefs of royal ceremonies, conveys an idea of the pomp and majesty of Achaemenid court ceremony and sumptuary arts. Sasanid brick architecture was enormous in scale, as the ruins of the palace of Shapur I (250 CE) at Ctesiphon, with its huge catenary vault, suggest. Sasanid architectural and sculptural remains at Sarvistan, Taq-i Bustan, and Nakhsh-i-Rustam near Persepolis, and their iconography of Sasanid kings as warriors, hunters, and lawgivers, attest to the political importance of art under the Sasanians. Numerous objects in precious metals likewise demonstrate the rich Sasanid royal iconography, while Sasanid silk weaving was in its time the epitome of beauty, luxury, and technical virtuosity in both the East and West.

Greek, Roman, and Byzantine Art in Anatolia

The Hellenic colonizers in Ionia spread the Hellenic visual culture to much of West Asia; like Greek philosophy, much of Greek art appears to have taken form in the Ionian colonies. The succession of Greek classical architectural orders—Doric, Ionic, and Corinthian—and the full repertoire of classical and Hellenistic art is reflected in the excavations of Anatolian cities, from early sites such as Assos and Priene, to later Helleno-Roman sites such as Ephesus (whose temple of Artemis was one of the seven wonders of the ancient world),

This ninth-century earthenware bowl is one of the earliest examples to incorporate calligraphy as the main element of decoration. The Arabic word *ghibta* (happiness) is repeated in the center. Collection of the Metropolitan Museum of Fine Art.

A 2004 view of the courtyard of Jameh Mosque in Isfahan, looking toward the north iwan. Photo by Alex O. Holcombe.

Halicarnassus (site of another of the seven wonders), and Pergamon, whose magnificent Altar of Zeus (c. 180 BCE) is now in Berlin. Both in the realms of architecture and sculpture, Ionia influenced the art of mainland Greece, and its great temples were far more splendid, and constructed on a much larger scale, than most of those of mainland Greece.

Under Roman dominance westernmost Asia underwent impressive urban expansion, and prosperity led to massive investment in art and architecture. The Romans spread the Helleno-Roman style to Syria and Palestine as well as to southern Anatolia and Egypt, and cities such as Palmyra, Baalbek, and Roman Ephesus display today the most impressive remains of the art and architecture of the ancient world. The Helleno-Roman cultural sphere encompassed indigenous peoples as well. Among these, perhaps the most famous were the Arab Nabataeans, whose great fourth-century BCE city of Petra, with its rock-cut monuments in Hellenistic style, demonstrates the pervasiveness of the classical artistic tradition. Archaeological remains from this period are found elsewhere as well, as far south as the Arabian Peninsula.

The establishment in the early fourth century CE of the capital of the Eastern Roman Empire at Constantinople was instrumental in the development of a new Christian artistic style in West Asia, especially in Anatolia and greater Syria. Drawing heavily on the technical and stylistic legacy of Rome, including the media of mosaic and classical architectural design, the Byzantine artistic style evolved from late classicism into the Middle Byzantine style by the ninth and tenth centuries. Roman and Byzantine engineering advances, such as the barrel and groin vaults and the pendentive (the concave triangular section of wall that forms the transition between a square or polygonal space and the circular base of a dome), greatly expanded possibilities for architectural interiors; the six-domed early Byzantine church of St. John at Ephesus (c. 525) and the famous Hagia Sophia in Istanbul (c. 537) exploited that new mathematical engineering. Byzantine Syria and Palestine saw the building of such monuments as the monastery of Simeon Stylites (c. 490) and the sixth-century structures associated with the Holy Sepulchre in Jerusalem. Around the same time the Armenian states in eastern and later in southern Anatolia began a centuries-long development of their own artistic tradition of exquisite cut-stone buildings and sculpture, as well as distinctive traditions of wall painting and manuscript painting. The Church of the Holy Cross at Achtamar, from the early tenth century, is perhaps the most famous of many sculpture-covered Armenian masonry churches of the Middle Ages, and the ruins of the Bagratid capital of Ani, ravaged by an earthquake in the eleventh century, still impress visitors to this day.

Early Islam in West Asia

With the explosive spreading of Islam from the Arabian Peninsula into the Middle East, North Africa, and Central Asia following the death of the Prophet Muhammad in 632, the arts of West Asia underwent major changes. Unlike the cultures of the Byzantine and Sasanid empires, which had deeply rooted traditions of artistic images of both kings and religious figures, Islamic culture reflected the Prophet's deep distrust of figural art as potentially idolatrous and symbolic of luxury. The art of West Asia after the coming of Islam, as one might expect, therefore represents a syncretism of preexisting traditions adapted to new needs and beliefs. The first great

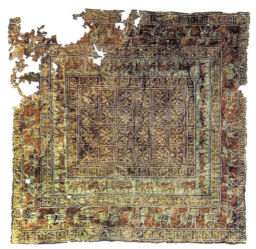

The Pazyryk Carpet, the oldest known surviving carpet in the world, dating from the fifth century BCE. By the late fourteenth century Islamic carpets had become an essential aspect of Europe's material culture.

Islamic building, the Dome of the Rock in Jerusalem (c. 680), reflects centralized church plans of Syria in its form and uses the Roman-Byzantine technique of mosaic in its decoration. The Great Mosque of Damascus, constructed in the early eighth century under the Umayyad dynasty (661–750), is in fact a recycled Christian edifice that was in turn converted from a Roman temple precinct. Scorning human and animal images in its public and religious art, early Islamic civilization developed the repertoire of Arabic calligraphy associated with the Qur'an, together with new adaptations of late Roman vegetal, floral, and geometric ornamentation that eventually took on the distinctive Islamic forms we today sometimes refer to as arabesque.

At the same time, in their private rural hunting lodges and urban palaces, the new rulers of the Islamic polity quietly adopted the sumptuous luxury arts and the court iconography of the Sasanid and Byzantine empires. Early eighth-century desert palaces in Syria were covered with mosaics and paintings, in some cases even including depictions

Gaspare Fossati's lithograph print from 1852 shows the interior of the gynaeceum (space reserved for women) of Ayasofya Mosque, formerly the Church of Hagia Sophia in Constantinople (Istanbul), Turkey. Library of Congress.

of the hunt, genre scenes, and depictions of nude women as entertainers in the Islamic version of the Roman baths. The fall of the Umayyads to the Abbasids (749/750–1258), who moved the capital from Damascus to Baghdad, led to a period of artistic splendor chronicled in the *Arabian Nights*. The shift of the political center of gravity to Baghdad in the east also intensified the Persian cultural impact on the emerging Islamic style. At the same time, the importation of Turkic slave soldiers from Central Asia and trade with Tang dynasty (618–907) China over the Silk Roads opened the art of West Asia to influences from the north and east as well. In the prosperous towns and urban courts of east Persia in the tenth and eleventh centuries there developed an urban middle-class Islamic art of high taste and literary sophistication, in which familiar stories from narrative poetry were often reflected in the visual arts. The famous epigraphic ceramic wares of the period show the adaptation of the art of calligraphy to ceramic decoration, with the use of aphorisms and adages to ornament lovely tableware.

The destruction of much of the early Islamic art and architecture of the eastern Islamic world in the Mongol invasions of the thirteenth century has resulted in a relatively meager amount of early art surviving to our time, which makes the splendid material culture described in the surviving historical records of the era both less accessible and more intriguing.

The Dome of the Rock in Jerusalem (close-up showing the Dome of the Chain), in a photo taken between 1934 and 1939, uses the Roman-Byzantine technique of mosaic. Library of Congress.

Eastern Invasions and Art of the Later Islamic Empires

Beginning with the arrival of the Seljuk Turks in the eleventh century, West Asia was subject to periodic waves of invasion from the east. The Mongols in the thirteenth century, the Timurids in the late fourteenth century, and the Afghans in the eighteenth century all brought a mixture of destruction and renewal to the art of West Asia. Seljuk patronage in particular resulted in a very complex and rich expansion in all media; the four-iwan type of religious structure (an iwan is a vaulted space that opens out at one end) that later enveloped the entire Islamic world from Central Asia to Morocco, began in Seljuk Iran, the eleventh-century Great Mosque of Isfahan being its first major manifestation. Art under the Seljuks and their successors in Iran, the Jazira, and Anatolia frequently used human and animal imagery. Depictions of people, and both mythical and actual creatures, appeared in media as diverse as public stone sculpture, architectural decoration, and especially ceramics and arts of the book.

At the same time, East–West contacts developed through the crusades (beginning in 1095 and occurring periodically through 1291) further enriched both the development and the dissemination of Islamic art. Islamic media such as enameled glass, inlaid metalwork, and the ubiquitous knotted-pile carpet were traded and esteemed in Europe. By the second half of the fifteenth century, the art of West Asia had developed a truly international Islamic style found in Timurid, Uzbek, Turkmen, and Ottoman realms, manifested in the media of architectural decoration, arts of the

Every great work of art has two faces, one toward its own time and one toward the future, toward eternity. • **Daniel Barenboim (b. 1942)**

book, and luxury arts. From Samarqand to Istanbul in the north, and with reflections in the Mamluk art of Cairo and Damascus in the south, this international Islamic style flourished under court patronage. Artists and works of art moved along commercial routes with ease, and inspiration from trade with China and with Europe enriched the art of Islamic lands in many ways. By the late fourteenth century Islamic carpets had become an essential aspect of the material culture of Europe, while silk commerce between Iran and Europe via the Ottoman Empire, and trade by ship across the Mediterranean between North Africa and both the Ottoman and European worlds, resulted in an enhanced commerce of both art and artistic ideas. The Mamluk rulers of Egypt (1260–1517), with their Turkic ethnicity, language, and customs, forged artistic links with Islamic lands farther to the east, and artists freely traveled between Iran and the Ottoman lands. After 1500, the Islamic art of West Asia was dominated by two great court styles, those centered in Ottoman Istanbul and those centered in Tabriz, Qazvin, and Esfahan, the successive artistic capitals of the Safavid Empire (1501–1722/1736). Safavid Esfahan was a planned city that took form during the reign of Shah 'Abbas I (reigned 1588–1629). Among the great artistic personalities of the age were the Ottoman architect Sinan (1489–1588), whose greatest masterpiece was the mosque of Selim II in Edirne (c. 1572), and the Safavid court painters Sultan Muhammad (flourished 1520–1540) and Reza 'Abbasi (flourished 1590–1635). The miniature painting and other arts of the book practiced by professional artists in Islamic courts, originally intended for a very limited audience of wealthy patrons, gained wider importance because of their impact on other art forms, such as carpets and textiles with figural decoration, and architectural decoration employing the wealth of vegetal, floral, calligraphic and geometric motifs first invented in the royal painting ateliers.

Later Art in West Asia

Artistic development in West Asia from the eighteenth through the twentieth centuries was subjected to the effects of both Eastern invasions and Western culture and commerce. European influence appears in Ottoman and Safavid painting as early as the seventeenth century, and the interplay between revivals of traditional styles and European cultural incursions continues to the present day. The eighteenth and early nineteenth centuries constitute a great age of calligraphy in the Ottoman Empire, and nineteenth-century Iranian art under the Qajars (1794–1925) led to many interesting innovations, especially in painting. In the twentieth century, traditional artistic forms were revived while simultaneously West Asian artists began to achieve reputations working in international techniques and media in architecture, easel painting, and sculpture; many of the twenty-first century's most prominent West Asian artists attempt to achieve a fusion of Islamic tradition and modern genres and techniques.

Walter B. DENNY

University of Massachusetts, Amherst

Further Reading

Blair, S., & Bloom, J. (1994). *Islamic art and architecture, 1250–1800*. New Haven, CT: Yale University Press.

Ettinghausen, R., Grabar, O., & Jenkins-Madina, M. (2001). *Islamic art and architecture, 650–1250*. New Haven, CT: Yale University Press.

Grabar, O. (1987). *The formation of Islamic art* (Rev. and enlarged ed.). New Haven, CT: Yale University Press.

Lloyd, S. (1969). *The art of the ancient Near East*. New York: Oxford University Press.

Mellaart, J. (1965). *Earliest civilizations of the Near East*. New York: McGraw Hill

Pollitt, J. (1986). *Art in the Hellenistic age*. New York: Cambridge University Press

Porada, E., & Dyson, R. (1969). *The art of ancient Iran: Pre-Islamic cultures*. New York: Greystone.

Roaf, M. (1990). *Cultural atlas of Mesopotamia and the ancient Near East*. New York: Facts on File.

Art—World Art Studies

World art—the objects and techniques humans have created from their earliest days to the present—provides a visual reference to stimulate the thinking of art historians and world historians alike. This interdisciplinary field studies resources and technologies of various cultures and the transmission of styles and ideas from one culture to another.

The emerging field of *world art* encompasses the study of art humans have made from the dawn of the species to the present, and across the entire globe—from Africa to Oceania and from Eurasia to the Americas. *Art* has many definitions: here it refers both to objects and techniques, especially those that produce an aesthetic response and leave some trace of their existence in the archaeological or historical record. While conventional, historical theories and methods are useful in the study of world art, many scholars involved in what they consider a burgeoning "world art movement" use an interdisciplinary approach, mining such fields as archaeology, anthropology, art history, and, perhaps surprisingly but significantly, neurobiology.

Traditional art history has long been associated with "fine art" (often meaning "art created by renowned individuals from cultures of the West"), while anthropology has been left to study the "crafts" from "non-Western" cultures and anonymous "artisans." World art studies embrace diverse media: performance arts such as drama, dance, and music; literary arts of language and literature; installation and environmental arts; electronic arts; and visual arts such as painting, sculpture, architecture, ceramics, textiles, and jewelry. (Contemporary art history, of course, has broadened its own realm to include many visual genres once considered nontraditional.) Because items made from tangible materials provide evidence reaching furthest back in time, the examples

For many years traditional art historians studied "fine art," leaving the subject of "crafts" from "non-Western" cultures and anonymous "artisans" for anthropologists. Photo by Kevin Conners (www.morguefile.com).

> *Everything that has ever been called folk art has always reflected domination.* • Theodor Adorno (1903–1969)

used here, in a general survey of world art studies, are objects (or visual records of objects) that survive to been seen, examined, and appreciated.

Art historians address the content, context, and meaning of such objects, as well as how, why, when, and by whom they were made, but world art historians take this "see the art in context" approach further (and deeper) to make cross-cultural comparisons. For example, fiber arts comprise textiles—wall hangings, quilts, tapestries, rugs, and cloth—as well as ropes and nets. Each of these specialties involves processes or considerations that reflect social, economic, and cultural aspects of particular groups who made them: the method or sophistication of fiber manipulation and construction (including spinning, weaving, knitting, and patterns of braiding or twisting); the resources or material available (such as cotton, silk, hemp, or flax); and the purpose or occasion of an item's use (fishing, trading, everyday or ritual clothing). Breaking down a genre of art and analyzing the specific factors that shaped its creation can often make comparisons across cultures more significant for world historians.

Key Aspects of the Field

Since art is created everywhere in the world, world art first and foremost demonstrates the universality of human neurology and nature—our sophisticated hand-eye coordination and our ability to symbolize (that is, to have one thing "stand for" another). The historian David Christian is among those who have observed that accumulated collective learning via symbolic representation is a "driving variable" in human dominance of the planet. The field of world art examines and interprets this symbolic record: art as fact (*artifact*, from the Latin words *factum* and *arte*, literally "thing made by skill") provides ongoing evidence of multivalent symbolic behavior and meaning that is generated and put into context over time and space.

Humans made objects long before the relatively recent time of written records; world art provides a more complete story of humanity and extends our global, historic understanding by tens of thousands of years. As history began to unfold in text, world art continued to record evidence of human endeavors. Such visual media can be used to augment and enhance the understanding of any given historic period, and to test various historical hypotheses. World art is thus a lens through which historians can explore how individuals in a culture expressed themselves creatively, or how societies communicated values through visual representations. The world art movement's focus—the ancient and ongoing evidence of human material cultures (art objects) and technologies (the purposes and methods of art making)—can expand the scale of study (a principle advocated by David Christian's theory of big history) and to locate panhuman threads of inquiry.

Evolutionary psychologists have explored individual and social reasons for *why* humans made art—to signify wealth and status, to teach values or protest social norms, and to aid memory, for example—but they have also theorized that the artistic forms people originally used grew from views about the body's role in humankind's survival. These researchers propose that the widespread desirability of the hourglass-shaped female figure derived from its association with fertility—bearing offspring perpetuates the species—and thus spurred the earliest cultures to represent the female body using artistic materials. (Clay figurines with corpulent forms characterized by the so-called Venus of Willendorf and similar small sculptures of the Paleolithic era provide an example). Other scholars, notably Bethe Hagens (1991), dispute the idea of female fertility as the inspiration for prehistoric figurines and suggest, with convincing visual evidence, that they were modeled on animal brains

The particularity and diversity of the objects humans have created reflect the ways in which ideas, skills, materials, or modes of representation have (or have not) been transmitted, preserved, or transformed. Thus world art supports specific studies that compare and contrast cultures by examining contemporaneous genres and techniques. Looking at tomb paintings and low-relief sculptures from the Han dynasty (206 BCE–220 CE) in China and at wall mosaics

The so-called Venus of Willendorf (24,000–22,000 BCE), a small limestone figurine discovered in 1908 near Willendorf, Austria.

in classical Rome can illuminate how two different cultures in the second century CE understood and used the concept of perspective. Portraiture in general or ritual death masks in particular might be used to compare African civilizations such as those in Benin or Egypt to tribal societies such as the Yoruba. The field of world art can also support specific area or period studies: a scholar researching the year 1000 CE might find it useful to compare variations in Islamic and European medieval calligraphies by considering the surfaces on which the "lettering" was applied, the calligraphic styles, the colors used, or, especially relevant to a world historian, the purpose of the writing and what it revealed about attitudes toward creation and divinity.

The evolution of the Buddha image shows how Greco-Roman representations of deities were imported into the Gandhara region of India in the second through the sixth centuries CE and influenced the formation of a standardized (Gupta) Buddha image. In one fifth-century high-relief sculpture from Sarnath, Uttar Pradesh, India, for example, a slight but broad-shouldered figure stands in a relaxed, graceful position conveyed by the open-palmed gestures of his hands; the sculptural representation of a sheer, clinging robe accentuates the body's purity and perfection. This Gupta style was modified as it traveled through Asia, so that in different countries and at different points in time, the Buddha image also reflected individual Asian cultures and styles. The monumental Buddha carved into the rock caves at Yungang (c. 460 CE, one of the earliest examples in China's Shanxi Province), sits in a rigid pose with short, stylized "drapery" hung over his massive shoulders; these attributes exhibit a distinctly Central Asian aesthetic influence, although the elongated ears and a protuberance on the head are elements familiar to the Gupta figure.

World art thus serves as a vantage point from which historians can study resources and technologies of various cultures, the relationship of humans to the natural, spirit, or ancestral worlds, and, significantly for world historians, the transmission of styles and ideas from one culture to another.

Approaches and Resources in the Field

Thus far the emerging field of world art has relied mostly on the work of anthropologists and art historians, so interests and biases of these fields have influenced scholarship to date. The anthropologist Arnold Rubin (1989, 17) proposed his view of world art as technology: "a system of tools and techniques by means of which people relate to their environment and secure their survival." Rubin favored an eclectic, interdisciplinary approach to art historical surveys that would allow scholars to examine the structures in which art was produced and utilized in certain cultures, and then to "identify similarities and differences between them according to the types of social, political, and economic systems they embody" (1989, 11). The field of visual anthropology, which emphasizes the importance of visual symbols embedded in gestures, rituals, and ceremonies (as well as artifacts), focuses on the use of video and photography instead of text to document ethnography. Recently the British art historian John Onians edited the comprehensive *Atlas of World Art* (2004), a monumental landmark study that divides world art (from 40,000 BCE to the present) into seven periods, for which maps are his primary visual tools.

In addition to these approaches, world art studies benefit (and perhaps thrive the most) from the insights of neuroscientists and European social science and humanities scholars working on neuroaesthetics and neuro–art history, both of which inform world history. (Two of the key figures in this exploration are Onians and Wilfried van Damme of the Netherlands.) By starting with panhuman neurology, these researchers and scholars attempt to account for universal "givens" (for example, why shapes and color having meaning) to the variability of art in different times and places (why colors and shapes mean what they do in particular places and times). Onians uses research about mirror neurons (a biological explanation for mimesis), brain priming (when the brain sees an image and then automatically looks for it again), and neural plasticity (the brain's neural firing patterns are altered by the very act of perception) to explain how art is perceived and created.

A new journal that will represent the field of world art as a whole—and the research being done using world art approaches—is slated for publication by Routledge in 2011: *World Art* began in March 2010 to call for research articles, essays, visual presentations, and other dialogues from world art scholars and those in interrelated fields (Taylor and Francis 2010). Several other journals relevant to world art studies include *Res: Anthropology and Aesthetics* (from Harvard) and *Third Text: Critical Perspectives on Contemporary Art and Culture* (from Routledge). The most rapidly growing world art resources are online databases of image and text made available by museums and academic institutions, such as the collection and timeline of the Metropolitan Museum of Art in New York. For information about specific areas, scholars often turn to regional organizations. For example, to learn more about arts of Oceania, one might turn to the Pacific Arts Association or the Association of Social Anthropologists for Oceania.

Trends and Challenges

World art often dovetails with recent trends and challenges in world history, as the following three examples explain. First, both fields reject a Eurocentric approach. But the lingering influence of Eurocentrism in many traditional disciplines, and the predominant use of English and other European languages in their scholarship, often cause scholars to misinterpret the world art movement as just being about "non-Western" art made by "non-Western" peoples. Scholars even contest what it is that constitutes language and literacy in a non-Western culture. In 1450 CE, for example, the Incan Empire extended for about 5,500 kilometers and functioned, not with a phonetic writing system, but with a "language" of tied colored threads called *quipu*. The Inca communicated meanings by twisting, knotting, and manipulating the strings, as well as by denoting string color and placement. Debating, as some do, whether the art of *quipu* is a form of literacy or numeracy tends to downplay what can be learned from its use as a viable communication system.

Second, questions about how humans and their civilizations develop are central to world history and world art studies. To what extent do people borrow (or diffuse) ideas versus independently invent them? A "world art" answer to this query might be found by looking at any number of specific art objects or their constituent parts—by examining, for instance, the relations between image and text in medieval

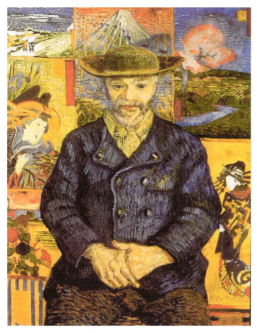

Vincent van Gogh, *Portrait of Père Tanguy* (1887). Oil on canvas. The rise of modernism in late nineteenth-century Europe embraced Japonisme. In the background van Gogh includes some of his *ukiyo-e* (woodblock) collection, or perhaps his take on the medium.

religious documents such as the Insular Gospels in western Eurasia and Buddhist sutra scrolls in eastern Eurasia. Scholars in both fields also ask, how reciprocal are the borrowings between groups? Historically Japanese culture was itself part of a reciprocal transformation over well more than a millennium as the nobility first adopted Buddhism and next the writing and other aesthetic styles from the Asian continent; those elements spread to and eventually were entirely transformed by indigenous culture. This reciprocity is reflected in the development and subsequent transformation of Japanese *ukiyo-e* "floating world" woodblock prints, a genre that embodied the principles of transformation and renewal inherent in ancient Buddhism and shamanism. Artists over time adapted familiar subjects to changing technologies, formats, tastes, and cross-cultural influences; cutters carved the drawings into wood; printers chose colors, inked the blocks, and transferred to paper what had essentially become a collaborative creation (Keyes 1999). Tracing the reciprocity further, Japanese *ukiyo-e* prints are widely recognized for influencing nineteenth-century European painting, but it is hard to quantify or qualify whether that influence equals the powerful impact of Western modernism on twentieth-century Japanese art.

Third, archaeologists and all art historians grapple with the same issues posed by the physical and chemical dating of artifacts (material culture) because they use the same, sometimes problematic, methodologies. Physical dating relies on finding objects "in context," that is, in stratigraphic layers or contiguous to other excavated remains; dendrochronology (tree-ring dating) is of use only on sites where trees exist. Chemical analysis may destroy at least a part of the object and is often costly, while carbon dating of objects has recently needed to be recalibrated. For these reasons many sites and objects are without firm dates. World art historians, who tend to look at greater numbers of non-Western objects, and who put their findings in a broader comparative, cross-cultural context than traditional art historians, can find their research just as hampered by these inadequacies in dating methods as archaeologists.

Comparative Aesthetics

Appreciating the aesthetics of world art requires getting beyond the familiar Western standards and habits of viewing—the most commonplace of which has the average museumgoer spending less than thirty seconds examining a work of art. Thus many museums today take a more interactive, contextual approach to their exhibitions, especially when displaying nontraditional art forms. (Opinions vary wildly, however, about the whether "guided tours" channeled through the headsets on offer at every blockbuster exhibit are enlightening or reductive.)

World art historians nevertheless have good reason to employ standard and time-tested methodologies of aesthetic appreciation. An analysis of formal elements and design, however traditional its approach, can still lead to the articulation and understanding of a particular style. Formal elements include line, shape (two dimensions), form (three dimensions), texture, space (types of perspective and negative spaces), colors (tints, tones, shades), and values (degrees of light and dark). Design principles include balance (bilateral or asymmetrical), figure–ground relations, texture, composition, pattern (repetition), rhythm, movement, contrast, emphasis, harmony, and unity. A formal analysis also addresses degrees of reality versus illusion, and naturalistic rendering versus abstraction. Comparisons of aesthetic styles between cultures—drawings by ancient Mesoamerican artists and those of the Egyptians, for instance, reveal a similar composite perspective of the human figure, in which the head, arms and legs appear in profile while the torso is depicted in a frontal view—can lead historians to explore whether such patterns across cultures developed independently or interactively.

Ideas of "beauty," (that is, what constitutes the aesthetic) have varied in different times and places. In the first century CE, Longinus's treatise "On the Sublime" proposed that aesthetics was the *experience* of beauty. Contemporary descriptions of aesthetics now include any emotional response to art and emphasize empathy between those who make the objects (or participate in events) and those who more passively view them. Beginning students and the general public might achieve this empathy by exploring another art form related to the object or the culture that produced it. For example, Western eyes may be unfamiliar with Australian "dreamings" paintings in which hundreds (even thousands) of dots are arranged in circles, spirals, and lines that evoke an aerial (if not spiritual) view of the Australian landscape as it was once traveled by Aboriginal ancestors or otherworldly beings. Such viewers might enhance (or possibly diffuse) the visual sense of "otherness" in these "dot" paintings by using their ears—that is, by listening to music played on a didgeridoo (an indigenous wind instrument developed at least 1,500 years ago). Such cross-sensory exposure, especially when it involves an aural art form capable of eliciting an emotional response, can serve as a tool to sharpen awareness

Contemporary Australian "dreamings" paintings, inspired by cave drawings such as this, use dotted circles, spirals, and lines to evoke an aerial (if not spiritual) view of the landscape traveled by Aboriginal ancestors or otherworldly beings. Photo by Kevin Conners (www.morguefile.com).

> *Art is a kind of innate drive that seizes a human being and makes him its instrument. To perform this difficult office it is sometimes necessary for him to sacrifice happiness and everything that makes life worth living for the ordinary human being.* • **Carl Jung (1875–1961)**

of other unfamiliar customs, practices, and traditions of an indigenous culture.

The Future of World Art Studies

Encouragement for the field of world art as an expressive communication and/or information movement is accelerating and expanding through both widespread tourism (actual and virtual) and other online resources. Visual and auditory global exchanges are commonplace, and new art fields, such as "visual culture and world art," are growing. Art education and organizations around the world show an increasing interest as public art (art displayed and performed in public places), community art (art made collaboratively within and by communities of people), and individual artists in their studios increase their use of technology in the twenty-first century. World art thus fits the temper of the postmodern age as it supports teaching diversity and accommodates multiple intelligences. (See Howard Gardner's *Multiple Intelligences* [1993], which explores the theory that individuals possess a unique blend of several types of intelligences—linguistic, musical, and body-kinesthetic, to name a few.)

The most fervent of world art supporters believe that the field has the potential to become an educational axis mundi. In the meantime, world art studies can stimulate the thinking of both art historians and world historians.

Kathleen I. KIMBALL

Independent scholar, Barrington, New Hampshire

See also Art—Paleolithic; Art—World History and Art; Museums

Further Reading

Adams, L. S. (2004). *World views: Topics in non-Western art.* Boston: McGraw-Hill.

Anati, E. (1993). *World rock art: The primordial language.* Capo di Ponti, Italy: Edizioni del Centro.

Bahn, P. G. (1998). *The Cambridge illustrated history of prehistoric art.* Cambridge, U.K.: Cambridge University Press.

Campbell, J. (1988). *Historical atlas of world mythology.* (Vols. I and II.). New York: Perennial Library.

Christian, D. (2005). *Maps of time: An introduction to big history.* Berkeley: University of California Press.

Dissanayake, E. (1992). *Homo aestheticus: Where art comes from and why.* New York: Free Press.

Eliade, M. (1991). *Images and symbols* (P. Mairet, Trans.). Princeton, NJ: Princeton University Press. (Original work published 1952)

Gardner, H. (1993). *Multiple intelligences: The theory in practice.* New York: Basic Books.

Hagens, B. (1991). Venuses, turtles, and other hand-held cosmic models. In M. Anderson & F. Merrell (Eds.), *On Semiotic Modeling* (pp. 47–60). New York: Mouton de Gruyter.

Holly, M. A. & Moxey, K. (Eds.). (2002). *Art history, aesthetics, visual studies.* Williamstown, MA: Sterling and Francine Clark Art Institute.

Keyes, R. F. (1999). Creative transformations: Japanese prints from the collection of William Green [catalog essay]. Amherst, MA: Amherst College, Mead Museum of Art.

Kleiner, F.; Mamiya, C. J.; & Tansey, R. G.. (2001). *Gardner's art through the ages*, (11th ed.). Fort Worth, TX: Harcourt College Publishers.

Lazzari, M., & Schlesier, D. (2001). *Exploring art: A global, thematic approach.* Fort Worth, TX: Harcourt College Publishers.

Lewis-Williams, D. (2002). *The mind in the cave: Consciousness and the origins of art.* London: Thames and Hudson.

Lowenfeld, V., & Brittain, W. L. (1987). *Creative and mental growth*, (8th Ed.). New York: MacMillan.

Nochlin, L. (1999). *Representing women.* New York: Thames & Hudson.

Ochoa, G., & Corey. M. (1995) *The timeline book of the arts.* New York: Ballantine.

Ohnuki-Tierney, E. (Ed.). (1990). *Culture through time: anthropological approaches.* Stanford, CA: Stanford University Press,

Onians, J. (Ed.). (2004). *Atlas of world art.* London: Laurence King Publishing.

Onians, J. (2006). A Brief Natural History of Art. In J. Onians (Ed.), *Compression vs. expression: Containing and explaining the world's art* (pp 235–249). New Haven, CT: Yale University Press.

Roughley, N. (Ed.). (2000). *Being humans: anthropological universality and particularity in transdisciplinary perspectives.* New York: Walter de Gruyter.

Rubin, A. (1989) *Art as technology: The arts of Africa, Oceania, Native America, Southern California.* Beverly Hills, CA: Hillcrest Press.

Schuster, C., & Carpenter, E. (1996). *Patterns that connect: Social symbolism in ancient & tribal art.* New York: Harry N. Abrams.

Shlain, L. (1991). *Art & physics: Parallel visions in space, time, and light.* New York: Quill/W. Morrow.

Stafford, B. M. (2001). *Visual analogy: Consciousness as the art of connecting.* Cambridge, MA: MIT Press.

Taylor & Francis. (2010). Journal Details. *World Art.* Retrieved April 18, 2010, from http://www.tandf.co.uk/journals/RWOR

Urton, G. (2003). *Signs of the Inka Khipu: Binary coding in the Andean knotted-string records.* Austin: University of Texas Press.

Van Damme, W. (1996) *Beauty in context: Towards an anthropological approach to aesthetics.* New York: E. J. Brill.

Venbrux, E.; Scheffield Rosi, P.; & Welsch, R. (2006). *Exploring world art.* Long Grove, IL: Waveland Press.

Werness, H. B. (2000). *The Continuum encyclopedia of native art: worldview, symbolism, and culture in Africa, Oceania, and native North America.* New York: Continuum.

Westermann, M. (Ed.). (2005). *Anthropologies of art.* Williamstown, MA: Sterling and Francine Clark Art Institute.

Zijlmans, K., & Van Damme, W. (Eds.). (2008). *World art studies: Exploring concepts and approaches.* Amsterdam: Valiz.

Leonardo da Vinci
(1452–1519)
Renaissance artist, scientist, and engineer

Leonardo da Vinci, one of the universal geniuses of Western history, made contributions to art, mathematics, and science that anticipated the ideas and inventions of future centuries. Most significantly for world history, Leonardo's curiosity and his belief in the power of observation spurred him to investigate and record the forces that drive the natural universe and define man's place within it.

A true "Renaissance man," Leonardo da Vinci achieved renown in painting, architecture, engineering, science, and anatomy. He was born in the Tuscan countryside, the illegitimate son of a notary, and trained in the Florentine workshop of Andrea del Verrocchio (1435–1488). By 1472 he was recorded as member of the guild of painters in his own right, and evidence of his growing reputation began to build. Works from this early period include the *Adoration of the Magi* (1481–1482), a painting left unfinished, as were so many of Leonardo's projects.

In 1482 or 1483 Leonardo left Florence for Milan to serve in the court of Duke Lodovico Sforza (1452–1508). His duties at the court were wide and included not only painting, sculpture, and architecture, but also military and civil engineering, stage design, and interior decoration. The life of a courtier allowed Leonardo time to pursue his interests in the natural world and mathematics. His notebooks, kept throughout his life and written in mirror writing, reflect his wide-ranging interests. Studies of human anatomy, wind and water, plants and animals, machines, and optics occupied his restless mind. Heavily illustrated, these notebooks constitute a document of Leonardo's curiosity and his ingenious investigation of mysteries such as flight.

In addition to creating some of his most famous paintings during this period—for example, *The Last Supper* (1495–1497) in Santa Maria delle Grazie—Leonardo worked to fulfill the commissions provided by his master, such as an enormous bronze horse honoring Lodovico's father, Francesco

Leonardo da Vinci, *Self-portrait*. National Gallery, Turin, Italy.

152 · ART IN WORLD HISTORY

Anyone who conducts an argument by appealing to authority is not using his intelligence; he is just using his memory. • **Leonardo da Vinci (1452–1519)**

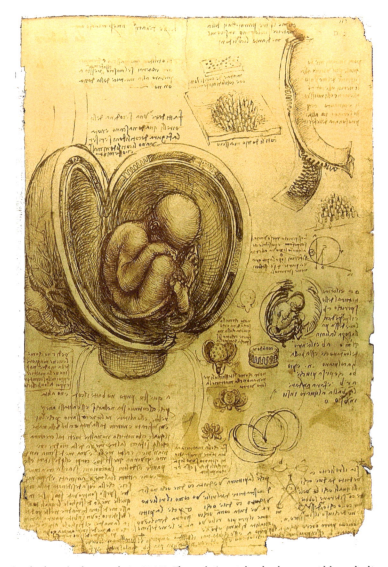

Leonardo's study of a fetus in the womb (c. 1510). The artist's notebooks document his curiosity and his ingenious investigation of mysteries such as flight. Royal Library, Windsor Castle. Photo of notebook by Luc Viatour.

Sforza. Although Leonardo managed to produce a clay model, the horse was never cast; Milan fell to King Louis XII of France in 1499, and Leonardo fled the city.

He accepted in 1502 a position as military engineer for the infamous Cesare Borgia (c. 1475–1507), but his hopes for Borgia patronage did not fully materialize, and Leonardo returned to Florence. There

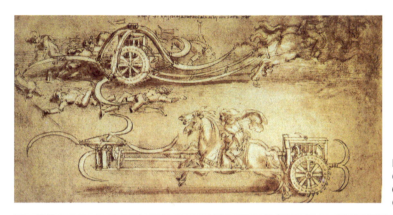

Leonardo da Vinci, *Assault Chariot with Scythes* (n.d.). **Charcoal drawing.** National Gallery, Turin.

he perfected his *sfumato* style (subtly shaded figures blending into the composition) in his *Virgin, Child and St Anne* (begun in 1502 but not completed until 1516), and attempted a new fresco technique for *The Battle of Anghiari* (1502–1503), commissioned for the Hall of the Great Council, the central deliberative chamber of the Florentine Republic. Unfortunately, the work is altogether lost as his experimental technique failed: the plaster did not dry evenly and the paint did not adhere.

Leonardo's second residence in Florence was consequently not very productive, although he did begin the portrait that would become perhaps the most famous painting in the world, the *Mona Lisa* (1503–1506). Returning to Milan in 1508, Leonardo resumed his responsibilities at court, but this time for the French, who were masters of the city until 1512, when the Sforza dynasty briefly returned. Again, most of his artistic projects were never carried to fruition (an exception is his *Virgin of the Rocks*, 1503–1506), in part because of his growing interest in scientific pursuits, especially anatomy.

In 1513 Leonardo set out for Rome. He served the Medici family, who had returned as rulers of Florence in 1512, including the head of the family, Pope Leo X. It is probable that Leonardo accompanied Leo to Bologna to meet with King Francis I of France. The young king recognized Leonardo's genius and convinced him to come to France in late 1516 or 1517, where Leonardo was presented with a small chateau at Cloux (Clos-Lucé), near the king's residence at Amboise. Leonardo continued his theoretical work and engaged in specific commissions for Francis, including designs for elaborate entertainments and grand royal palaces (which were never built). He also completed some of the unfinished paintings he had brought with

Leonardo da Vinci. *Virgin of the Rocks* (1506). **Oil on wood.** National Gallery, London.

Leonardo da Vinci, *Last Supper* (1498). Fresco. "Restorations" made to Leonardo's frescos over the years often obscured the artist's original intention. In 1997 scientific treatment to the *Last Supper* revealed that a platter on the table, long thought to contain bread, actually held grilled eel and orange slices. Judeo-Christian iconography provides no evidence that eels were served at religious feasts, but the dish was a popular delicacy during Renaissance Italy.

him. Leonardo's health had already begun to decline, perhaps the result of a stroke; in August 1519 he was dead, and was buried in Amboise.

The contribution of Leonardo to the culture of the West was enormous. His wide-ranging genius united many aspects of technical and creative skill (such as designs for a parachute and flying machines) to establish new heights of High Renaissance art; indeed, the art historian Giorgio Vasari (1511–1574) saw in Leonardo the moment when the ancients were at last surpassed. Most significantly for world history, Leonardo believed in the power of human observation. His curiosity about nature and the world spurred him to investigate and record the forces that drive the natural universe and define man's place within it.

Kenneth R. BARTLETT
University of Toronto

See also Art—Europe

Further Reading

Chastel, A. (1961). *The genius of Leonardo da Vinci: Leonardo da Vinci on art and the artist.* New York: Orion Press.

Clark, K. (1988). *Leonardo da Vinci: An account of his development as an artist* (Rev. ed.). London: Viking. (Original work published 1939)

Kemp, M. (1981). *Leonardo da Vinci: The marvellous works of nature and man.* Cambridge, MA: Harvard University Press.

Muntz, E. (2006). *Leonardo da Vinci: Artist, thinker, and man of science* (2 Vols.). New York: Parkstone Press.

Pedretti, C. (1973). *Leonardo da Vinci: A study in chronology and style.* Berkeley and Los Angeles: University of California Press.

Turner, R. (1993). *Inventing Leonardo.* New York: Knopf.

Museums

A museum is a place for housing, conserving, restoring, and displaying objects and collections of artistic, scientific, or historical significance. These collections are generally selected, arranged, and presented by a curator and made available for public viewing through exhibitions. The museum is an institution with an important role for conserving cultural heritage and in educating the public about the items in its care.

The museum, or institute of the Muses (the goddesses of song, poetry, and the arts and sciences more generally), has been with us for millennia, since the time of the ancients. Plato's library in Athens is thought of as one of the first, while the Musaeum at Alexandria, including the great Library of Alexandria, is considered one of the most famous. Today museums take all shapes and sizes; some are housed in magnificent monuments to preservation, while others are virtual and only accessible online. Museums contain and display all manner of objects and artifacts, from the ancient to the near new, from the conventional to the bizarre. Often thought of as dedicated to archeological, anthropological, and natural history preservations, museums are also dedicated to various themes, places, and peoples: from maritime to space, from science to fashion, from wars to sports, and from Goethe to Elvis.

From "Curiosities" to "Ethnographica"

Starting in the second half of the nineteenth century, anthropological museums began to flourish in virtually all major European and American cities. Through the 1920s these institutions became major centers for the construction of global narratives, whose rise and fall can be charted over the course of this period. Such an investigation also reveals that museums and global narratives are by no means exclusively Western phenomena.

In the Western world, museums developed out of an impetus to understand and categorize the world. It was during the Renaissance that a combination of mercantile wealth and human inquisitiveness created the first "curiosity cabinets" in Italy. Initial curators of such cabinets had few organizing principles, and they listed the relics of saints along with "curios" of animal and plant remains. Frequently such cabinets presented little more than mementos retrieved from long-distance voyages undertaken in the 1500s and 1600s. Yet already within these cabinets a clear separation between *artificialia* (or human-made artifacts) and *naturalia* (or natural objects) soon appeared. This distinction became more pronounced with the development of the natural sciences in the 1700s. The most significant development was the publication of the *Systema Naturae* (1735) by the Swedish naturalist Carolus Linnaeus (1707–1778). Linnaeus's system classified plants by reproductive apparatus and created a taxonomy that accommodated new plant types encountered during exploratory voyages. While Linnaean categories functioned well in the realm of *naturalia*, one could not extend them to indigenous artifacts. Over the next century, however, scholars invested considerable time and effort in replicating Linnaeus's system for the realm of human artifacts. Their endeavors became even more pronounced as Westerners increasingly encountered non-European peoples following 1750. Expeditions into the African continent or the watery expanse of the Pacific

Give me a museum and I'll fill it. • **Pablo Picasso (1881–1973)**

A museum in Tirupati, India, specializes in temple art. Photo by Klaus Klostermaier.

Ocean returned thousands of objects that stimulated not only curiosity about indigenous peoples but also attempts to classify the world's diversity into well-ordered epistemological systems.

By the 1800s, this search for organizing principles received additional currency from the field of archaeology. Conceived to support the available Greco-Roman literature, archaeology provided additional findings that extended and reinterpreted the humanist traditions. While classical archaeologists operated within the framework of an existing body of Greek and Roman literature, anthropologists were free to conceive histories from the material cultures of so-called nonliterate societies of Africa and Oceania. At the same time, however, there emerged a growing concern about the availability of indigenous artifacts. Early anthropologists argued that Western expansion brought about the transformation of indigenous cultures around the world. They believed that Western commerce, diseases, and theology reshaped indigenous societies to such an extent that material culture became tainted with Western influence or, in the worst case, ceased to exist. Either way, there emerged a need for an "anthropology of salvage," which ultimately called for storage houses for indigenous artifacts and established their value as historical sources. This salvage anthropology became instrumental in the creation and sustenance of anthropological museums, which were thus conceived as a thesaurus of human cultures.

The Rise of World History in Anthropological Museums

Armed with new perspectives on the importance of indigenous artifacts, anthropological museums flourished throughout the second half of the nineteenth century. Skilled anthropologists employed the salvage agenda to mobilize civic pride in their respective cities in an attempt to create leading anthropological institutions. Concern over disappearing non-Western heritages enlisted patrons and established networks of collectors. Over the next decades, there also emerged increasing pressure to impose a coherent, orderly framework on the artifacts amassed that could be displayed in the museums' hallways. The concern about vanishing indigenous peoples was nowhere more pronounced than in the United States, whose westward expansion to the Pacific Ocean often conflicted with the interests of Native Americans. The emerging Smithsonian Institution, created by the U.S. Congress in the 1840s, provided a museological example for other institutions to follow in dealing with indigenous artifacts. Within the United States, a number of other anthropological museums emerged, and the competitive atmosphere with regard to indigenous artifacts soon spread to such countries as Germany, Great Britain, and, later, France.

The Fall of World History in Anthropological Museums

A number of important factors contributed to the decline of world historical narratives within anthropological museums. Most telling were novel methodological approaches in anthropology. By the first decade of the twentieth century, museum practitioners began to venture into the wider world. While formerly relying on collectors such as colonial officials, missionaries, and traders, museum anthropologists decried the paucity of indigenous information accompanying the artifacts they obtained. To remedy such omissions, museum anthropologists organized expeditions to particular regions of the world. While the primary objective of such expeditions was still the collection and study of indigenous artifacts, many expedition participants, dissatisfied with the superficiality of previous data collection, argued for a more localized understanding of cultures, something that could be accomplished only by long-term residence among the members of a particular society. Such considerations, however, could not be easily accommodated in museum displays.

Anthropology's turn from global to local or regional methodology was under way before the outbreak of World War I. This conflict, however, greatly facilitated matters. It disrupted supply lines of collectors around the world, realigned colonial territories, and decimated the scholarly community. Similarly, certain practitioners were stranded as foreign nationals and by default restructured their studies around specific locations. The most prominent example was Bronislaw Malinowski, who as a national of the Austro-Hungarian Empire, ran into complications in the Australian colony of Papua. His ensuing research among the Trobriand Islanders resulted in a number of influential monographs. Although Malinowski did not invent the anthropological method of participant observation, his work enshrined anthropology's turn away from material culture. Museums continued to exist, but theoretical innovation shifted to the university setting. Anthropology's attempts at universal histories gave way to more localized studies that have dominated the discipline ever since.

Non-Western Museums and Their Global Narratives

By 1930, global historical narratives had departed from the hallways of anthropological museums. These institutions still served as important training and employment stations for generations of anthropologists, but novel theoretical constructs emerged elsewhere. Hence emerged the stereotype of anthropological museums as relics of a bygone era so popular in postmodern and postcolonial literature. There exists, however, an interesting byproduct of historical investigations into anthropological museums. Legitimate questions emerged about whether or not

European explorers and colonists in the early 1600s often brought indigenous peoples of the Americas to European cities, treating them as museum pieces, or objects of curiosity. In the 1800s museums became storage houses for indigenous artifacts and established the value of such objects as historical sources.

anthropological museums were indeed Western institutions. While it is difficult to generalize in this context, there seems to be ample evidence that similar processes existed in other societies. Just as Western societies appropriated indigenous material culture to construct historical narratives, so an indigenous appropriation of Western artifacts was a frequent occurrence. Material culture is once again indicative in this case. During the height of the collecting frenzy (three decades before World War I) a number of suspect artifacts started to arrive in anthropological museums. These were things that incorporated Western materials and colors, and whose production involved iron tools. Museum curators generally instructed collectors to abstain from such "tainted" artifacts, yet their numbers started to increase by the 1900s. Deemed inauthentic at the turn of the century, these artifacts are currently restudied to reveal indigenous counternarratives (or, as some historians put it, counterethnographies) to museum world histories. There are even some accounts of indigenous museums, one of the most famous, perhaps, located on the island of Tahiti in the Pacific Ocean. There, inside a *marae* (religious structure) located at Tarahoi, Captain William Bligh (of *Bounty* fame) discovered an odd collection of artifacts that included mementos hailing from the *Bounty* mutineers—British symbols of power—and a portrait of James Cook. The last was usually carried to arriving ships, whereupon the captains were asked to add their signatures on the back. Bligh did not make much of Tarahoi, but historians now recognize here the emergence of a museum narrating the encounters between Tahitian and foreign societies.

Controversies

A significant issue for any museum is the means by which its artifacts or displays are acquired: were they acquired legally and ethically, or is there some dispute over their acquisition? A series of relatively recent cases have served to bring these issues to the fore. Perhaps the most famous case is that of the Elgin or Parthenon Marbles, a series of classical Greek marble sculptures that have been housed in the British Museum in London since the early nineteenth century, but which are very much wanted by many to be returned to their original home in the Acropolis of Athens. Even today the theft and trafficking of antiquities is an increasingly common and serious transnational crime. It gained significant international attention following the pillaging and looting of the Iraqi National Museum in the wake of the United States' invasion and war in 2003. In recent years a number of prominent American art museums, including the Cleveland Museum of Art, Metropolitan Museum of Art in New York, the J. Paul Getty Museum in Los Angeles, the Museum of Fine Arts in Boston, and the Princeton University Art Museum have all returned works of art to Italy that were found to be stolen or looted by third parties and sold on. Similarly, the bones of Australian Aboriginals acquired on voyages in the early nineteenth century and long held by National Museums Scotland, the Royal College of Surgeons in London, and the National Museum of Ethnology in Leiden, the Netherlands, have recently been returned to their tribal descendants for reburial. While there have been some successes in winning the return of artifacts, particularly human remains, the very nature of many museums and the means by which their numerous artifacts were collected means that this contentious issue will likely remain unresolved as long as there are museums.

Rainer F. BUSCHMANN
California State University, Channel Islands

See also Art—World Art Studies

Further Reading

Bennett T. (1995). *Birth of the museum: History, theory, and politics.* New York: Routledge.

Coombes, A. (1994). *Reinventing Africa: Museums, material culture, and popular imagination in late Victorian and Edwardian England.* New Haven, CT: Yale University Press.

Dias, N. (1991). Le musée d'ethnographie du Trocadero, 1878–1908: Anthropologie et museologie en France. Paris: Editions du CNRS.

Findlen, P. (1994). *Possessing nature: Museums, collecting, and scientific culture in early modern Italy.* Los Angeles: University of California Press.

Foucault, M. (1970). *The order of things: An archaeology of the human sciences.* New York: Random House.

Helms, M. (1988). *Ulysses' sail: An ethnographic odyssey of power, knowledge, and geographical distance.* Princeton, NJ: Princeton University Press.

Hinsley, C. (1981). *Savages and scientists: The Smithsonian Institution and the development of American anthropology, 1846–1910.* Washington D.C.: Smithsonian Institution Press.

Penny, H. G. (2002). *Objects of culture: Ethnology and ethnographic museums in imperial Germany.* Chapel Hill: University of North Carolina Press.

Stocking, G. (1992). *The ethnographer's magic and other essays.* Madison: University of Wisconsin Press.

Thomas, N. (1991). *Entangled objects: Exchange, material culture, and colonialism in the Pacific.* Cambridge, MA: Harvard University Press.

Porcelain

Porcelain was first made in China about 850 CE. The essential ingredient is kaolin, white clay that when fired at an extremely high temperature acquires a glassy surface. Porcelain wares were first exported to Europe during the twelfth century. By 1700 trade in Chinese porcelain was immense, with Ming dynasty wares (characterized by cobalt-blue-painted motifs) highly prized.

Porcelain is a type of ceramic that is white, rock hard, translucent when thin, and resonant when struck. Made from quartz and either kaolin (china clay) or porcelain stone (and later from all three) it is fired at around 1,350°C. The ingredients for porcelain are found in abundance in China but do not exist in West Asia and occur only in isolated deposits in Europe. West Asian potters produced earthenware—made from various clays and fired at 600–1,100°C, while Europeans turned out earthenware and, from the fourteenth century, limited amounts of stoneware, a ceramic produced at 1,100–1,250°C. In contrast, China produced stoneware as early as the Shang period (1766–1045 BCE) and porcelain by the Tang (618–907 CE). During the Song dynasty (960–1279), artisans at Jingdezhen in Jiangxi Province created a superior form of porcelain, made by combining kaolin and porcelain stone.

China had a monopoly on porcelain for a thousand years, until the Meissen manufactory of Augustus II (1670–1733), elector of Saxony and king of Poland, turned out a close facsimile in 1708. Indeed, the success of Chinese porcelain closely tracks that of China's economy and China's international reputation. Triumphant for a millennium, porcelain, Chinese industry, and Chinese prestige all went into steep decline in the last half of the eighteenth century, giving way to British pottery (which came to overshadow mainland European pottery) and Western imperialism.

Before that historic turnabout, China dominated the international ceramic trade, exporting untold numbers of ceramic vessels to Japan, Southeast Asia, India, western Asia, and eastern Africa. After the Portuguese opened trade with China in the sixteenth century, Europe also became a premier market for porcelain, with perhaps 250 million pieces being imported by 1800. Jingdezhen used mass production techniques to manufacture wares for wide-ranging markets, with a single piece of porcelain passing through the hands of over seventy workers during its manufacture and decoration. Other regions could not compete with the massive Chinese economy, nor could their potters create vessels as lustrous as porcelain. Porcelain surpassed all ceramic ware before it, whether monochromatic whiteware in the Song, or blue-decorated pieces from the Yuan dynasty (1279–1368). In Borneo and Java, local ceramic traditions died out when huge quantities of porcelain were imported. Peoples in the hills of Sumatra and the islands of the Philippines incorporated porcelain into their fertility, divination, and headhunting rituals; they adopted Chinese "dragon jars," each seen to possess a personality and embody supernatural power, into lineages and passed them down through generations. On the coast of eastern Africa and the littoral of North Africa, porcelain adorned mosques and religious shrines.

In Iran, Iraq, and Egypt in the eleventh century, potters imitated gleaming white porcelain by applying a tin glaze surface to their earthenware. Discontent with the dull result, they used cobalt oxide pigment to paint blue designs on the earthenware. By the fourteenth century, under the influence of Muslim merchants in China and

A pen-and-ink representation of a Chinese porcelain dragon jar decorated with an intricate floral motif.

Mongol rulers in Beijing, potters in Jingdezhen also began producing vessels in blue and white, the ceramic style destined to conquer the world, imprinting them with images of elegance and refinement.

Rulers of Mughal India (1526–1857), Safavid Iran (1501–1722/1736), Mamluk Egypt (1250–1517), and Ottoman Turkey (c. 1300–1922) collected blue-and-white porcelain, while potters in those kingdoms replicated and transformed Chinese designs on their own blue-and-white earthenware. When porcelain reached the West in large quantities after 1600, the same thing happened: the elite amassed blue-and-white porcelain, and potters in Holland, Germany, France, and Italy copied the Chinese ceramics, combining their own traditional motifs with imaginative versions of Chinese pagodas, Buddhist symbols, and urbane mandarins. At the same time, European princes, influenced by mercantilist doctrine, aimed to staunch the flow of silver bullion to Asia to pay for exotic commodities, including porcelain. In the end, the race to find a formula for porcelain was won by Augustus II, although within a few years, absconding artisans carried the secret to other manufactories.

Still, neither Meissen nor its great competitor, the Sèvres manufactory outside Paris, could compete internationally with Chinese porcelain. That was the achievement of Josiah Wedgwood (1730–1795), the pottery baron of Great Britain. He produced an innovative glazed earthenware, christened "creamware," that was as durable and thin as porcelain. Equipping his manufactory with steam power and employing mass production methods (modeled on Jingdezhen's), and being attentive to the latest fashion styles and promotion techniques, Wedgwood aggressively sold his pottery, driving Chinese porcelain from markets around the world. Just as veneration for China in Western intellectual and ruling circles began declining precipitously after 1750, so too Chinese porcelain fell from its age-old pedestal.

Robert FINLAY
University of Arkansas

See also Art—East Asian and European Connections

Further Reading

Atterbury, P. (Ed.). (1982). *The history of porcelain*. London: Orbis.

Carswell, J. (1985). *Blue and white Chinese porcelain and its impact on the Western world*. Chicago: David and Alfred Smart Gallery.

Emerson, J., Chen, J., & Gardner-Gates, M. (2000). *Porcelain stories: From China to Europe*. Seattle, WA: Seattle Art Museum.

Finlay, R. (2010). *The pilgrim art: Cultures of porcelain in world history*. Berkeley: University of California Press.

Finlay, R. (1998). The pilgrim art: The culture of porcelain in world history. *Journal of World History, 9*(2), 141–187.

Vainker, S. J. (1991). *Chinese pottery and porcelain*. London: British Museum Press.

Textiles

Textiles, the broad term used to encompass the range of material objects created from fiber, cord, fabric and/or string—and manipulated by weaving, tying, sewing, knitting, braiding, and other techniques—have been a part of human culture since prehistoric times. Textiles can be studied to examine not only a peoples' aesthetic sense and development, but to provide insight about socioeconomic, political, and cultural aspects of their lives.

Prehistoric people all over the world twisted fibers from animals or plants into cordage to bind objects together, knot fishnets, sew skins, and string beads. In many different locations, they looped or interlaced the cordage into fabrics for both utilitarian and decorative purposes. They incorporated designs within the fabric construction or decorated the surface with embroidery or pigments. When worn, these fabrics provided protection from foul weather, insects, and perhaps evil spirits. Cloth also offered wearers many possibilities to express identity and individuality.

Archaeology and linguistics provide evidence of early textile production. Early spinners in many locations developed techniques to make cordage or yarns by twisting animal hair or bundles of fibers from plant stems and leaves. They invented the spindle, a shaped stick with a weight at the larger end, to twist the fibers uniformly and store the spun yarn. Archaeologists seldom find spindle sticks, but often clay or stone weights have survived. Spinners in many countries still hand-spin yarns with a spindle, although some twist long plant fibers into yarn by rolling them on their bare thighs as their ancestors did.

Looms

Early people found a number of ways to arrange the spun yarns into fabric. The earliest extant examples, which date from around 6000 BCE came from a cave in present-day Israel at Nahal Hemar and archaeological excavations in Turkey at Catal Huyuk. The fabrics from these and other early sites contain fibers, like flax, from plant stems. Mesopotamian weavers along the Tigris and Euphrates Rivers wove flax fabrics on

Four-harness floor loom, Saunderstown (Rhode Island) Weaving School.

Embroidery from Bulgaria. University of Rhode Island Historic Textile and Costume Collection, Whitlock Collection 1962.99.293.

horizontal looms. Wall paintings in tombs and three-dimensional funerary models also show Egyptians controlling stiff flax yarns on a horizontal ground loom. Basically this loom had two wooden beams spaced apart with yarns wrapped back and forth between the two beams, which were held in place by pegs beaten into the ground. This set of yarns is called the warp. The Egyptians interlaced another yarn over and under the tightly stretched warp yarns to produce a woven fabric. This intersecting set of crosswise yarns is called the weft. The width and length of the loom determined the size of the fabric. Plant fibers contain mostly cellulose, which does not dye easily, so Egyptians most often used undyed linens. They showed wealth and prestige by the fineness of the yarns and the whiteness of the fabric.

Early weavers north of the Mediterranean developed a vertical loom by suspending the warp yarns from a horizontal beam held by upright supports on either side. The warp yarns hung down from the beam. To provide order and tension, the weavers tied the lower ends of the warps to clay or stone weights. The weaver then interlaced the weft yarns beginning at the top of this warp-weighted loom. Archaeologists have found loom weights dating as early as Neolithic times in Crete, Greece, Switzerland, Hungary, Romania, Bulgaria, and Yugoslavia. Discovering a row of weights between two postholes provides clear evidence that people wove on vertical looms even when no yarn or fabric remains.

Figurines, wall paintings, pendants, and extant textiles from Egypt to China show the development of other types of looms. Most often the spinners and weavers depicted are women, who could combine these tasks with childcare. Over time in many locations, women produced textiles for domestic use; men became more involved when the cloth had potential for trade. Textiles have been a major trade commodity since ancient times, making a significant contribution to the economy of many areas.

Fibers

As sheep became domesticated around 4000 BCE, weavers produced fabrics containing wool yarns. Sumerian cuneiform tablets recorded information about sheep breeds. Wool is a protein fiber and is easily dyed, and Mesopotamian figures and wall paintings show colorful fabric patterns. Wool had limited use by pharonic Egyptians, but in the New Kingdom, they wove hieroglyphic designs in linen fabrics. The tomb of Thutmose IV contained examples of this tapestry weaving with weft yarns woven in only where their color is needed. They are tightly packed, obscuring the warp yarns. Later Egyptian Christian Coptic weavers expertly used this discontinuous weft-faced tapestry weave to create pictorial textiles. The Coptic influence is particularly obvious in surviving Syrian, Byzantine, and Persian textiles. Far Eastern weavers also produced tapestry and figured weaves, but they used different fibers.

Spinners in Tibet and China spun fibers from the stems of hemp plants. People also cultivated hemp (*Cannabis*) in Europe, but whether they used it for cordage or narcotic smoke is undetermined. Wild silkworm grew many places in Europe and Asia, but the moths cut through the cocoons damaging the fine filaments they had spun and leaving very short fibers that made yarn construction difficult. In the production of cultivated silk from *Bombyx mori* moths, the Chinese killed the moths before they could harm the filaments in the cocoons. They unwound many yards of filament from undamaged cocoons. Raising silkworms and their food source, mulberry leaves, is a

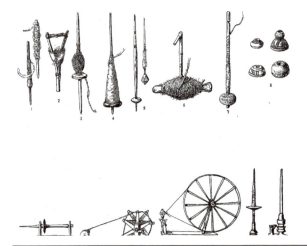

This series of drawings shows the variety of implements used over time and across cultures to twist fibers: (1) wooden peg; (2) silk winder (China); (3) spindle with whorl (Native Americans of British Columbia); (4) spindle (Mesoamerica); (5) spindle (Peru); (6) spindle for yak wool (Tibet); (7) spindle (Tibet); (8) simple spinning wheel; (9) early machine spindle (Finland); (10) flywheel spindle (China); (11) simple cotton and wool spinning wheel; (12) saxon spindle of a spinning wheel; (13) spindle commonly used on nineteenth-century cotton-spinning machines (United States).

very labor-intensive enterprise; the process is called sericulture.

The trade of colorful, patterned silk fabrics expanded westward by the late fifth century BCE, and trade routes developed into the renowned Silk Roads. The Chinese traded their silk fabrics but not their production secrets, although by the sixth century CE weavers in the Byzantine Empire were producing *Bombyx mori* silk textiles that all of Europe envied. Mosaics in Ravenna, Italy, show that lavish patterned fabrics were worn in the court of Emperor Justinian and Empress Theodora.

The other natural fiber that clothed East and West, royalty and peasant, male and female was cotton.

Originating in the Indus Valley by the third millennium BCE, cotton is the seed-hair fiber of a bush or tree (*Gossypium*). Like they did with silk, traders took cotton fabrics westward, and archaeologists have found examples at Egyptian and Mesopotamian sites. A number of classical writers described a plant on which "wool" grew and explained that gardeners chose cotton plants because they have blossoms of two different colors, depending on their maturity. Cotton grows in a variety of colors and is easier to dye than flax. Indian dyers perfected the art of coloring cotton. Beginning earlier than 2000 BCE, they made dyes that were colorfast by using mordants, metallic salts that minimize the fading of dyes by light or

Winslow Homer, *The Cotton Pickers* (1876). Oil on canvas. Los Angeles County Museum of Art.

Silkworms eating mulberry leaves. Photo by Paul and Bernice Noll.

laundering. Textile workers in other early civilizations shared the knowledge of mordants, most often using iron and aluminum salts.

Dyes

A significant trade of dyestuffs occurred along the Silk Roads and many other Old World routes. Coloring wool, silk, and cotton yarns and fabrics made them more valuable economically. Dyers played a major role in textile production, although they and their dye pots often had to exist on the fringes of settlements because the fermentation required for plant dyes as well as the use of urine and dung in the dyeing and printing processes gave off unpleasant odors. Early plant dyes included madder—orange-red to purple, depending on the mordant; indigo—blue; safflower—red or yellow; saffron—yellow; and weld—yellow. Like mulberry trees left from futile efforts at sericulture, madder and indigo plants, once a valuable commodity, now grow wild in many places.

Two animal dyes that produced vibrant reds came from a Mediterranean sea snail and a female shield louse that grew on trees. The Minoans of Crete probably perfected and certainly distributed the production of dye from the sea snails around the Mediterranean, although the Phoenicians are given credit for this dye, which is called Tyrian purple. The most expensive ancient dye, it is the color associated with emperors and royal courts. Kermes, the dye from the shield louse, excelled in dyeing silk and wool. Central and South American dyers also used two similar dyes. They perfected the process of dyeing with the color from a small sac in sea snails and from a louse that lives on cactus plants. The latter, cochineal, replaced kermes and became one of the most valuable New World exports until synthetic dyes began to replace natural dyes in the last half of the nineteenth century.

Historically the dyeing process has not been as simple as dunking a piece of fabric into a pot of dye. Sun-bleaching fabrics to reduce the natural off-white colors required time and space. Dyes and mordants needed preparation, and the multistep dyeing process took days to complete. Dyers were among the earliest chemists, the earliest herbal doctors, and the earliest artists. They colored not only pieces of cloth but also skeins of yarn, which were then woven or braided into colorful patterns.

Patterned Fabrics

Many cultures have produced patterned fabrics for centuries by applying a resist in chosen areas to prevent dye absorption. Resists can be wound around yarns or fixed to a fabric. The Indonesian word for patterned fabrics woven of yarns that have been wrapped in sections to prevent dye penetration is *ikat*. Asian, African, and Guatemalan ikats are internationally fashionable today. Japanese dyers produce a very marketable product called *shibori*, an expertly patterned tie-dyed cloth. African dyers create large tie-dye designs, popular in T-shirts today. Wax or paste resists paint. When blocked onto a cloth before dyeing, it produces a patterned fabric

Illustration of a murex shell, the source of a red-purple dye first made by Phoenicians. University of Toronto Wenceslaus Hollar Digital Collection.

Weft ikat from Cambodia. University of Rhode Island Historic Textile and Costume Collection, Donor: Lois Berney, 1999.05.01.

called by the Indonesian word *batik*. Indonesians traditionally use wax to make their batiks; Africans use cassava paste while Japanese make a rice paste. In the eighteenth century, resist pastes included chemicals that prevented a dye from fixing to a fabric. Popular indigo-resist prints in colonial America had large floral patterns influenced by the imported Indian calicoes.

A patterned fabric, even a plaid, offers marketable variations. From the earliest times, weavers devised methods of raising sets of warp yarns before inserting a weft yarn between the warps on a loom. When the weaver raised every other warp yarn, inserted a weft yarn across the width of the fabric, raised the alternate set of warps, and laid in another weft yarn, she produced a plain weave. By varying the pattern in which she raised each warp, she made other weave structures such as twills. The earliest hand-operated mechanism for selectively raising warp yarns was a string that encircled alternate warps connecting them to a rod that could pull them up away from the other set of yarns. The term for the string loops controlling the warp yarns is *heddles*. Over time, improvements to this use of heddles allowed weavers to construct fabrics with complex patterns.

The loom with the most complicated control over warp patterning was developed in the Middle East and Far East, although the Chinese often receive credit for it. The operation of this loom, called a *drawloom*, required two people: one controlled the frames or harnesses that held the heddles to make a plain-weave base structure and inserted the weft yarns; the other sat above the loom to control the patterning warps. This second person was often a child; child labor has been prevalent worldwide in the textile industry—in homes, workshops, and mills.

Tapestry-woven fabrics, such as cashmere shawls from Kashmir, are very labor intensive and cannot be made by machines. Weaving mechanically-controlled patterns required less time than tapestry weaving and produced a very marketable product, particularly if made of silk. For a thousand years, Chinese, Japanese, Syrian, Byzantine, and Persian workshops produced exotic figured silks on variations of the drawloom. Competition from Palermo, Sicily, and Lucca, Italy, by the thirteenth century introduced fabrics that evolved into the luxurious velvets of the Italian Renaissance from Florence and other Italian city-states. Many of these fabrics are portrayed in fifteenth-century paintings and tapestries.

The Italians dominated figured-silk production through the sixteenth century, when instead of velvets, fashionable silks had patterns created by colored supplementary weft yarns. Under the guidance of Jean-Baptist Colbert, finance minister under Louis XIV, drawloom weaving in Lyon expanded. By the eighteenth century, Lyon's damasks and brocaded fabrics surpassed Italian production, with some competition from weavers in Spitalfields outside of

Italian silk velvet (c. 1500). University of Rhode Island Historic Textile and Costume Collection, Whitlock Collection 1962.99.331.

Brocaded head ribbon (*cinta*) with supplementary weft yarns. San Martin Sacatepequez, Guatemala. University of Rhode Island Historic Textile and Costume Collection 1997.99.17.

London. Many Spitalfields textile workers had fled persecution after the revocation of the Edict of Nantes in France, and the demise of textile production in Palermo, Spain, and Flanders was also the result of worker migration caused by political unrest and religious persecution.

Jacquard attachments on looms, a nineteenth century English invention, revolutionized figured-silk weaving, as well as the production of carpets, imitation Kashmir shawls, coverlets, knits, and machine-made laces. Lyon apartment houses with excessively tall ceilings on the top floors reflect the height and light requirements of these looms. This early computerized system used a series of punched cards that determined which warp yarns were raised to create a pattern. This basic system provides control for looms, lace, and knitting machines today.

Jacquard's invention also affected the production of lace, first made by hand in the sixteenth century. Like figured silks, bobbin and needle laces reflected conspicuous consumption by the wealthy. The English development of machines to make knits (sixteenth century) and fine net (late eighteenth century) came before more complicated equipment that imitated handmade lace. Leavers lace machines with Jacquard attachments made the best imitations and still do today in England and France. Raschel knitting machines make the least expensive modern laces, which are not as durable as other laces because of their looped construction.

Printed Cottons

Another fabric became as valuable as lace and patterned-silk cloth during the seventeenth century. Brightly painted and printed cottons from India appealed to Europeans, and various Western trade companies set up the production of these calicoes or chintzes in East India. To obtain a share of the profits being made on the Indian prints, entrepreneurs in England and France began printing imported cotton fabric. The popularity of the imported and domestically printed calicoes forced silk and wool producers to seek legislative restraints on the importation, local

Cylinder-printed cotton dresses (colored with madder, a plant dye), mid-nineteenth century. University of Rhode Island Textile Gallery exhibition on natural dyes.

Pigment-printed cotton, Senegal. University of Rhode Island Historic Textile and Costume Collection 2008.04.02.

production, and use of the prints. After the bans were lifted in the mid-eighteenth century, printers, having perfected the use of mordants, sold many yards of block-printed cottons to a public whose desire had not been abated by the legislation.

Laws passed to govern consumer expenditures, called sumptuary laws, have seldom been effective, especially in regulating printed cottons, lace, and figured silks. Whether to protect local production, as in this case, to maintain social order by limiting consumption based on income, or to limit worldly excesses as determined by religious groups, sumptuary laws often fostered the development of illegal methods for consumers to obtain a product.

Christophe-Philippe Oberkampf of Jouy near Paris was the most successful early calico printer. Fast dyes and well-cut blocks brought his manufactory fame and fortune. He was one of the printers in the latter eighteenth century who experimented with faster methods of printing. The result was printing cloth with an engraved copper plate on which the design was incised into the metal surface. Copperplate printing produced large-scale monochromatic patterns with very fine lines, which were not possible with wood blocks. Ever-seeking to increase production, inventors finally perfected an engraved copper cylinder printing machine through which fabric moved continuously.

By the 1820s European and American shops produced printed cottons at price levels all could afford. Inventions by Englishmen John Kay (1733), James Hargreaves (1767), Richard Arkwright (1770s), and Samuel Crompton (1779) greatly increased the production of spun cotton yarn in England. Two Americans also made significant contributions. Eli Whitney's 1793 cotton gin made large-scale cotton production economically feasible. Samuel Slater, who had worked for Arkwright, partnered with two Providence, Rhode Island, merchants and set up a cotton spinning factory in Pawtucket. This manufactory, now the Slater Mill Historic Site, was the beginning of the Industrial Revolution in America.

The Nineteenth Century and After

By the beginning of the nineteenth century, spinning was no longer the rate-determining step in cloth production. Spinning mills in England and southern New England had thousands of spindles. With the perfection of water-powered looms after 1815 and cylinder printing in the twenties, printed cotton cloth that had been available only to the rich in the previous century sold for as little as ten cents per yard. Hand-production of cloth diminished significantly in western Europe and the United States. Dye technology also kept pace with other advancements, the most significant being the discovery in 1856 by William Perkin of mauve, the first synthetic dye. By the end of the century, most classes of dyes recognized today had been developed. Cylinder-printing technology changed little after the mid-nineteenth century and remained the backbone of the industry until rotary-screen printing took over in the 1990s.

An additional change in the 150 years of printing with dyes also occurred then. Improvements in formulations to print pigments that are insoluble in water increased the amount of pigment printing significantly. In the twenty-first century, rotary screen-printing with pigments is economically and environmentally expedient.

The textile world changed irrevocably around 1910 with the commercial production of a filament regenerated from cellulose that came to be known as

> Work on good prose has three steps: a musical stage when it is composed, an architectonic one when it is built, and a textile one when it is woven. • Walter Benjamin (1892–1940)

rayon. With improvements in the strength of rayon filaments and the introduction of acetate in the mid 1920s, the quest for an inexpensive silk-like fiber was accomplished. In the late 1930s, the accidental discovery of nylon led to the first synthetic fiber, which played a significant role in World War II. Polyester in the early 1950s, followed by wrinkle-resistant finishes on cotton, introduced the "wash-and-wear" era. A succession of new fibers, dyes to color them, and finishes to alter their properties continued to invigorate the textile market. New polymers and finishes offer elasticity, superior strength, antimicrobial properties, ultraviolet-light protection, and flame, soil, water, and impact resistance. The future is bright for consumer products and also new applications in the fields of medicine, electronics, aeronautics, and geotextiles.

Textiles have influenced economics, technology, art, religion, government, customs, and many other human endeavors. The production, design, and use of textiles are also a mirror held up to history.

Margaret ORDOÑEZ
University of Rhode Island

Further Reading

Balfour-Paul, J. (1998). *Indigo.* London: British Museum Press.

Barber, E. J. W. (1991). *Prehistoric textiles: The development of cloth in the Neolithic and Bronze Ages.* Princeton, NJ: Princeton University Press.

Barber, E. W. (1994). *Women's work: The first 20,000 years.* New York: W. W. Norton.

Brédif, J. (1989). *Printed French fabrics: Toiles de Jouy.* New York: Rizzoli.

de'Marinis, F., ed. (1994). *Velvet: History, techniques, fashions.* New York: Idea Books.

Collier, B. J., Bide, M. J., & Tortora, P. G. (2009). *Understanding textiles.* Upper Saddle River, NJ: Pearson Prentice Hall.

Geiger, A. (1979). *A History of textile art.* Leeds: W. S. Maney & Son.

Harris, J., ed. (1993). *Textiles: 5,000 years.* New York: Harry N. Abrams.

Phillips, B. (1994). *Tapestry.* London: Phaidon Press.

Sandberg, G. (1994). *The red dyes: Cochineal, madder, and murex purple, A world tour of textile techniques.* Asheville, NC: Lark Books.

Schoeser, M. (2003). *World textiles: A concise history.* New York: Thames & Hudson.

Seiler-Baldinger, A. (1994). *Textiles: A classification of techniques.* Washington, DC: Smithsonian Institution Press.

Toomer, H. (2001). *Antique lace: Identifying types and techniques.* Atglen, PA: Schiffer Publishing.

Wada, Y., Rice, M. K. & Barton, J. (1983). *Shibori, The inventive art of Japanese shaped resist dyeing: Tradition, techniques, innovation.* Tokyo: Kodansha International.

Wilson, K. (1979). *A History of textiles.* Boulder, CO: Westview Press.

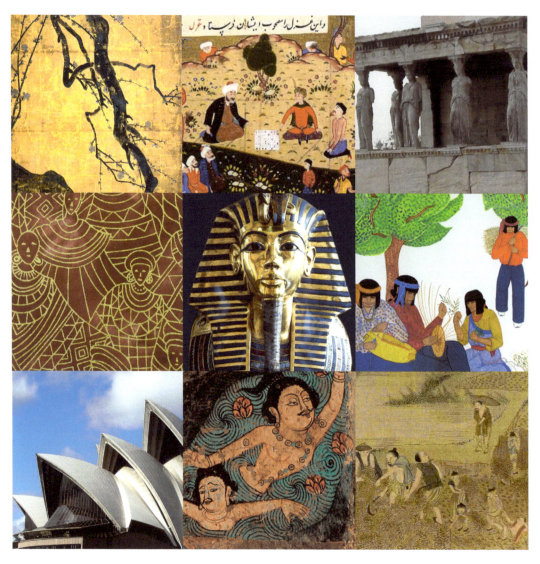

Top left: Ogata Korin, *White Plum Blossoms* (Edo period). Ink, color, and gold and silver leaf on paper. One of a pair of twofold screens. Museum of Art, Atami.

Second row left: Pigment-printed cotton, Senegal. University of Rhode Island Historic Textile and Costume Collection 2008.04.02.

Bottom left: Sydney Opera House. Photo by Kevin Conners (www.morguefile.com).

Center top: Rumi's teacher, Shams-i Tabrizi, portrayed in an illustrated copy of Rumi's poem, the "Diwan-e Shams-i Tabriz-i," circa 1502–1504. Bibliothèque Nationale de France.

Center: Solid gold death mask of the Egyptian pharaoh Tutankhamun. The Egyptian Museum, Cairo.

Center bottom: Fragment from the "Swimmers" wall fresco in Kizil, Cave of the Seafarers (c. 500 CE). Collection of the Museum of Asian Art, Berlin.

Top right: Caryatids, sculpted female figures serving as architectural supports, take the place of a columns or pillars on many ancient Greek buildings.

Second row right: Pablita Velarde, *Basketmaking* (1940). Casein paint on board. The Bandelier National Monument in New Mexico commissioned this painting under the Works Progress Administration (WPA).

Bottom right: Illustration from a Qing-dynasty version of *Gengzhi tu* (Pictures of Tilling and Weaving, first printed in 1210), a series of twenty-three scenes celebrating the development of farming technology in the Song dynasty (960–1179).

Index

Notes: 1) Names, terms, and page-number ranges in **bold** denote chapter entries.

A

Abbasid caliphate, art, 140
Achaemenids, 33–34, 137
Acropolis, 25–26, 29
Adam, Robert, 7
Aestheticism, 117
Afghanistan
    art, 31–38 (*See also* **Art—South Asia**)
    Bamiyan Buddhas, 37
Africa
    architecture, 18
    art of (*See* **Art—Africa**)
Africa—colonial, art and, 20
African religions
    Christianity, 18
    Islam, 18
African states, ancient
    Benin, 18
    Zimbabwe, Great, 18
Akbar, 125, 127
Akkadia. *See* **Art—South Asia**
Alberti, Leon Battista, 6, 68
Alexander the Great
    Achaeminids and, 33
    art, 121–122, 137
Alexis I (czar), 113
Alhambra, Granada, Spain, 5
Altar of Peace (*Ara pacis*), 28
Americas, the, *See* **Art—Pre-Columbian Central and South America**
Amida Buddha, 77, 78
Anasazi culture, 2, 84
Anatolia, art, 135, 137
Andean states. *See* **Art—Pre-Columbian Central and South America**
Andes, art in. *See* **Art—Pre-Columbian Central and South America**
Angkor Thom, 132
Angkor Wat, 133
Apartheid, art and, 20
Archaeology, Bactrian-Margiana archaeological complex, 31
Architecture, 1–11
    ancient temple ziggurats, tombs, and palaces, 2–3, 23–24
    Art Noveau, 8
    Baroque, 6
    Christian, 4, 63–65
    historic revivals, 7
    Islamic, 4, 18, 124–125
    Middle Ages, 4–5, 65
    modernism, 8–9
    prehistoric and nonurban, 1–2
    Renaissance, 5–6
    Roman innovations, 3–4
    twenty-first century, 9–10
    See also **Art—Ancient Greece and Rome; Art—Europe; Art—Japan; Art—Pre-Columbian Central and South America**
Architecture, vernacular, 12–16
Argunov, Ivan, 115
Armenia, art, 139
Art Bulletin, xv
Art History, xv
Art—Africa, 17–22
    ancient, 17–18
    European modernism influenced by, 70, 71–72
    Paleolithic, 92–96
Art—ancient Greece and Rome, 23–30
    classical period, 25–26
    Egyptian influences, 24–25
    evolving balance in Roman art, 27–29
    Greek influence on Rome, 26–27
    temples, architecture of, 3–4, 23–24
    West Asian art, influence on, 137

171

Art—Central Asia, **31–39**
  Achaemenids and Greeks, 33–34
  first millennium ce, 36–37
  Kushans, 34–36
  modern era, 37–38
  pre-Achaemenid, 31–33
Art—China, **40–56**
  Buddhism and, 43–46
  early imperial artifacts (Qin and Han), 41–43
  emergence of literati art (Song), 46–50
  Qing period (1644–1911/12), 50–52
  painting and calligraphy, 43
  post-imperial, modern China, 52–56
  pre-imperial era (circa 3000–221 bce), 40–41
  See also **Art—East Asian and European connections; Porcelain**
Art—East Asian and European connections, **57–62**
  Chinese blue and white, 57–58
  Chinoiserie, 58–59
  influence of Asian spiritual systems, 61–62
  influential role of museums, 60–61
  Japonisme, 59–60
  See also **Art—China; Porcelain**
Art—Europe, **63–73**
  Baroque, 68
  early Christian art, 63–65
  medieval art, Eastern and Western, 65–67
  modern, 68–69
  Native North American art, influence of, 86
  Paleolithic art, 97
  Renaissance, 67–68
  tribal migration, 65
  West Asian art, influence on, 141–142
Art—Japan, **74–83**
  Asuka period, 75–76
  Edo period, 80–81
  Heian period, 77
  Jōmon culture, 74
  Kamakura period, 77–78
  Kofun period, 75
  modern period, 81–82
  Momoyama period, 78–80
  Muromachi period, 78
  Nara period, 76–77
  Yayoi culture, 74–75
Art—Native North American, **84–91**
  early European/indigenous interactions, 85–86

Notes: 1) Names, terms, and page-number ranges in **bold** denote chapter entries.

  cultural evolutionism (19th c.), 86
  modern influences, 86–88
  pre-European contact, 84
  present-day identities and artists, 88–90
Art—Paleolithic, **92–100**
  aesthetics and meaning, origins of, 92–94
  beyond Africa, 96–97
  Blombos cave, 93–95
  icons, 95–96
  interdisciplinary studies, 99–100
  interpretations, 97–99
  See also **Art—world art studies; Introduction: Art in world history**
Art—Pre-Columbian Central and South America, **101–111**
  overview, 101–102
  Mesoamerica, 102–108
  South America, 107–111
Art—Russia, **112–120**
  early religious art, 112–113
  eighteenth century, 113–115
  modern, 116–118
  revolution and Soviet Socialist Realism, 118–120
Art—South Asia, **121–129**
  painting, 125–129
  sculpture, 120–125
Art—Southeast Asia, **130–135**
  Chinese influences, 134
  earliest art, 130
  Indian influences, 131–134
  modern art, 135
  tribal arts, 134–135
Art—West Asia, **136–142**
  earliest artifacts, 136–137
  early Islam, 139–141
  Eastern influences, 141–142
  Greek influences, 137–139
  Persian traditions, 137
Art—world art studies, **143–150**
  comparative aesthetics, 147–149
  field, key aspects, 144–145
  field, resources and approaches in, 145–146
  future, 149
  trends and challenges, 146–147
  See also **Art—Paleolithic; Introduction: Art in world history; Museums**
Arts and Crafts Movement, 8, 86
Ashikaga Takauji, 78
Ashikaga Yoshimasa, 78
Ashikaga Yoshimitsu, 78

Asia,
   architecture, 1
   art, 31–39, 112–120, 121–129, 130–135 (*See also* **Art—Central Asia**; **Art—Russia**; **Art—South Asia**; **Art—Southeast Asia**)
Asoka, 121, 122
Assyrian Empire, Palace of King Sargon II, 3
Asuka period, 75–76
Atahualpa, 110
Athens, Acropolis and Parthenon, 3
Aurangzeb, 127–128
Australia,
   paleolithic art, 96
   petroglyphs, 84
   Aztec Empire, 85–86
   See also **Art—Pre-Columbian Central and South America**

B
Babylon, art, 137
Bactria, 34
Bactrian-Margiana archaeological complex (BMAC), 31
Bailey, Gauvin Alexander, xviii
Bangladesh
   vernacular architecture, 14
   See also **Art—South Asia**
Baroque era, 6, 67–68, 112
Basilicas, 4, 6, 64
Beijing
   architecture, 10, 45
   Forbidden City, 6
   Olympics (2008), 56, 109
Belgium, architecture, 9
Benin, 18
Bingen, Hildegard von, 73
Bligh, Captain William, 158
BMAC (Bactrian-Margiana archaeological complex), 31
Boccioni, Umberto, 71
Boffrand, Germain, 7
Book of Kells, The, 65
Boone, Elizabeth, 107
Bottger, Johann Friedrich, 58
Boucher, Francois, 58
Boullée, Étienne-Louis, 7
Bramante, Donato, 6
Brancaccio, Pia, xii
Braque, Georges, 70
Bricks, building with
   ancient Greece and Rome, 28–29
   Aztec Empire, 134, 137

Mesopotamia, 2–3, 4
Southeast Asia, 109
vernacular architecture and, 12, 15
west African Islamic architecture, 19
Bridge, Anne (Lady O'Malley), xvii
Britain,
   architecture, 6, 8, 9, 58, 59
   porcelain, 160, 161
British Empire, Asian colonies, 125, 128
Briullov, Karl, 115
Bronze Age,
   China, art of, 40–41
   migration and Tarim Basin mummies, 37
   Southeast Asia, art of, 130
Brook, Timothy, xii
Brunelleschi, Filippo, 5, 68
Brutalist movement, 9
Buddhism,
   architecture, 4, 5
   art, 35–37, 43–46, 122, 131–134, xvi–xviii
   Bamiyan Buddhas, 37
   Indus Valley, pre-Achaemid, 32
Bulatov, Eric, 119
Byzantine Empire, art, 64–65, 137, 139

C
Cahill, James, 48, 49
Cai Guo-Qiang, 56
Calendars, Mayan, 104–105
Calligraphy, 43, 48, 50, 61, 80, 139, 142
Cambodia, 132
   art, 130, 132
Cameroon, 2
Campidoglio, 6
   art, 84–88
Capac, Huayna, 110
Capac, Manco, 110
Capitoline Triad, 27
Caravaggio, 68
Caravaque, Louis, 113
Caribbean region, vernacular architecture, 14
Cassatt, Mary, 59, 69
Castiglione, Giuseppe, 51
Castles, architecture of, 5
Catacombs, painting in, 63
Catal Huyuk (Turkey), 162
Catherine the Great, 114
Chagall, Marc, 118
Chartres Cathedral, 67
Chavín de Huántar, 102, 108–109

Chicago, Judy, 72–73
China
    architecture, 5, 6, 10, 45
    art, 145, xiii, xvii–xviii (*See also* **Art—China**;
        Art—East Asian and European Connections;
        Porcelain)
    porcelain, 51 (*See also* **Porcelain**)
    Southeast Asian art, influence on, 134, 140
    vernacular architecture, 14
Chinoiserie, 58–59
Christian, David, xii, xiv, 144
Christianity
    architecture, 4, 63–65
    early Christian art, 63–65, 112
    Russia, 112
Clothing and costume. See Textiles
Coinage
    Achaemenidean/Graeco-Bactrian, 33
    Kushan, 35
Colbert, Jean-Baptist, 166
Colosseum amphitheater, Rome, 4, 28
Columbus, Christopher, 101
Communication media. *See* **Art—Paleolithic**
Congo [Kongo], Democratic Republic of, art, 18, 19, 20
Constantine the Great, 64–65
Cook, James, 158
Corinth, architecture of, 23–24, 26
Cortés, Hernan, 86, 101, 107
Cubism, 70, 117
Cubo-Futurism, 117
Cultural Revolution, 54–55

D
Damaratus, 26
Daoists, 43
Davidson, Robert, 88, 89
Degas, Edgar, 69
Deineka, Alexander, 118
Delaunay, Robert, 71
Delaunay, Sonia, 71
Dexter, Miriam Robbins, xiv
Dipylon pots, 23
Dogon (Mali), architecture, 2
Dome of the Rock (Jerusalem), 139
Dong Qichang, 49–50
Dong Xiwen, 54
Doric architecture, 23–26
Doryphoros, 28

Notes: 1) Names, terms, and page-number ranges in **bold** denote chapter entries.

Dōtaku bells, 75
Durer, Albrecht, 85, 86
Dutch Empire, Japanese trade, 58
Dyak peoples of Borneo, 13

E
Earthquakes, vernacular architecture and, 15
East African Hadza, 13
Edo period, 80–81
Egypt
    architecture, 2, 3
    art, 18, 137
    Greek and Roman art influenced by, 23–24
Eiffel Tower, 8, 118
El Salvador, art, 104
Elizabeth Petrovna, empress of Russia, 114
Elkins, James, xv, xvi
Ethiopia
    art, 18
    religions, 29, 37
Etruscans, 26, 27
Eurasia, art, 84–86
Europe
    architecture, 4, 5, 8–9
    art (*See* **Art—Europe**)
Evenki of Siberia, 13

F
Fabrics. *See* **Textiles**
Fan Kuan, 47
Fang Congyi, 49
Fenollosa, Ernest, 60, 61, 81
Finlay, Robert, xii
First American art. *See* **Art—Native North American**
First Nations art. *See* **Art—Native North American**
Florence, Cathedral of, 5–6
France
    architecture, 6–7
    Paleolithic art in, 93, 97, 99
Frank, Andre Gunder, xiv
Freer, Charles Lang, 61
French Empire, Southeast Asia, influence in, 43 (*See also* Vietnam)
Fry, Roger, 61
Fujiwara Yorimichi, 77
Futurism, Russia, 117

G
Gaozong, 48
Gauguin, Paul, 59

Gerasimov, Sergei, 118
Germany
  architecture, 6
  Paleolithic art in, 97
Ghana, Akan people, art of, 19
Giza, Great Pyramids of, 2
Glazunov, Ilya, 119
Golden House (Domus Aurea), 28–29
Goncharova, Nathalia, 71
Gothic architecture, 5, 7, 66, 67
Graves, Morris, 61
Great Mosque, Córdoba, Spain, 4
Great Mosque of Damascus, 139
Great Stupa, Sanchi, India, 4
  Achaemenids and, 33
  architecture of, 2–3, 23–29
  art (*See* **Art—ancient Greece and Rome**)
Green architecture, 10
Green ware (*qingci*), 57
Gris, Juan, 70
Gu Kaishi, 43
Gu Wenda, 55
Guatemala, art, 102, 104, 111
Guo Xi, 48
Guptas, sculpture under, 123–124

H

Hadrian, emperor, 29
Hagens, Bethe, 144
Hagia Sophia, 4, 66, 139, 140
Hamada, Shoji, 61
Hammurabi, art, 135
Han dynasty, 41, 43, 47, 75, 144
  Shiji, xviii
Handscrolls, 43, 77
Haniwa, 75
Harappan state and Indus civilization, art, pre-Achaeminid, 32
Hasegawa Tōhaku, 79
Hearn, Lafcadio, 60
Heian period, 77
Hemp, 163
Hidemichi Tanaka, xvii
Hildegard, St., 73
Hinduism,
  architecture, 5, 14
  art of, 121–129, 131–133
Hiroshige, 60
HIV/AIDS, art and, 20
Hokusai, 59–60

Hon'ami Kōetsu, 80, 81
Honduras, art in, 102, 104
Hōnen, 78
Hōryū-ji, 75, 76
Huang Binhong, 53
Huizong, 48

I

Ibn Battuta, 57
Iconoclasm, period of, 66
Iconography, 63–64
Impressionism, 68
  Japonisme and, 59–60, 69 (*See also* Ukiyo-e)
  Russia, 117
Inca Empire, 146
  art, 109–110
  See also **Art—Pre-Columbian Central and South America**
India, art, 33, 131–134, 145 (*See also* **Art—South Asia**)
Indigenous peoples, exploited by museums, 156
Indonesia, art, 131–132
Industrial Revolution. *See* **Textiles**
Industrialization, Arts and Crafts Movement and, 8
Installation art, 21, 55, 82, 84, 120, 144
  Dinner Party, the 72–73
Intergenerational learning, 99
Iran
  Central Asian art, role in, 32, 33
  Great Britain, influence of, xv
Iraq, 136, 2–3
Ishtar Gate, 137
Islamic world
  art, 124–125, 139–142
  mosque, architecture of, 4
Israel, Paleolithic art in, 96
Italy
  modern art, 70
  Renaisssance art in, 68–68
Ivan IV (Ivan the Terrible), 113
Ivanov, Alexander, 115

J

Jahangir, 127
Jainism, 125–126
Japan
  architecture, 6, 8, 9
  art, 58–60, 147, xviii (*See also* **Art—Japan**)
  minka houses, 15
Japonisme, 59–60, 69
Jenne-Jeno, 17–18

Jerusalem, 139
Jōmon culture, 74
Journal of Global History, xii
Justinian I, 66

K

Kabakov, Ilya, 119
Kaihō Yōshō, 79
Kairouan, Great Mosque at, 18
Kamakura period, 77–78
Kandinsky, Wassily, 117, 118
Kanmu, Emperor, 77
Kano Eitoku, 79
Kashmir, 14–15
Keyser, Louisa, 88
Khmer kingdom, 132
Khrushchev, Nikita, 119
Khubilai Khan, 58
Kiprensky, Orest, 115
Kofun period, 75
Kokubunji system, 76
Kollowitz, Kathe, 54
Kongo [Congo], Democratic Republic of the, art, 18, 19, 20
Korovin, Konstantin, 116
Kramskoi, Ivan, 115
Krishna, 127, 128
Kudara Kannon, 76
Kushan Empire
    art, 122–123
    Gandharan and Mathuran art, 34–36
Kuznetsov, Pavel, 117
Kyrgyz, 13
Kyrgyzstan, 31, 38

L

Lace making, 167
Larionov, Mikhail, 117
Le Corbusier, 9
Leach, Bernard, 61–62
Lee, Dat So La, 88
Lenin, Vladimir Ilyich, art and, 118
Leonardo da Vinci, 151–154
    See also **Art—Europe**
Levitan, Isaak, 116
Levitsky, Dmitry, 114

Notes: 1) Names, terms, and page-number ranges in **bold** denote chapter entries.

Li Tang, 48
Li Zhaodao, 46
Lin Fengmian, 53
Linnaeus, Carolus, 155
Lissitsky, El, 118
Literature, 98
Liu Haisu, 52–53
Liu Shaoqi, 54–55
Longhouses, 13
Longinus, "On the Sublime," 148
Looms, 162–163
Losenko, Anton, 114
Louis XIV, king of France, 6
Lu Xun, 53

M

Mahayana Buddhism, 36
Mair, Victor, xiv
Malevich, Kazimir, 117
Mali,
    ancient art, 18
    Bamana people, art of, 19
Mamluk Empire, 161
Mamontov, Savva, 116
Manchu rule, and art, 50–51
Mandala, 5
Manor houses, architecture of, 5
Mao Zedong, 54–55
Markets of Trajan, 29
Masaccio, 68
Matulu, Tshimbumba Kanda, 21
Mauryan Empire, 121–122
Maya, 104–105
McNeill, William H., xi, xiv
Meissen porcelain, 58, 161
Mesoamerica, 101
    art, 148 (*See also* **Art—Pre-Colombian Central and South America**)
Mesopotamia
    architecture, 1
    art, 136
Mexica people, 101, 105–108
Mexico, art in, 102, 104, 105, 107, 109
Michelangelo, 6, 68
Middle Ages, architecture, 4–5
Miller, Mary Ellen, 103
Ming dynasty, 49
    architecture, 6
Minka houses, 15

Missionaries
  in China, xvii
  in Central and South America, 110–111
Modernism
  architecture, 7–9
  art, 18–21, 38, 52–56, 68–70, 81–82, 86–87, 116–118, 135, 142
Momoyama period (Japan), 78–80
Monet, Claude, 59
Morisot, Berthe, 69
Morocco, Paleolithic art in, 92
Morris, William, 8
Mughal Empire
  painting, 127
  sculpture, 125
Muhammad, figural art and, 139
Mukhina, Vera, 118
Mummies and mummification, 37
Muromachi period (Japan), 78
Museums, 155–159
  See also **Art—world art studies**
Myanmar (Burma), art of, 130
Mycenae, Treasury of Atreus, 2

N
Nainsukh, 128
Nampeyo, 89
Nara period (Japan), 76–77
Native American religions. *See* **Art—Native North America**
Native Americans, art, 84–90
Naukratis, 24
Neolithic era
  architecture, 1
  art, 33–34, 136
Nepal, art, 31–39 (*See also* **Art—South Asia**)
Nero, 28–29
Neumann, Johann Balthasar, 6
New Testament, catacomb paintings, 63–64
New York City, as Western art capital (20th c.), 72
New Zealand, art, 87
Newton, Isaac, Cenotaph to, 7
Nguyen Phan Chanh, 133
Ni Zan, 48, 49
Nigeria, art of, 21
Nihonga, 81
Nikitin, Ivan, 113
Nitten, 82
Nok culture, 17

North America, art, of indigenous populations, 84–90

O
Oceania, 156
  art, 85–86
Ogata Kenzan, 81
Okeke, Uche, 21
Olmec civilization, 101–104, 109
Olympic games, Beijing (2008), 56, 89
O'Malley, John W., xviii
Onians, John, xvi, 146
Onobrakpeya, Bruce, 21
Open Door policy (U.S.), 56
Orang Asli, 12
Orozco, Jose Clemente, 107
Ottoman Empire, art, 140, 141

P
Pakistan, art, 31–38 (*See also* **Art—South Asia**)
Paleolithic (foraging) era
  art, 92–96
  habitation, 2
Palestine, art, 138
Palladio, Andrea, 6
Pang Xunqin, 53
Pantheon, 4, 29
Parthenon, 3, 25, 28
Pastoral nomadic societies
  architecture, 1
  art, 65, 135
Performance art, 55, 72, 82, 84, 143
Peristyle, 24–25
Perov, Vasily, 116
Perry, Matthew, 58
Persian Empire, art, 34, 135, 137
Peru, Andean art, 103, 107–109
Peter the Great (Czar Peter I), 113
Petheo, Bela, xi
Petrarch (Francesco Petrarca)
  Indus Valley, 32–34
  North America, 84
Petroglyphs, 33–34, 103
Phidias, 25
Picasso, Pablo, 20, 70
Pictographs, 103
Piranesi, Giambattista, 7
Pissarro, Camille, 69
Pizarro, Francisco, 101, 110
Polenov, Vasily, 116

Polo, Marco, 57
Pomerantz, Kenneth, xiv
Popova, Liubov, 71, 118
Porcelain, 57, **160–161**
  See also **Art—East Asian and European connections**
Prehistoric art, 98
Primitivism, 86, 117
Propaganda, People's Republic of China and, 54
Propylaia, 29
Puccini, Giacomo, 60
Pueblo architecture, 86
Pushkin, Alexander, 115
Pyramids, 2, 102, 108, 109, xix

Q
Qi Baishi, 53
Qin dynasty, 41
Qingci (green ware), 57
Qing dynasty, art during, 50–52
Qur'an, calligraphy, 142

R
Raku techniques, 61
Raphael, 68
Rastrelli, Carlo, 114
Reilly, Kevin, xiii
Rembrandt, 68
Renaissance
  architecture, 5–6, 67–68
  See also **Art—Europe; Leonardo da Vinci**
Renoir, Auguste, 69
Repin, Ilya, 116
Revolution—Mexico, 117
Revolution—Russia, art, 118
Richardson, Henry H., 8
Ringgold, Faith, 73
Rivera, Diego, 107
Robie, F. C., House, 8
Rococo style, 7
Rodchenko, Alexander, 118
Roman Empire
  architecture, 3–4, 26–29
  art (*See* **Art—ancient Greece and Rome**)
  catacombs, 63
Romanesque architecture, 4, 66
Roupp, Heidi, xiii
Rowland, Benjamin, xix

Rubin, Arnold, 145–146
Rublev, Andrei, 113
Russian Soviet Empire
  modern art, 70, 71
  See also **Art—Russia**

S
Sahara Desert, art, 17
Saint Petersburg, Russia, 113–114
St. Paul's Cathedral, London, 6
St. Peter, Basilica of, 6
Ste-Geneviève, Church of, 7
Samokhvalov, Alexander, 118
Sant'Andrea, church of, 6
Scientific instruments. *See* **Museums**
Scythian era, 32
Seleucid era, 33–34
Selim II, Mosque of, 6
Sen Rikyō, 80
Sesshō Tōyō, 78
Sèvres porcelain, 161
Shah, Muhammad, 128
Shang dynasty, 40–41
Shen Zhou, 49
Shi Huangdi, 41
Shi Lu, 54
Shikibu, Lady Murasaki, 77
Shoji Hamada, 61
Shōmu, Emperor, 76
Shunga dynasty, sculpture during, 122
Silk
  handscrolls and hanging scrolls (*See* **Art—China**)
  production of, 164
Sinan, 6
Siva, 123, 131–132
Smithsonian Institution, 61, 157
Socialist Realism
  in Chinese art, 54, 55
  in Russian art, 118–120
Sogdia, 33
Song dynasty, 78
  Song–Yuan period (and literati art), 46–50
Soufflot, Jacques-Germain, 7
South Africa, Zulu people, art of, 20
South American art, pre-Columbian
  Chavín, 108
  early origin, 108
  European conquerors, aftermath, 110–111
  Inca, 109–110
  Moche, 109

Notes: 1) Names, terms, and page-number ranges in **bold** denote chapter entries.

Nazca, 108–109
Southeast Asia. *See* **Art—Southeast Asia**
Spengler, Oswald, xi
Spirituality, Asian, 61–62
Sri Lanka (Ceylon), art (*See* **Art—South Asia**)
Stavrianos, Leften, xii
Stepanova, Varvara, 118
Stonehenge, 2
Stupas, Buddhist, 4, 121–122
    Indonesia, 131
    Schwe Dagon stupa, Myanmar, 133
Sui dynasty, 43, 45
Sullivan, Louis, 9
Sullivan, Michael, xviii
Sumatra, 131
Sumerian civilization, 136,
Summers, David, xvi
Sunga dynasty, sculpture during, 122
Supreme Harmony, Hall of, 6
Surikov, Vasily, 116
Symbols, Paleolithic origins (visual symbolism and iconography), 92–96
Syria, art, 138, 139

T

Tagore, Rabindranath, 128
Tajikistan, 31–38
Taj Mahal, 125
Tale of Genji, The, 77
Tang dynasty, art, 36, 45–46, 47, 76
Tange, Kenzo, 9
Tankha, Brij, xviii
Tannhauer, Gottfried, 113
Tarquinias Priscus, Lucius, 27
Tatlin, Vladimir, 117, 118
Tawaraya Sōtatsu, 80, 81
Temples
    Angkor Empire, 132–133
    architecture of, 1–3, 23–24
    Emerald Buddha, Temple of, Thailand, 134
    Hindu, 123
    Ionia, hellenic temples in, 137
Tenochtitlán, 107
    art and pyramids, 2, 105–106
Textiles, 37, 84, **162–169**
    damask, 166
    dyes and, 165–168
    lace, 166
    looms and, 162
    nineteenth century and after, 168–169

    patterned fabrics, 165–167
    printed cottons, 167–168
    yarns and, 163–165
Thailand,
    art, 129, 133–135
    Khmer kingdom, 133
Tibet, art, 37
Tobey, Mark, 61
Tōdai-ji, 76
Tokugawa Ieyasu, 78–79, 80
Toulouse-Lautrec, Henri, 60
Toynbee, Arnold, xi
Toyotomi Hideyoshi, 78
Trading patterns, ancient American. *See* **Art—Pre-Columbian Central and South America**
Trajan, emperor, 29
Tretiakov, Pavel, 116
Tunisia, architecture, 18
Turkmenistan, 31–38

U

Ukiyo-e ("floating world" prints), xviii, 60, 69, 81, 147
Umayyad caliphate, 139
United States
    architecture, 7–8, 9, 10
    art, 58, 60, 72–73, 84, 86–90
    Japanese trade, 57, 58
Unkei, 78
    archeological excavations at, 136
    Ziggurat of Ur-Namu, 2
Ushakov, Simon, 113
Uzbekistan, artifacts and art in present-day region, 31–38

V

Van Damme, Wilfried, xvi
van der Rohe, Ludwig Mies, 9, 71
van Gogh, Vincent, 59–60, 61, 117, 147
Vedas and vedic culture, art, 121
Venetsianov, Aleksei, 115
Vermeer, Johannes, xii
Versailles, 6
Vespasian, Emperor, 28
Vietnam
    art, 130
    Khmer kingdom, 134
Vishnu, 123–124, 127, 131–132
Visual arts/communication, 92–96, 143–144
Visvanatha Temple to Shiva, Khajuraho, India, 5
Vrubel, Mikhail, 116

W

Walpole, Horace, 7
Wang Hui, 51
Wang Jian, 51
Wang Meng, 49
Wang Shimin, 51
Wang Xichi, 43
Wang Yuanqi, 51
Warburg, Aby, 86
Warham, William, 57
Wedgwood, Josiah, 161
Wei dynasty, 44
Whistler, James McNeill, 60
Whitney, Eli, 168
Wong, Aida, xviii
Wong, R. Bin, xiv
World art. *See* **Art—world art studies**
World History Association, xii, xiii, xiv
World War I, Eastern Europe, 15
World War II, Eastern Europe, 15
Wren, Christopher, 6
Wright, Frank Lloyd, 8, 86
Wu Guanzhong, 51

X

Xinru Liu, xii
Xu Bing, 55

Y

Yang Guifei, 46
Yayoi culture, 74–75
Yoshihara Jirō, 82
Yuan dynasty, 48

Z

Zapotecs, 101, 102, 105, 111
Zhang Daqian, 53
Zhou dynasty, 41
Zhu Da, 50
Zhu Ruoji, 50–51
Ziggurats, 2
Zijlmans, Kitty, xvi
Zimbabwe, Great, 18
Zimbabwe, art of, 21
Zverev, Anatoly, 119

Editorial Board and Staff

Editors
William H McNeill, *University of Chicago, Emeritus*
Jerry H. Bentley, *University of Hawaii, Manoa*
David Christian, *Macquarie University, Sydney*
Ralph C. Croizier, *University of Victoria*
J. R. McNeill, *Georgetown University*
Heidi Roupp, *World History Center*
Judith P. Zinsser, *Miami University*

Associate Editor
Brett Bowden, *University of Western Sydney*

Advisory Board
Ross E. Dunn, *San Diego State University*
Ryba Epstein, *Rich East High School*
Brian Fagan, *University of California, Santa Barbara*
Daniel R. Headrick, *Roosevelt University, Emeritus*
Kailai Huang, *Massachusetts College of Liberal Arts*
Marnie Hughes-Warrington, *Macquarie University*
Tom Laichas, *Crossroads School*
Craig Lockard, *University of Wisconsin, Green Bay*
Pamela McVay, *Ursuline College*
Carl Nightingale, *University of Wisconsin, Milwaukee*
Patrick O'Brien, *London School of Economics*
Hugh Page Jr., *University of Notre Dame*
Paul Philip, *Lancaster High School*
Mrinalini Sinha, *Pennsylvania State University*
Peer Vries, *Leiden University*

Publisher
Karen Christensen

Senior Staff Editor
Mary Bagg

Editorial Staff
Kathy Brock
Rachel Christensen
Hillary Cox
David Gagne
Ginger Nielsen
Barbara Resch
Ashley Winseck
Chris Yurko

Design and Photo Research
Anna Myers

Cover Art
Cave-art illustration: Lisa Clark

Front cover images, left-to-right:
1. Petrogylph in Kazakhstan. Photo by Jeff Frame.
2. Xia Gui (c. 1180–1230), *Twelve Views from a Thatched Hut* (detail). Handscroll, ink on silk.
3. Claude Monet, *La Japonaise: Madame Monet in Japanese Costume* (1876). Oil on canvas. Museum of Fine Arts, Boston.

Back cover images, left-to-right:
1. Johannes Vermeer, *Officer and Laughing Girl* (c. 1655–1660). The Frick Collection, New York.
2. Coyolxauhqui Stone, Mexica (Aztec). Photo by Danielle L. Pierce.
3. Ceramic Mammoth figurine, Pavlov (Czech Republic).

Author Credits

Introduction: Art in World History
by **Ralph C. Croizier**
University of Victoria

Architecture
by **David M. Breiner**
Philadelphia University

Architecture, Vernacular
by **Paul Oliver**
University of Huddersfield

Art—Africa
by **Kate Ezra**
Columbia College, Chicago

Art—Ancient Greece and Rome
by **Robin F. Rhodes**
University of Notre Dame

Art—Central Asia
by **Craig Benjamin**
Grand Valley State University

Art—China
by **Joan Lebold Cohen**
Independent scholar, Fairbank Center for East Asian Studies
and **Ralph C. Croizier**
University of Victoria

Art—East Asian and European Connections
by **Robert J. Poor**
University of Minnesota

Art—Europe
by **Mara R. Witzling**
University of New Hampshire

Art—Japan
by **Andrew L. Maske**
University of Kentucky

Art—Native North America
by **Lea S. McChesney**
Independent scholar, Rochester, New York

AUTHOR CREDITS

Art—Paleolithic
by **Wilfried Van Damme**
Leiden University and Ghent University

Art—Pre-Columbian Central and South America
by **Danielle L. Pierce**
University of North Texas

Art—Russia
by **Lindsey Hughes**
Deceased, formerly of the School of Slavonic and East European Studies

Art—South Asia
by **Debashish Banerji**
University of California, Los Angeles

Art—Southeast Asia
by **Jerome Feldman**
Hawaii Pacific University

Art—West Asia
by **Walter B. Denny**
University of Massachusetts, Amherst

Art—World Art Studies
by **Kathleen I. Kimball**
Independent scholar, Barrington, New Hampshire

Leonardo da Vinci
Kenneth R. Bartlett
University of Toronto

Museums
by **Rainer F. Buschmann**
California State University, Channel Islands

Porcelain
by **Robert Finlay**
University of Arkansas

Textiles
by **Margaret Ordoñez**
University of Rhode Island

This  book was distilled from the

BERKSHIRE ENCYCLOPEDIA OF WORLD HISTORY 2ND EDITION

AWARDS
Library Journal Best Reference Source
Booklist Editor's Choice
Choice Outstanding Academic Title

William H. McNeill

Jerry H. Bentley, David Christian,

Ralph C. Croizier, J. R. McNeill,

Heidi Roupp, and Judith P. Zinsser

Editors

Brett Bowden

Associate Editor

This landmark work has grown from 5 to 6 volumes and includes over 100 new articles on environmental history, world art, global communications, and information technology, as well as updates on events such as earthquakes and the global economic crisis. Hundreds of new illustrations enhance visual appeal, while updated Further Reading sections guide readers toward continued study.

6 VOLUMES • 978-1-933782-65-2
Price: US$875 • 3,152 pages • 8½ × 11"

CHOICE

"Challenging traditional encyclopedias that offer the standard who, what, when, and where, the second edition of the *Berkshire Encyclopedia of World History* continues to focus on cultural comparisons and interactions using broad themes. The second edition offers much more material on such distinctive and interdisciplinary entries. Groups of entries, such as the nine on trading patterns and the nine on revolutions, allow for easy comparisons between cultures. The big, traditional encyclopedias lack much of the unique content offered in this work, and do not focus on the historical significance of topics such as sweet potatoes and trees or discuss emerging trends such as "big history" and trade cycles. **Summing Up: Highly recommended. Lower-division undergraduates and above; general readers.**"

Booklist

"One of the great strengths of this unique resource is that although it is accessible to novices and younger users, it is still useful to more advanced researchers and scholars. It succeeds in tying specific and local histories to larger patterns and movements. Overall, this magnificent set provides an interconnected and holistic perspective on human history and is recommended for most libraries."

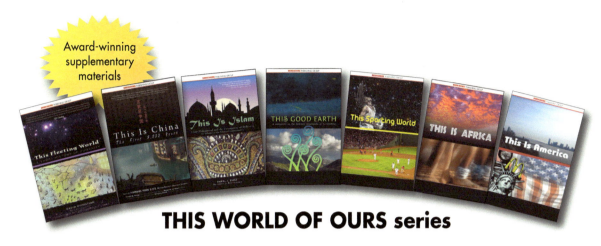

THIS WORLD OF OURS series

"I became an avid student of David Christian by watching his course, *Big History*, on DVD, so I am very happy to see his enlightening presentation of the world's history captured in these essays. I hope it will introduce a wider audience to this gifted scientist and teacher."
—Bill Gates

"It is hard to imagine that such a short book can cover such a vast span of time and space. *This Is China: The First 5,000 Years* will help teachers, students, and general readers alike, as they seek for a preliminary guide to the contexts and complexities of Chinese culture."
—Jonathan Spence, Yale University

"I only wish I had had *This Is China* available during my 15 years of teaching Chinese at the college level. A tremendous resource for both Chinese language students and teachers."
—Scott McGinnis, Defense Language Institute, Washington DC

Berkshire's series of very short books on very big topics in world history are designed to help teachers and students get the big picture on big, challenging aspects of history and culture. The books, written by well-known scholars, include illustrations, discussion questions, "thought experiments," and suggestions for further readings. Digital versions are also available.

MULTIPLE COPIES DISCOUNTS

2–10 copies, **10% off**

11–20 copies, **20% off**

21–30 copies, **30% off**

Order two or more copies of any title or combination of titles in the "This World of Ours" series for a multiple copies discount (when shipped to the same address). Orders for *This Fleeting World*, *This Is China*, and *This Is Islam* will ship immediately. Orders that include *This Is Africa*, *This Good Earth*, or *This Sporting World*, will ship upon publication.

This Fleeting World

BESTSELLER

A Short History of Humanity

David Christian, *Macquarie University, Sydney*

Available now : 978-1-933782-04-1
http://bit.ly/thisfleetingworld

This Is China

The First 5,000 Years

Editors: **Haiwang Yuan,** *Western Kentucky University Libraries,* **Ronald G. Knapp, Margot E. Landman, Gregory Veeck**

Available Now : 978-1-933782-20-1
http://bit.ly/thisischina

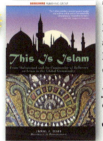

This Is Islam

From Muhammad and the Community of Believers to Islam in the Global Community

Jamal J. Elias, *University of Pennsylvannia*

This is Islam offers readers an introduction to one of the world's major religions, its philosophies, and how it affects the world today. Geared to those unfamiliar with the religion and its rituals and customs—and written in clear and simple terms by one of the United States' leading scholars of religion—this volume explains Islamic law, major figures and sects, and the role of mysticism.

Available Now : 978-1-933782-81-2
http://bit.ly/thisisislam

FORTHCOMING

This Good Earth
978-1-933782-86-7

This Sporting World
978-1-933782-91-1

This Is Africa
978-1-933782-93-5

This Is America
978-1-933782-95-9

EACH: $14.95 : 6x9" : 152 pages : Paperback : Hardcover and Digital editions also available

CPSIA information can be obtained
at www.ICGtesting.com
Printed in the USA
BVHW021919070719
552721BV00012BA/51/P